14.95

THE DREAMER'S WO[

D0406653

THE DREAMER'S
WORKBOOK

A Complete Guide to Interpreting and Understanding Dreams

NERYS DEE

Sterling Publishing Co., Inc.   New York

9 10

Published in 1990 by Sterling Publishing Company, Inc.
387 Park Avenue South, New York, N.Y. 10016
Originally published in Great Britain by The Aquarian Press
© 1989 by Nerys Dee
Distributed in Canada by Sterling Publishing
⅞ Canadian Manda Group, P.O. Box 920, Station U
Toronto, Ontario, Canada M8Z 5P9
Manufactured in the United States of America
All rights reserved

ISBN 0-85030-705-8

Contents

Preface

I am writing this preamble to justify writing on the subject of dreaming, a subject about which, despite the fact humanity has been doing it for thousands of years, very little is still known. In addition to this, they are very personal experiences, so interpreting another's dream is akin to reading their private letters.

I began working with dreams 30 years ago when I discovered that many of my dreams came true. I soon realized I was not unique and that everyone had dreams that came true, even though they did not always realize it. Next time you hear someone say 'That's broken my dream' you will know what I mean.

You have probably noticed that when you are really interested in a subject you do not have to go looking for information about it—it looks for you. This is how it was with me and dreams. I discovered a Jungian study group, talks on dreams and even a dream-workshop, or 'Dream Weekend' as it was then called, right on my doorstep. In addition to this I was working in a psychiatric hospital where I heard many remarkable dreams from the patients and staff.

It was not long before I was writing about dreams in daily papers and magazines in Britain and abroad, as well as discussing them on the radio and television. Then, 15 years ago, I became *Prediction* magazine's dream interpreter. This gave me the unique opportunity to investigate an endless supply of dreams, from action replay domestic dreams to the most outrageously bizarre nightmares imaginable. I have now collected over 20,000 of these.

Since a dream is a message from the dreamer to the dreamer, it follows that the only person to truly understand it is the creator of the dream—namely the dreamer himself. All a dream interpreter can offer is the meaning of traditional, cultural and social signs and symbols that appear in dreams. When dreamers apply these meanings to what they alone know of their own situation and circumstances, they immediately understand what it is they are trying to tell themselves through their own dreams.

If experience counts, I like to think I have had sufficient to at least recognize whether a dream is a warning, encouraging, admonishing or predictive dream. But what these relate to specifically is another matter. The interpreter can only guess at this—and rightly so, for this is the secret known to the dreamer alone. As a catalyst, I hope that what I have to say in the following pages will help you, the dreamer, to discover your own innermost secrets.

Introduction

If we do not understand the messages and instructions hidden in our dreams, we do not understand ourselves; but understanding ourselves (and, of course others) is what life is all about—and where better to begin than with our dreams?

Life is made up of one experience after another. Two-thirds of these take place during the 16-hour day which on average we spend awake, and the other third is experienced during the eight hours we spend sleeping. Daytime experiences provide practical lessons from which we can learn how to deal with similar experiences, if and when they occur again in the future. From our night-time experiences, which are equally important although in an entirely different way, we are offered the opportunity to understand life from a psychological, psychic and spiritual point of view—a view that can only be expressed in dreams either literally or through symbols, analogy and metaphor.

Impressions, whether received when we are awake or when we are asleep, all arise from inner images. Realistic images are those originating from contact with outer objects and events, perceived through the five senses. As stimuli from the outer world, they are transformed into images, which are then recognized in terms of sight, sound, taste, smell and touch. These images are stored as memories, to be recalled later. Non-realistic or conceptual images, by comparison, consist of recalled memory-images which may consist of realistic objects, sounds, tastes and smells, plus abstract images which represent emotions, pain, desire, fear, love or hate.

Dreams are made of all these images but it is the interpreting of the abstract, symbolic and metaphoric images that usually causes most of the problems. A shape, for example, may well represent a fear; a tree with fallen branches may stand for family problems; a bird could be showing the dreamer which direction in life to take. However, once it is recognized that dreams use a different language to communicate their messages from the one used when we are awake, these messages are readily revealed.

Since our inner world is reflected in this way through its own special language, it is not surprising that on waking many dreams appear to make little sense. It is a sobering thought to realize that *we* have created these elaborate scenes, full of unknown characters and events, apparently unrelated to anything we have done in the past. We could, however, be forgiven for believing that, perhaps temporarily, someone else is manipulating our dreaming mind during sleep. True, we can be influenced by others when awake, but it is really up to us to what degree we allow the impressions of others to control us while asleep. Protection is the answer, and this will be dealt with later in the book.

Dreams are messages from ourselves, to ourselves. Some are more literal than others, offering obvious, literal messages; others seem to be full of hidden symbolism and have to be translated from the language of sleep into the language of everyday wakefulness. By converting these messages into practical terms it is then possible to be guided along a path that leads to peace of mind, healing, acceptance, understanding and achievements in life that will benefit not only the dreamer but others too. In this way we can cast our bread on the waters and receive threefold blessings in return.

Discovering the messages in our dreams is obviously important but this is only half the story. Having found out what these are, we must then put them into action. Unless we do this, we are not making full use of the power of dreams, nor understanding their real purpose, namely to bring improvement and evolution into our lives through change. And change is the name of the game of life.

In the final analysis, it is the practical application of dream-messages that matters, to be able to do this we need to have control over the dreams our dreaming minds conjure up for recall on waking. The exercises in this book are, therefore, designed to encourage the right dream at the right time.

Dreams are fragile and transient so working with them is an art. Like all arts, it needs patience and commitment, but with determination the scenes created each night will be unique reminders of what we were in the past, what we are now, and what we can become in the future.

PART ONE

The World of Dreams

1.

What Are Dreams?

Defining dreams as 'visions during sleep' may describe what occurs but this does not explain what they are. Undoubtedly, they are experiences which are real enough to produce strong psychological and physiological responses in a sleeping person. The nightmare, for example, produces the flight or fight mechanism, with its accompanying increase in blood pressure and heart rate, and even sleep-walking in readiness for physical action. The passionate dream of a lover, renowned for its emotional and biological effects, is a further example, yet these dreams are not reality.

Imagination, those inner scenes responsible for every thought, emotion, word and deed, is the underlying phenomenon of dreaming. If we close our eyes, it is possible to conjure up a particular scene or image at will. This is a daydream—under our conscious control. During sleep, scenes and images are likewise conjured up, but these are *not* consciously controlled. They are spontaneous.

Sometimes events from the previous day are in our thoughts as we drop off to sleep, so not surprisingly these scenes are re-enacted as literal dreams, in the hope of extracting further information from what has already happened. Reliving events in this way has been suggested as the reason for dreaming, but this is only one aspect. The dream reflecting a foreign land the dreamer has never heard of, or the weird and wonderful mansion to which the dreamer returns night after night, demolishes any such simplistic explanation.

Dreams can be as complicated or simplistic, mysterious or pragmatic as life itself—which is not surprising since it is life, with its innumerable facets, they reflect. Yet dreams do far more than reflect life; they provide inspiration, information and solutions that can be revealed to us in no other way. Inspiration, information and solutions received in this way have been responsible for determining the destiny of countless individuals, as well as shaping the history of nations, to an almost unbelievable degree. In this context, dreams are recognized as both prophetic and powerful.

The Power of Dreams

An excellent example of the power of dreams and their subsequent influence on the world is to be found in the biblical Pharaoh's dream concerning the 'seven fat and seven lean kine', followed by the dream of 'seven full and seven

11

empty ears of corn'. If this Pharaoh had not had these dreams, and Joseph, one of the 12 sons of Jacob whom he had imprisoned, had not correctly interpreted them as seven years of plenty followed by seven years of famine, Joseph would almost certainly have perished in gaol.

Without Joseph's prophetic interpretation of the Pharaoh's dreams, and his release as a reward, the 12 sons of Jacob could not possibly have been reunited. These 12 brothers were to become the fathers of the Twelve Tribes of Israel, so without them there would have been no Old Testament story with its exodus, Promised Land and Judaic beliefs, and no New Testament story heralding the birth of Christianity. The entire world would most certainly be a very different place today were it not for these dreams so long ago.

The Pharaoh's dreams and Joseph's interpretation undoubtedly set in motion a train of events which is still affecting our lives today, but in addition to these dreams there are countless others, dreamed by famous and infamous people, which have also swayed the course of history. Alexander the Great, Julius Caesar, Joan of Arc, Napoleon and Bismarck are just a few of those who shaped national and international destinies in this way.

A particular nightmare that initiated one of the most devastating chains of events ever to affect humanity is said to have been experienced by Adolf Hitler. In November 1917, as the German and French armies faced each other across the Somme, the sleeping Corporal Hitler had a terrifying dream in which debris and molten earth crushingly and suffocatingly descended upon him. He awoke suddenly and dashed outside into the cold night air, thankful to discover that it had only been a bad nightmare. Seconds later, a shell landed on the bunker he had just left and killed all the sleeping occupants. Again, how different the world would be had this nightmare not saved Hitler's life.

Dream Messages

Whether destined to determine the history of the world, or a simple action-replay of a trivial event, all dreams have one thing in common—they contain a message. A dream-message should not only be interpreted but also be put to good use—either acted upon practically, by taking certain steps which alter the dreamer's direction in life for the better, or understood in such a way that it increases their knowledge and wisdom.

In the case of certain dreams experienced by those in power, the effect these have not only on the dreamer but on countless others as well can usually be seen in retrospect. Hitler's dream which saved his life is an example of this. In this light, a dream can be compared with the dropping of a stone into a pool and watching the ripples radiating away from the centre, eventually affecting the entire pool. Individually, dreams influence our lives and those of people around us, even though the reverberations may not be noticed at the time, nor perhaps will they be as world-shattering as the dreams of the famous and the infamous.

Every dreamer has the potential to become an inventor and many inventors' dreams have become reality and have, as a result, revolutionized the way we live. The sewing machine, lead shot, ball-bearings, canned food and even the atomic bomb were all first viewed in dreams, and all have made an impression in one way or another, for better or worse, on society and history.

The experience from a single dream can shape our destiny, irrespective of whether we are inventors or powerful public figures. Many rewarding dreams of this nature which bring success and achievement, comfort and healing, occur spontaneously, although without realizing it the dreamer has, in fact, already been working towards that end. The groundwork has been done consciously, through intelligent, carefully-controlled thinking and planning, but the final touches which bring about that success and achievement, comfort and healing, are added unconsciously with the help of a dream.

To receive a meaningful and helpful dream-message it is therefore necessary to possess the conscious counterpart as well as the unconscious contribution. This means we must know precisely what it is we want to invent, achieve, win or overcome. It would, for example, have been a waste of time if an unsciential dreamer had received the dream of a snake chasing its own tail. To Kekule, the 19th-century chemist, this provided the answer he had intelligently been seeking for years. His dream-scene symbolically represented the missing link in his research—the benzine ring, a discovery that led into the age of the motor car and the aeroplane.

Dreams reflect that which needs to be reflected because they are created by an aspect of ourselves which knows, or has access to, precisely that which we need. The advice 'sleep on it' exemplifies this. Dreams also respond to requests for help, healing guidance and comfort, but unless we make requests such help may not be forthcoming.

The Exercise

This exercise is conscious and intellectual; it is none the less very important because without a conscious realization of precisely what it is that you seek in life, there is little point of recording, interpreting or working with your dreams.

The dreaming mind, that unconscious aspect within, is capable of relaying incredible information to its counterpart, the conscious self, but without acknowledgement and recognition of its existence and ability, it cannot be relied upon to deliver the right dream at the right time. It needs requests and instructions. Knowing that a dream can help is the first step towards receiving that help, so once an aim, ambition, hope, fear or desire is clearly formulated, a conscious request can then be made, for this is the signal your dreaming mind expects and awaits.

Exercise 1—Your Worries, Fears, Needs & Aims

From the list overleaf indicate your innermost feelings, negative and positive. Try also to decide on a short-term aim and a long-term aim.

Problems & worries

Fears & phobias

Lack of confidence

Relationships causing unrest

Difficult circumstances

Health problems

Emotional needs

Hopes for the future

Short-term aims

Long-term aims

Now re-write this list in order of importance:

1.

2.

3.

4.

5.

6.

7.

8.

9.

10.

Summary

Dreams   — are messages from yourself, to yourself.
— are created by you, for you.
— are as important as real events.
— bring about physiological changes during sleep.
— can heal.
— even bad ones can be beneficial.
— reveal the truth and original ideas.
— highlight problems and circumstances.
— warn, enlighten, strengthen emotionally, and inform.
— influence the dreamer, and subsequently others.
— bring hope.
— need to be requested, recognized and respected.

2.

Sleep and Dreams

We sleep on average for eight hours each night. This means that one third of our life is spent sleeping, so by the time we are 75 years old we have slept for 25 years. And during these years we have probably been dreaming, in one form or another, for most of that time even though we remember only a fraction of them.

After working during the day we look forward to lying down in a warm, comfortable bed at night and slipping off into that strange unconscious state called sleep. Until this century very little was known about sleep and the only knowledge concerning it came from legends and remembered dreams; but the introduction of electronic monitoring has led to the discovery of brainwaves, rapid eye movements and physical changes which take place during sleep.

Sleep and the Immune System

Recently a biochemical link has been found between deep sleep and a strong healthy immune system. The compounds that trigger restful deeper sleep, as opposed to lighter sleep, also play a part in recharging the body's chemical defence mechanism.

The chain of events that induce sleep and spur the immune system into action begins in the digestive system, in particular the intestines, where bacteria produce sleep-inducing chemicals called muramyl peptides. These are so potent that it is said that one billionth of a gramme is sufficient to add several hours to a night's sleep.

These peptides find their way to the brain where they trigger off the production of interleukins which in turn stimulate the immune system's lymphocytes, the defensive cells that destroy invading bacteria and any rogue host cells which can cause cancer.

Originally it was believed that the only purpose of sleep was to allow the body to rest and repair itself physically. This belief was soon discounted when it was discovered that resting for 24 hours, yet remaining awake, still physically rested the body. From experiments involving the deprivation of sleep it was discovered that lack of sleep mentally disturbed and disoriented a person. It was then assumed that sleep was essential to rest the brain, but again researchers were to be proved wrong.

Electronic monitoring revealed that the brain was far from resting and inactive during sleep. In fact it was more active than when awake, but a difference in the nature of the brainwaves was noticed. Impulses altered from a fast, low amplitude when awake, to a slow, high amplitude when asleep. Through electroencephalograms (EEGs for short) these waves can now be identified as Alpha, Beta, Gamma, Delta, Theta, Mu, Vertex, and 'k' waves.

Two distinct sleep states were also discovered and individual researchers gave these two states the following different names: 'deep and light', 'active and passive', 'quiet and active', 'desynchronized and synchronized', 'high and low', and the commonest of all for a time in the 1960's, 'paradoxical and orthodox'.

REM Sleep State

Further experiments carried out on volunteers revealed that the brainwaves altered when an awake subject cut out visual messages to the brain by closing his or her eyes. It was further observed that sleep could be divided into six distinct types or levels. These were labelled A,B,C,D,E and F, and each night we progress from sleep state A to sleep state F.

It was in the level of sleep labelled F that unusually rapid eye movements, under closed eyelids, were noticed. These rapid eye movements became known as REM, and for a time, it was thought that dreams occurred only in the REM sleep state. This was assumed because when subjects were woken up during REM sleep, they reported that they were dreaming visually. When, however, subjects were woken up during non-REM sleep, they also reported that they were dreaming, although not always visually.

The Purpose of Sleep

It is now recognized that the purpose of sleep is not only to rest the physical body and the mind. It is to dream. To deprive a person of sleep, and consequently their dreams, was found to be dangerous, so—whether dreams are remembered or not—they are vital for our well-being. During sleep, problems, fears and hopes are viewed from an entirely different standpoint and information is assessed in a different language from that used by the conscious mind. The sleeping mind does not communicate in words—it uses scenes, actions and symbols, and it is this other language that has to be learned if the message is to be understood at the conscious awake level.

It is generally assumed that problems can only be assessed and solved when we are awake, through logical reasoning and the intellect. It is not recognized that during sleep symbolic vision, intuition and inspiration take over, yet the old saying 'sleep on it' is based on the belief that something extraordinary occurs during the night. Most of us have experienced the truth of this saying, having gone to sleep with indecision and fear running through our heads, only to find that in the morning, the cloud has lifted and hope has returned. This improved new outlook did not develop by chance; it was due to a complete reassessment of values from that other standpoint.

The Source

In sleep, our awareness reaches out into undiscovered realms—the source. Maybe this is the prime state of existence, for when asleep it is possible not only to come to terms with the real world and the unthinkable, but to see things in a far more profound way than when awake. On occasions it is even possible to see into the future.

Sleep is the state we enter when we are ill and when we are weary of the everyday world, so maybe the sleep of death is but a short step beyond that of a good night's rest. 'To sleep, to sleep, perchance to dream—ay, there's the rub; for in that sleep of death what dream may come when we have shuffled off this mortal coil?' was how William Shakespeare expressed this.

New-born babies, having just taken on that mortal coil, sleep for 90 per cent of a 24-hour day and during this sleep they are dreaming. And, according to dream researchers, they were dreaming even before they were born. As they grow older and experience more and more in the outer world, they are weaned off so much sleep until eventually, as adults, they sleep and contact the source from which they sprang for only one third of each day.

When we return at night to the source, the Land of Dreams, we enter an inner dimension that is far more expansive than the limited outer world. Here we are recharged with vitality, but if our physical output during the day is greater than our psychic input during the night, a deficit develops, and this deficit is recognized as chronic tiredness. Although in the present fast-moving age stress is often blamed for this condition, it is not in itself the problem. The problem is not being able to cope with stress.

It has been discovered that those who cannot cope with life tend to be drained of energy, do not sleep well, and feel permanently tired. Before modern drugs, the treatment for those suffering from 'a nervous breakdown', namely a lack of ability to cope, was *sleep*. This was sometimes induced with the help of a mild sleeping drug, but on waking the world seemed a much more hospitable place because copability had returned. As a follow-up to this simple treatment, it was advised that if life became too much, the patient should opt out and escape into healing sleep.

Today, relaxation and meditation are often resorted to when life is too stressful, but these practices do not remove stress. Stress results from circumstances. In this context, relaxation and meditation are apologies, attempts to compensate for a lifestyle that does not make provision for sufficient sleep. Few adults have enough sleep each night, except at weekends and holiday-time, when they take the opportunity to catch up on this. Unfortunately, few realize that what is lacking in their life is sleep and that it is impossible to recharge when awake; only in sleep can we contact the source, and receive that essential vitality.

While it is true that some people require less than eight hours sleep each night, they are in the minority. 'Early to bed, early to rise, makes a man healthy, wealthy and wise' may sound old-fashioned but it still offers advice that is ignored at our peril; the remedy for so many emotional upsets is, quite simply, more sleep.

During a night's sleep a recurring 90-minute pattern, divided into phases of non-REM and REM sleep, is repeated, five or six times. Towards morning, periods of non-REM sleep decrease and periods of REM sleep increase, so it is at the end of a long session of REM sleep that we wake up. When sleep is looked at from this standpoint, it can be seen how wrong it is to disrupt this important pattern before the cycles have been completed. For many, this is precisely what happens when their alarm clock rudely awakens them.

The Exercise

The purpose of this exercise is to encourage sleep that benefits you most. When your sleep-programme is complete, you wake automatically but difficulties often arise in getting to sleep initially, and returning to sleep if you are disturbed in the middle of the night. Inability to sleep when first going to bed is usually due to worry or over-excitement. Both these states, negative worry and positive excitement, produce powerful images reflecting activity in the outer world. These overshadow and prevent passive images, which precede and invite sleep, from manifesting in the mind's eye.

Insomnia may also be due to sleeping during the day. Many older people indulge in this, then wonder why they cannot sleep at night. Apart from not being tired, sleeping during the day breaks up their sleeping pattern to such an extent that day turns into night, and night into a wakeful nightmare.

Returning to sleep in the middle of the night, having been disturbed, can be difficult, especially if you wake up half-way through one of those 90-minute phases. Again, thoughts from the real world tend to take over, and if these are allowed to dominate, passive thoughts leading to the inner realm of sleep and dreams cannot manifest.

The following exercises will help you benefit fully from your sleep. If you already sleep well and do not have to be woken up with an alarm clock which deprives you of valuable sleep-time, these exercises will not apply to you. Consider, however, if you really *do* have sufficient sleep, if your level of sleep is deep enough to recharge you fully, and if further benefit could be reaped from an improved sleeping pattern.

If you have difficulty in getting to sleep, yet you are tired, this is almost certainly due to an over-active state of mind. Bedtime is not the time to think intelligently about the real world and its problems; this belongs to the acutely awake state during the day. Thoughts anchored on the outer world make it impossible to sleep, until mental exhaustion takes over. By focusing on a passive symbol it is possible to overcome this form of insomnia, which is due to uncontrolled thoughts.

Cheese and heavy meals are often blamed for bad dreams. There are some people who can eat cheese and partake of enormous meals and still sleep soundly. Others, however, suffer a disturbed night if they eat in this way. The high fat content in cheese is not easily digested by everyone and those who have this digestive problem will find their sleep is disturbed. It is over-activity of the digestive system that is incorporated into dreams, not the cheese or other food, and it is this that causes the trouble.

Good quality sleep results from good sleeping habits, but these habits sometimes have to be cultivated. By practising the following exercises, and trying to get to bed earlier if you feel you are suffering from lack of sleep, you will soon discover that you can control your sleeping pattern. In return, you will find your days will be much more productive, harmonious and happier in every way.

Exercise 2—Your Sleeping Pattern

The following suggestions will help to induce good quality sleep and encourage a good sleeping pattern.

If heavy meals prevent you from sleeping peacefully, try to have your last meal of the day earlier in the evening.

Do not eat fatty food, such as cheese, last thing at night. Instead, eat an apple or a few grapes, and have a drink of water.

Discover precisely how many hours sleep you need each night.

Set yourself a 'going to sleep time,' as well as a 'waking-up time'.

If you have to get up at a certain time, set the alarm for this, then count back the number of hours sleep you need. This will tell you the exact time you need to go to sleep.

Discipline yourself to be in bed 30 minutes before your 'going to sleep' time.

Read a book to detract your thoughts away from worries or exciting circumstances which belong to the outside world.

To prepare yourself for sleep, your attention must be withdrawn from the outer world and focused within yourself.

Repeat the following message, to yourself:
'I have tried to solve my problems intelligently while awake; now I am going to see them from another standpoint while asleep, so over to you, dreaming mind.'

Having completed this, and other exercises, you are now ready to go to sleep. Select one of the following passive images which will lead you into the Land of Dreams: *a gold cross, a tree, a bird in flight.*

Summary

Sleep   — allows you to dream.
            — relaxes you.
            — has many different phases and levels.
            — has a definite pattern which should not be broken.
            — occupies one-third of your life.
            — recharges you physically and psychologically.
            — is elusive when thoughts become anchored on worry and the outer world.
            — is disturbed by over-activity of the digestive system.
            — is an escape route.
            — is nature's great healer.

3.

Dream Recall and the Dream Diary

We all dream but not everyone remembers their dreams. Unless you are really interested in your dreams and are prepared to think about them the moment you wake up, they tend to fade from memory very quickly indeed. It is for this reason that many people believe they do not dream. The first step towards remembering, therefore, is to become sincerely interested in what your dreams are trying to tell you, for undoubtedly this is what they are attempting to do.

An excellent way to remember dreams is to positively programme yourself just before going to sleep through the power of your creative imagination. By creating an inner vision, a day-dream, of yourself waking up in the morning, going over every detail of the night's dreaming, and then remembering it clearly, is an approach that tells your dreaming mind exactly what your intentions are. And since your dreaming mind is always ready to receive suggestions and instructions, a link is forged between that aspect of yourself and your conscious, awake state, thus allowing a two-way system of communication to develop.

Having decided on this positive approach to your dreams, the next priority is to make sure that the dreams, once remembered, are recorded. Passing them on verbally to a partner helps, but a permanent record is essential. And the simplest and best method is to write down the memory of a dream or dreams immediately on waking, or to record them on a small tape recorder. This, however, will have to be transcribed later and permanently recorded in your Dream Diary.

Your Dream Diary

It was Hugh Lynn, Edgar Cayce's son, who said that the most informative book you will ever read on dreams is the one you write yourself. He was referring to the personal Dream Diary conscientiously kept by those interested in receiving unique messages and help from their dreams. The importance of a Dream Diary cannot be overestimated, especially when it is realized that—since many dreams are prophetic—often they cannot be proved to be so until several years have elapsed.

The Diary

The first rule in keeping a dream diary is practicality, yet at the same time it has a ritualistic value and significance. This entails purchasing an attractive notebook and pen, to be kept exclusively as your Dream Diary. Simple though this first step is, it is a commitment, an act of faith which informs and reminds your dreaming mind—that aspect of yourself responsible for producing dreams—that you really are serious in your quest for self-help and self-knowledge from this source.

Having purchased a pen and special notebook for your Dream Diary, place them by your bedside where they must, at all costs, remain because there will not be time to look for them when they are needed.

The Day, Date, Time and Number

The second rule in keeping a Dream Diary is a further practical consideration, and concerns the day, the date, the time and the number of the dream. It is important that the day as well as the date is written at the top of the page because certain dreams have a habit of appearing, say, on Mondays or on Saturdays. These entries should be done each night in readiness before going to sleep.

Dating reveals many things, especially sequences and serial-dreams, which are far more common than is often realized. It also reveals that the dreaming mind is a fantastic clock and calendar, which remembers birthdays, anniversaries and memorable events from the past. Dreams recurring at regular intervals can also be easily spotted through this system of dating.

If the time of a dream is known it should be recorded; this usually coincides with the waking time. Numbering dreams in the order of appearance for a year at a time is important too, and applies especially to a series of dreams occurring on the same night or on consecutive nights. Serial dreaming can be encouraged and is particularly valuable to writers and poets.

Speed

The third rule in keeping a Dream Diary is that you write down all you can remember about your night's dreaming as speedily and as soon as possible after waking, before the images vanish. If you cannot remember anything at all, write instead the feeling or mood you have at that moment. These moods or feelings have been produced by your dreams, even though the dreams themselves may not be recalled consciously.

Any delay in recording the night's experiences will rob you of valuable information, so do not bother at this stage about the order in which you write down items, events, conversations, feelings and colours. All this will fall into place later when your dreams are rewritten in readiness for analysing. Since the initial recording of dreams is only a draft, it is a good practice to write them first on a scrap of paper, so keep a few loose sheets for this purpose in your dream diary.

Atmosphere, Mood and Feeling

The most important feature of every dream is the atmosphere, mood or feeling it leaves in its wake. These indicate the nature of the dream, and it is this that creates the backcloth in front of which the dream-scene is enacted, so deciding on this is really the first priority when it comes to recording the dream itself.

A haunting, happy, gloomy, romantic or bright atmosphere will give you considerable information concerning the origin and theme contained in the dream. And if you feel happy and contented on waking, you know your night's dreaming has offered you confidence, reassurance and encouragement to face whatever circumstances lie ahead. On the other hand, should you wake with a cloud of deep depression surrounding you, and you feel uneasy, it means your dreams, although perhaps not remembered, have none the less reflected problems relating to a particular situation.

Objects and Symbols

Next, make a note of any objects and symbols. These will include people, animals, creatures, monsters and plants, as well as objects such as houses, cars, trains, bicycles, tables, vases, and so on. Geometrical shapes, numbers and archetypal symbols representing ideals, religious messages and those with mystical significance should also be noted.

Journeys and Travel

Long and short journeys are commonly experienced in dreams. They denote your way through life—your destinational journey. The mode of transport in your dream symbolizes this. Walking, for example, shows efforts made at present are entirely self-generated and self-supporting, whereas travelling by public transport tends to suggest that the dreamer is being carried along with the rest of humanity. A railway station or bus-stop tells the dreamer to decide in which direction he wants to travel next. Actually missing a bus or train indicates that he does not make the most of his chances when they arise so tends to lose opportunities to achieve or succeed.

Colours and Conversations

Most dreams are in colour, but—along with the memory of a dream—these fade quickly with a result that many people believe they dream only in black and white. Grey atmospheres or dull scenes are part of the dream's attempt to draw special attention to a particularly grey or dull situation, so it is not a question of them being in simply black or white rather than colour.

Conversations can be, metaphorically speaking, very colourful, and in dreams these include puns, poems, rhymes, songs, keywords, and apparently meaningless messages. These messages are often in code and, since it is the dreamer who concocted them, it is the dreamer who, after sifting through all the clues, discovers what it is that he is trying to say to himself.

Previous Associations

Since a dream reflects a problem, aim, or a situation requiring careful and maybe serious consideration, it often includes references to previous events. These may originate from television programmes the night before, newspaper items, encounters from the previous day, and past events generally, so noting these can be very valuable indeed when it comes to piecing together the component parts that go to make up the entire dream.

The Dream Itself

Having recorded all the details and aspects of a dream as suggested, you will then be in possession of a rough sketch covering your nocturnal adventures. At a convenient time during the following day this will have to be re-written in readiness for interpretation. The final account of your night's dreaming should therefore be similar in format (but not in content) to the following examples (if possible, give your dream a title—this usually reflects the theme of the dream).

Dream 1

Day and Date:	Friday, 2 March 1990.
Time:	Between 6.00 a.m. and 7.30 a.m.
Number:	125.
Atmosphere:	Intellectual.
Mood:	Aware and alert.
Objects and Symbols:	A lecturer. A hall or classroom. Other people although they were insignificant.
Journeys or Travel:	None.
Colour and Conversations:	The place was bright and light. A lecture.
Previous Associations:	TV programme on education.

The Dream—'The Lesson'
I was at a lecture in a school hall or classroom but I did not really understand what was being said. The subject was important to me and even in the dream I tried very hard to hear every word and try to make it into some form of sense.

Dream 2

Day and Date:	Tuesday, 3 April 1990.
Time:	4.00 a.m.
Number:	201.
Atmosphere:	Dark, spooky.
Mood:	Frightening.
Objects and Symbols:	Steps, cellar, table, cup.
Journeys and Travel:	Walking down steps.
Colour and Conversations:	None:
Previous Associations:	None recalled.

The Dream—'The Cellar'
There was a flight of stone steps descending into a basement or cellar. I went down them and found it to be frightening and spooky. In the half-light I could see an old table with an empty cup standing in the middle. On waking this left me with a worried, disturbed feeling which stayed with me throughout the next day.

The Exercise

To work with your dreams it is necessary to collect as many as possible, so having taken the practical step of purchasing a book to be used exclusively as a Dream Diary, the next step is to make sure they are remembered.

Since the language of dreams is pictorial and symbolic, and not verbal and literal, requests for remembering them meet with more success when made through the power of the imagination. By using this form of communication, namely imagery or visualization, the dreaming mind understands and responds to that which you consciously need, so on waking you will discover that the memory of your dreams is sharp and clear. They should, none the less, be recorded speedily because once the events of the day commence, they are easily overshadowed and forgotten.

Exercise 3—Remembering Your Dreams

You can positively programme yourself into remembering your dreams in the following way:

Make sure you are warm and comfortable in bed.

Close your eyes in readiness to use the power of your creative imagination.

Relax by breathing in to the count of *three*, and then out to the count of *ten*.

Repeat this twice more.

Without moving, *imagine* you have just woken up in the morning.

With your eyes still closed, imagine and experience what it feels like to remember a dream.

See yourself, again in your creative imagination, writing an account of your night's activities.

Relax for a few minutes by looking at a beautiful *tree*, in your mind's eye.

On waking next morning, try not to move or think of the day ahead, but cast your thoughts back over the night's dreaming.

As soon as possible, reach for your pen and notebook and write down every detail you can remember of your dreams.

Summary

Dreams — are not always remembered, although everyone dreams.
— need to be recognized as unique sources of wisdom and understanding.
— can be recalled on waking by positively programming yourself, before going to sleep, into remembering them.
— should be recorded in a Dream Diary.
— fade in the light of day.
— sometimes occur in serial form, unfolding a story episode-by-episode.
— all have an atmosphere which sets the backcloth to the dream.
— leave behind a mood or feeling, even though the dream itself may not be remembered.
— have themes and these can be used as titles for your dreams.

4.

The Incubation of Dreams

Dreams were once looked upon as oracles and interpreting them was considered to be a form of divination. Today, in the light of modern psychology, they are still regarded as unique sources of enlightenment but are also viewed more as personal psychic experiences which offer the dreamer opportunities to expand his awareness and understanding of life. Maybe it is only the terminology that has changed—after all, a dream is still a dream and still has powers which defy logical explanation.

To ensure that they received answers to their problems in this way, the ancients incubated their dreams. Incubation, from the Latin *incubare*—to lie down upon, involved lying down in a special shrine upon a dream bed. Once asleep, angelic hosts or messengers of the gods would visit the dreamer and deliver a special dream offering solutions, help, comfort or healing.

Greek literature describes how those with problems travelled to such shrines, leaving votive inscriptions, testifying that problems had been solved and cures had taken place. Some of these inscriptions can still be seen today. Delphi, the shrine of Apollo, and the Temple of Epidauros in Greece, and the Ascelpienon of Memphis in Egypt, were famous for their dream sancturies.

Indian and Japanese literature describe shrines similar to those found in the Middle East. Long before Buddhism came to the East, there was one such Shinto temple at Usa in Kyushi where Japanese emperors incubated dreams in order to solve problems of State. Dreams were considered to be part of the ruler's religious duty and so in his palace there was a dream-hall, with a special incubation bed, known as a *kamudoko*. Made of polished stone, it would have been most uncomfortable yet it was upon this that the emperors slept and received their enlightening dreams.

Seeking dreams through invoking the power of the gods was widely practised throughout the world from at least 4000 BC down to 2000 BC. At Abusir, on the fringe of the western desert to the south of Cairo, there once stood the great temple of the healing god, Imhotep. An explorer writing in the 10th century AD described this shrine in detail and in particular the oracular dream cavern itself. In this cavern, 900 years ago, there was, according to this explorer, a seated statue of Joseph, the son of Jacob, who interpreted the Pharaoh's dreams. The reason this statue was placed here, in the dream sanctuary of Imhotep, was that this sacred place later became the prison where Joseph was incarcerated by the pharaoh. In this atmosphere, it was not surprising that the baker and the butcher, both prisoners along with Joseph, dreamed such prophetic dreams, which Joseph interpreted correctly. It was the interpretation of these prisoners' dreams that drew the pharoah's attention to Joseph, so had it not been for them, Joseph would almost certainly have remained in prison.

Inducing dreams through incubation was an accepted practice of the Hebrew Fathers. In Genesis 28:10–22 details are given of the ancient Canaanite sanctuary which Jacob created and retreated to in order to communicate with divine forces in sleep through his dreams. His stone pillow, like that of the Japanese kamudoko dream bed, seems to have played an important role in the incubation of his dreams, including the most famous of these, the 'Jacob's Ladder' dream.

The importance of stone in the incubation ritual and its significance as the foundation of the corner stone of the Temple is shown in the account of the Jacob's Ladder dream which he experienced in Canaan, prior to building the Temple. 'Then Jacob rose early in the morning and took the stone that he had put at his head, set it up as a pillar and poured oil on top of it. And this stone which I have set as a pillar shall be God's house and of all that you give me I will surely give a tenth to thee' (Genesis 28:18). In addition there is, perhaps, also the question of a near dream pun with the play upon the words 'pillar' and 'pillow'.

In I Samuel 3 it transpires that it was a regular practice of Samuel to 'lay down and sleep in the temple at Shiloh before the Ark and receive the word of the Lord'. And in I Kings 3:5, Solomon follows the recognized custom when he sleeps and dreams in the hill shrine of Gideon. 'In Gideon the Lord appeared to Solomon in a dream by night and God said "Ask what I shall give thee".'

Messengers of Dreams

It is clearly stated in the Bible that God speaks to us through our dreams. 'For God speaketh once, yea twice yet man perceiveth it not. In a dream, in a vision of the night when deep sleep falleth upon men slumbering upon their bed, then He openeth their ears and sealeth in their instructions' (Job 33:14–16). According to Greek legend, it was Hypnos, the god of sleep, and Morpheus, the god of dreams, with the help of Hermes their messenger, who sent warnings, inspirations and prophecies to mortals as they slept in dream temples and shrines.

Today, religious practices do not include the incubation of dreams as a way of seeking God's help, nor are there temples or shrines dedicated to Hypnos and Morpheus in which to sleep, 'perchance to dream'. But this does not mean the age of miraculous dreaming is past, nor that the divine messengers who convey dreams have deserted us. The temples and shrines we seek are still to be found, but they are within, not without, and the gods of old are there too, although they are now perceived more in the Jungian sense and recognized as universal principles and archetypal forces.

So the divine angelic hosts are still here, along with the gods, but as of old they will not necessarily present themselves unless an effort is made to communicate with them first. It is true that all dreams have messages, but it is also true that the right dream does not always appear at the right time, unless a specific request is made. Incubating a dream is making that specific request.

Incubating a Dream

In present-day language, incubating a dream simply means requesting a dream relating to a particular problem, aim, hope or fear, along with advice, an answer or a solution. The contribution of the gods is still important, and this is reflected in the incubation process itself, which begins with self-hypnotic programming—Hypnos's influence—followed by a special dream—Morpheus's response.

The time to incubate a dream is just before going to sleep, and the place is a warm, comfortable bed. But before making your request it is necessary to become physically relaxed yet at the same time mentally alert. To achieve this relaxed state of concentration, those who incubated their dreams centuries ago paid particular attention to this aspect, so not only did they sleep and dream in a special shrine, they carried out a sequence of rituals beforehand as well.

Principally, this was a sacrifical act of purification and dedication, involving abstinence from sex, refraining from eating flesh, fish or fowl, and drinking water only, for 48 hours prior to making a request. An offering was also made to the deity to be invoked in the form of a gift or service. In today's terms, this ritual is seen as psychological conditioning—a commitment and a payment by way of a donation to charity or by being of service to others.

The response from dreaming is only half the story—the unconscious half. The other half, the conscious counterpart, is just as important and this is why relaxing, positively programming yourself, and formulating a clear request before going to sleep is necessary if the incubation of a dream is to be of any value.

The Exercise

Having accepted the basic principles underlying the incubation of dreams, the way in which a dream is incubated—and its success—depends on individual beliefs and the degree to which you are prepared to dedicate and commit yourself to carrying out the procedure. If your religious beliefs are such that you rely entirely on God for support and help, then the request for a special dream should be made in the form of an invocative prayer. On the other hand, if you believe that God helps those who help themselves, the request should be made directly to your dreaming mind, that aspect of yourself which is capable of contacting archetypal forces and is responsible for projecting dreams.

Each request will be different but whatever the nature of the problem or question, the more concise the plea, the clearer will be the responding dream.

Rambling requests receive rambling replies, so having decided on the problem or question, it then has to be succinctly included in a requesting prayer, or incorporated into a personal affirmation.

An invocative prayer on the following lines is suggested:

'Almighty God, from whom all good things come, please send me a dream to show me how to accept the situation; help me to understand; make me well again; make someone else better; know which way to go. I shall accept this advice and act upon it as best I can. Thank you, God. Amen.'

A positive affirmation, where you speak directly to yourself, should be more authoritative and instructive, and so the following lines are suggested:

'Dreaming mind, please send me a clear dream to show me precisely how to accept the situation; help me to understand; get well again; make someone else better; or, know which way to go. I am ready to receive this information, I will write down every detail on waking and I will act upon it in the future. Thank you, dreaming mind.'

Write down your prayer or personal affirmation during the day before you incubate your dream. This ensures that all the necessary details are included in your request; it also represents the conscious, intellectual counterpart to the unconscious and inspirational dream aspect. Finally, this written declaration should, according to ancient dream-lore, be placed under your pillow on the night you incubate your dream.

Exercise 4—Incubation of your Dreams

From the list you made in 'Exercise 1—Your Worries, Fears, Needs and Aims', select the worry, fear, need or aim that is uppermost in your thoughts at present.

Read through your written declaration, which will be in the form of a prayer or a personal affirmation. Now place this under your pillow.

Having carried out the exercise which enables you to remember your dreams on waking, proceed now with the following exercise which begins with a progressive relaxation. You will then be ready to incubate a helpful, positive dream:

Relax further by lying flat on your back and tensing up your toes, and then letting them relax.

Turn your toes up towards your head, and then relax them down again.

Now clench both fists, and then let them relax.

Breathe in to the count of three, and let it out to the count of ten.

Repeat this exercise twice more.

Become aware of your physically relaxed state and of your mental alertness, enabling you to concentrate and control your thoughts.

You will now be able to think of your problem, aim, hope or fear without emotion.

Go over your problem, aim, hope or fear in your thoughts, seeing it as a scene in your imagination.

Now speak your request in the form of a prayer or as a personal affirmation, silently but positively, to yourself.

Take a deep breath, stretch a little, and prepare to go to sleep.

Think no more about your problem or hope until tomorrow. The ball is now out of your court.

Summary

Dreams
— were once incubated in sacred shrines.
— can still be incubated through an invocative prayer or a personal affirmation.
— are only half the story—they need a conscious counterpart.
— respond to a written request.
— provide help, information and ideas from unique sources, if specifically requested to do so.
— can be successfully incubated following relaxation and self-instruction in your own bed.
— reflect the request: concise instructions produce concise dreams, rambling instructions result in rambling dreams.
— are created by you.

5.

Lucid Dreaming

The term 'lucid dreaming', the realization that you *are* dreaming during a dream, was first introduced into the language of dreams early this century by a Dutchman named van Eeden. Until recently, this awareness was believed to be so rare and unimportant that even psychiatrists interested in dreams did not consider them worth investigating. Witness Freud, Jung and Adler's virtual lack of interest in lucid dreams. When, however, a cross-section of the community was asked if they had ever had a dream in which they knew they were dreaming, 73 per cent said they had.

Van Eeden, himself a prolific lucid dreamer, found these dreams were sometimes preceded a few nights previously with flying dreams but the most important thing he discovered about them was that he was able to say during a dream 'this is a dream'.

During the 1980s Dr Keith Hearne from Hull has extensively studied lucid dreamers and their dreams. In his dream laboratory he uses his own apparatus to measure ocular signalling, REM, which establishes communication between the sleeping subject and the dream investigator. A further aspect of his work is directed towards encouraging lucid dreaming by externally stimulating the dreamer with another of his devices, the dream machine.

From this work further information has been discovered concerning the electro-physiological function of the brain and the type of sleep associated with lucid dreaming. These discoveries have physiological, psychological and psychic implications which not only add academically to the understanding of dreams, but open up an entirely new avenue of exploration.

Apart from dreamers knowing they are dreaming, another characteristic of lucid dreaming is that colours and details are far more vivid than when awake. Furthermore, it is often the fantastic nature of the imagery that causes the dreamer to say 'this is impossible, it must be a dream'.

Accepting that it is an aspect of our totality that creates dreams, and accepting too that we have little control over this aspect, it makes sense to at least try to become familiar with it. 'Know thyself' is the recognized goal of those who go to extremes to seek what they call Englightenment, and it is also the unrecognized goal of those who simply want to understand themselves, others, and the purpose of life generally, so where better to begin than with the personal inner-instigator of dreams?

To know you are dreaming is the first step; the next step is to *alter* a dream. Control, therefore, is the important issue when considering lucid dreaming. In effect, the question is not can you create your dreams (because you do this already) but can you *control* them?

Dreams reflect and draw attention to many things in life we have failed to notice when awake—they point out our faults honestly, alert us of danger, admonish us for our bad behaviour and reactions, caution us about ill-health, and present us with visions of the future. Thus they are already fulfilling an invaluable, indispensable role. There is therefore no point in controlling them in this respect—indeed to do so would interfere with the essential, natural, psychological processing of information.

Dreaming lucidly nevertheless has three important functions in addition to the above-mentioned attributes. The first is that if we consciously become aware of the unconscious aspect of ourselves that creates dreams, we are discovering something new about ourselves. The second is that if we can consciously alter a dream-scene in sleep, it helps us to alter our lives by consciously controlling imaging, thinking and actions when awake. The third function of lucid dreaming, and this is the most important of all, is that since some dreams are premonitions, and come true, it is possible to create a dream-situation which can, in fact, come true.

The implications of this are enormous. Not only is a link forged with the conscious and unconscious, a state hoped to be achieved through endless meditation, but an entirely new perspective of life and destiny is revealed. In theory and in practice it is possible to attain aims and goals in this way and—more importantly—self-help and self-healing become distinct possibilities.

Becoming a successful lucid dreamer introduces the question of ethics. If it is possible to produce positive consequences, then it is possible to produce negative consequences too. An individual who attempts to negatively programme a dream adversely involving or affecting another person already harbours ill-thoughts and would put them into action when awake, anyway. Through action and re-action they can only reap that which they have sown, so on every level—awake and asleep—such manipulation would be disastrous for them.

To achieve results, a combination of dream-incubation, lucidity and positive programming is necessary. This is a step-by-step process, but before attempting it you must decide whether or not you really want to do this and, if you do, for what good purpose. 73 per cent of people, if not everyone, has had a spontaneous lucid dream, so this in itself is not unique. Becoming lucid in a dream *at will* on the other hand, and then manipulating it, is.

Assuming you have a problem or are in circumstances which you feel could be helped by dreaming about it lucidly, the next step is to incubate this dream-state before going to sleep. You may be successful the first time you request this, but it usually takes a little practice. Having achieved it, however, which you will if you are sincere in your desire, you will find yourself transported into a world which is truly your own. From personal experience, I have found that sometimes there is a fear of being trapped in this ultra-real yet at the same time unreal world, but once you become immersed in the surrounding scene and action, this palls into insignificance!

Initially, the scene in which you find yourself will have been created involuntarily and you will be a lucid spectator. As this realization crystalizes you will be motivated to carry out certain feats, if only to prove to yourself that you really do have power over your own unique dream world. It is said, however, that even in this self-created situation it is impossible to break a wine glass. And hard as a glass is thrown to the floor, it always remains intact. Another feat said to be impossible of performance is that of switching a light on or off, so when the opportunity arises, as it will, try this to prove or disprove it.

Having satisfied yourself that you can achieve lucidity and possess abilities in this state you do not have when awake, you can then begin to consider altering the dream-setting and the action. At this stage it is only an additional step to freeing yourself and flying astrally up to the ceiling. During this feat you will be able to view yourself objectively, standing or sitting below. The only valid reason for doing this, however, is if you wish to heal yourself.

Health is not the only problem to be helped through lucid dreaming. Consider a forthcoming interview for a much desired job. By creating this interview in a lucid dream, inventing the circumstances and the characters, and then producing a harmonious meeting with a satisfactory outcome, your unconscious self is already programmed for success.

The Exercise

It is possible to become conscious of the fact that you are dreaming in a dream, and once having accomplished this you will then be in a position to begin to manipulate and control it. Not everyone wishes to do this but if you do, this exercise will lay down safe foundations allowing you to know yourself better, discover the aspect of yourself that is in control, develop self-confidence, and help the natural processes of healing, should you need it.

Self-control is the major issue in lucid dreamwork, as indeed it should be in life as a whole. No one has the right to dominate or control another, nor indeed should circumstances weigh so heavily upon a person that these adversely affect their lives. If you feel threatened when awake, then by confronting whatever or whoever it is in a lucid dream—not aggressively but intelligently and objectively—amazing resolutions can be achieved.

If you misuse your creative power in a lucid dream, it will lead to further problems, so make sure you do not interfere with or harm anyone or anything. The simple rule to remember, for safety and a positive outcome is *'integrate, not eliminate'*.

Exercise 5 — Lucid Dreaming

Having decided you want to develop the ability to dream lucidly, at will, consider the ethics and valid reasons for doing this. Remind yourself that what you do and how you behave when awake complements your dreamwork when asleep. It is the combined effort of your conscious and unconscious efforts that brings about success.

Begin by incubating a dream before going to sleep, in which you will realize you are dreaming.

As soon as you become aware that you are dreaming, attempt a small feat. Make a cup and saucer appear on a table, or materialize a picture on a wall. Be creative and inventive.

The next phase is to use your ability to enhance your life in some way. If you write songs, sit down and write one, if not, see yourself achieving a small but positive aim.

If you have a problem, see yourself resolving this in a way that makes you, and anyone else involved, happy.

To heal yourself, see yourself as you would like to be, strong and well. Again, be creative and original in doing this.

The ability to dream lucidly and manipulate scenes and actions is progressive. The rules to follow are those of positivity and selflessness, never negativity and selfishness.

Summary

Lucid dreams   — are dreams in which you realize you are dreaming.
  — give dreamers the opportunity to control their dreams.
  — open up entirely new possibilities which help you to understand yourself and others.
  — combined with incubation and positive programming produce scenes of real problems, hopes, aims and ambitions.
  — offer the artist, writer, musician or otherwise creative person unique opportunities to realize their latent talents.
  — help to enhance self-healing.
  — can come true.

6.

When is a Dream Not a Dream?

During sleep, psychological and physiological changes take place. The brainwaves alter, muscles relax and contract, the heart-rate slows and quickens, the blood pressure decreases and increases, and the digestive system, except when coping with an indigestible meal, is less active. Sometimes these changes are incorporated into a dream—and are responsible for some nightmares. A high temperature, especially in children, frequently gives rise to hallucinations, and pain is often symbolized as appropriate traumatic action. An example of this is the dreamer who suffered from headaches and noted that when these occurred during sleep, they were represented in a disturbing dream of birds pecking at a loaf of bread.

Paralysis and Light Sleep Experiences

Most of us have dreamed at some time or other of being chased by someone or something and found we are unable to run or move. This feeling of immobility is not a dream; it is real, because during certain phases of sleep the muscular reflexes associated with the limbs disappear, and the sleeper is, in fact, paralysed. If the unconscious realization of this penetrates through to the conscious level, as it often does in light sleep, it is then incorporated into a dream where the dreamer finds him or herself rooted to the spot, unable to escape from some unknown pursuer.

This experience usually rouses the dreamer and on waking they discover they are unable to move, but only momentarily. Immediately they open their eyes the reflexes return and the muscles are once again under their conscious control.

Waking suddenly with the feeling you have just inadvertantly stepped off a kerb is another experience occuring in early sleep. This again is not a dream but is due to the sudden contraction of the limb-muscles, causing a 'myoclonic jerk'. Spasm of these muscles in this way is exactly what does happen when we do step off a kerb accidentally, so not surprisingly this action is associated with that feeling and incorporated into a dream which reminds us of this.

Another early sleep experience is that of falling. This is not to be confused with the exciting feeling of flying. The feeling of falling through space is due to the conscious appreciation of an altered state of awareness, namely moving from the awake state to the sleep state. 'Falling asleep' or 'dropping off to sleep' are common expressions originating from this experience.

During light sleep noises outside in the street and those in the home, especially the telephone ringing, are sometimes incorporated into a dream. Bells ringing—literally and symbolically—are alerting signals, so either way the interpretation amounts to a warning. Not every noise necessarily has a message, but all will play a role in the dream into which they have intruded.

False Awakenings

Since dreams are (among other things) memories, in retrospect it is often impossible to distinguish with absolute certainty if a memory reflects a real event or a dream. An example of this is the belief that we wake up in the middle of the night and see someone standing by the bed. The person is so real, as indeed they are in dreams, that in the morning we are convinced that we were awake and really saw them. Dreaming we are awake is known as a 'false awakening' and, although this explains some of the visions seen during the night, it does not account for all of them.

Sleep-Walking and Sleep-Talking

Somnambulism, better known as sleep-walking, occurs when the action in a dream is put into operation. Children do this far more than adults because they are less inhibited and more agile; it is therefore not a question of growing out of the habit, as has been suggested in the past, but rather that of psychological control and physical restriction. Sleep-walking in adults is most likely to occur when they are worried or ill, and especially when they have a fever. Unlike children, who often wander downstairs in a sleep-state, adults do not usually take more than a few steps.

Talking when asleep is an attempt to consciously express a dream verbally. It is possible to carry on a conversation with a sleeping person and ask them questions but their replies are not entirely reliable. When a dreamer recently uttered the name 'Anna' in his sleep, his wife became very suspicious, believing he had a girlfriend of this name. She began questioning him but his replies were mainly unintelligible and it was not until the morning when he was fully awake that he was able to convince his wife that 'Anna' was a character in a book he was reading.

Recurring Dreams

Certain dreams recur over and over again, some beginning in childhood. Other dreams repeat themselves over a few months, weeks, or perhaps only days, and they do this for just one reason—to draw attention to their message. Once this is recognized, and if necessary acted upon, that particular dream will never occur again. Why should it? It has fulfilled its function and informed the dreamer.

An example of this is the dreamer who, from early childhood, dreamed over and over again that she was in a lion's den where a lion was about to attack her. It has been explained that she had probably heard of such an event when she was a small child and had carried the memory of this as a frightening image for all those years, but this explanation did not stop the nightmares. It was not until it was suggested to her that she may have been one of those unfortunate victims in Roman times who had been thrown to the lions, and it was the memory of this, re-enacted in repetitive dreams, that the nightmare stopped. Whether this explanation was correct or not, it sufficed, for they never recurred again.

A Dream Within a Dream

Just as it is possible to dream we are awake, so too can we dream we are asleep, and also dream within *that* sleep. It has been suggested that in dreams within dreams a deeper level of awareness is reached but since few of these are of an illuminating nature, there is little evidence to support this theory. A more likely explanation is that a particular point is being emphasized in the hope that the dreamer will discover it.

Serial Dreams

Serial dreams are those dreams which advance the theme that ran through preceding dreams. It is possible to dream, wake up and then go back to sleep and continue with the same dream. At other times, serial dreams span two or three nights or even weeks and months, and it is then that literary masterpieces may be received.

In his book '*Across The Plains*' Robert Louis Stevenson described how complete stories came to him in a succession of dreams. Before going to sleep each night he would re-read the previous night's dream-script, go to sleep and progress the theme. Graham Greene is another great writer who apparently wakes up four or five times in a night to record storylines offered up to him by his unshackled dreaming mind.

Telepathy and Teleportation in Dreams

There is evidence to show that telepathic messages are exchanged in dreams. One dreamer recently dreamed he had won the pools and next morning he received a cheque for two hundred pounds—not from a pools win but from another unexpected source. Other telepathic dreams are not so happy, in particular those of relatives and friends who seem to be in trouble and, when contacted next day, confirm this to be the case.

An extension of telepathy is teleportation. This is where the dreamer is actually seen, either in a reciprocal dream or as a ghostly vision, by the person of whom they are dreaming. This happened to a mother in Britain who dreamed her daughter in Australia was very ill. On telephoning her daughter in the morning she not only discovered that her dream had proved correct, but that her daughter had actually seen her mother standing by her bedside. The vision of the mother may well have been seen by the daughter in a false awakening, but whatever the explanation it is an amazing experience showing that dreams and the unconscious have powers far beyond conscious recognition and reckoning.

Flying Dreams

When asked, seven out of ten people said they had experienced at some time or another a dream in which they were flying. By jumping into the air and then flapping their arms they were able to rise above the ground. Some even managed to fly outside into the streets, over houses and out into the countryside.

Practical theorists explain this experience as a dream reflecting an ancestral memory from the days when, according to Darwin, our ancestors were birds. Psychiatrists recognize flying in dreams as a form of depersonalization but, although this gives it a name, it fails to explain the mechanism supporting it. The psychic name for this is *astral projection*, a state whereby the spirit of the dreamer leaves his body and weightlessly flies free.

Every night apparently many dreamers 'ghosts' leave their bodies and are teleported to far away places on missions of healing. When Tudor Pole, a well-known pre-war archaeologist, writer and broadcaster, was in Egypt, he was taken ill with a tropical fever. As he dozed on a houseboat on the Nile he dreamed someone knocked on his cabin door and a British doctor entered dressed in a black coat, striped trousers and a top hat, the traditional dress for doctors in the 1930s. The doctor took off his top hat and placed it on a table beside Tudor Pole, who was fascinated by this because he could see right through it. The doctor prescribed something for the malady and then went on to say that he was in practice in Britain and often left his body in sleep to heal people who needed his help.

A feverish fancy, many may say, but Tudor Pole was soon well again, convinced the doctor had saved him. On returning to England, he appealed over the BBC radio for the doctor to come forward. He did. He was a Scottish general practitioner who confirmed that he regularly astrally travelled to heal the sick. He also confirmed that his daily attire, including the top hat, was just as Tudor Pole described it.

Health and Dreams

Certain illnesses have particular characteristics which manifest as bad dreams. As already mentioned, fevers may give rise to hallucinations and pain can be symbolized as an action or an object, but in addition to these, a sudden increase in the heart-beat frequently awakens the dreamer in a disturbed state. This is not usually associated with a heart problem but it may be a warning to take life a little easier.

Traditionally, it was believed that chest complaints manifested in dreams as fights and difficult journeys, kidney problems appeared as overful canals, stomach trouble presented as disputes, liver problems manifested as green grass, lawns and bushes, and anaemia was revealed as feelings of suffocation. Obviously, these experiences are unreliable indicators of ill-health, but if nightmares of this nature persist it would be wise to consult a doctor to put your mind at rest.

Prophetic Dreams and Premonitions

Dreams really do come true—at least, some of them do. The difference between a prophecy and a premonition is that a prophecy is due to unconscious deductions from subliminal perception, on a causal chain. Premonitions, on the other hand, result from what can only be called extra-sensory perception, which is acausal.

In true premonitions, names, places, and occasionally times, are given of a future event which may or may not involve the dreamer. Although premonitions are usually associated with catastrophes, by no means are all of them. The majority are extremely trivial—so trivial in fact that most of them pass unnoticed. Yet how often have we said 'that has broken my dream' when a word or incident re-enacts that which took place earlier in a dream?

Premonitions are, initially, warnings. Only when they come true are they premonitions. This means steps could be taken to avert a disaster but unfortunately few people heed such warnings. A mother, whose son was a weekend flyer, training for his pilot's licence, tried to warn her son when she dreamed his 'plane dived into the sea, by a seaside pier. On being told this he assured his mother that he never flew anywhere near the sea so her dream could not possibly come true. On arriving at the aerodrome on the following Saturday the dreamer's son was told he was going to fly along the south coast. Still ignoring his mother's warning, he took off and the 'plane flew into the sea to the west of one of the south coast piers. Both the instructor and the dreamer's son were drowned.

The Exercise

This exercise will help you to distinguish any physiological origin or involvement in your dreams. Not all experiences during sleep, as we have seen, are dreams in the strictest sense, so it is helpful to be able to recognize those arriving from physical changes. Dreams arising from these causes always produce the same experiences in everyone (such as the feeling of being rooted to the spot, falling through space and the myoclonic jerk).

Having said this, these experiences, when incorporated into a dream, often have a message as well. The physical changes are present each night but they are used only if and when they can play a useful role. Usually this is a warning role. Take the dream where you are rooted to the spot and cannot move—symbolically, this means you are in a situation about which you can do very little.

Flying experiences in sleep, whether an ancestral memory, psychological depersonalization or psychic astral projection, convey the happy message that the dreamer can rise above his problems. It has also been noted that the dreamer who can fly in this way rarely becomes depressed.

No experience when asleep is worthless; even the worst nightmares have their uses, but it is up to the individual dreamer to discover exactly what this is.

Exercise 6—When is a Dream Not a Dream?

Enquire from other people if they have nocturnal experiences or not—strictly dreams but nevertheless remembered experiences. Discover how many actually fly at night, have recurring dreams, serial dreams, dreams within a dream, and so on.

Read through your Dream Diary and note any dream which you think may have been due to physiological causes.

If you remember feeling rooted to the spot in a dream reconcile this with the normal immobilization occurring during certain stages of sleep.

In the nocturnal experience, where you think you are awake and see someone standing by your bedside, try to accept that this is a false awakening—a dream of being awake.

Dreams which recur should be reinterpreted in order to discover the message they are so insistently repeating.

Should you wish to write a story, suggest to your dreaming mind that it sends you a theme which will run through a series of dreams.

If a recurring dream disturbs you regularly, consider whether it is trying to warn you of a health problem. If necessary, heed its warning.

Summary

Dreams
— incorporate physiological changes which take place in sleep and sometimes use them to convey a message.
— known as false awakenings account for some apparitions seen in the night, but not all of them.
— when acted out physically produce sleep-walking and sleep-talking.
— which recur do so in order to draw attention to their important message.
— are so real they convince us we are awake when in fact we are dreaming.
— often carry a theme or story in serial form.

— convey telepathic messages.
— can be reciprocal.
— of flying and overcoming gravity are positive signs showing the dreamer can rise above their problems.
— reflect health problems.
— sometimes project into the future and in so doing can warn of and thus avert danger and catastrophes.

7.

Dreams and Their Language

To understand what our dreams are trying to tell us, we have to understand their language. They do not use words to express their meaning but communicate through visual imagery and, to a lesser extent, through the other four senses—hearing, smelling, tasting and touching. Once we know this and see our dreams as scenes and metaphorical word-pictures depicting various aspects of our life, we can begin to discover exactly what it is they are trying to say. Then all that is necessary is to translate the symbolic language of stand-ins into reality.

Imagery, whether pictures in the imagination when we are awake or scenes remembered from dreams when we were asleep, was once regarded as a primitive way of experiencing and expressing life compared with the later-developed spoken and written word. In the last ten years, however, it has been realized that not only is imagery superior and fundamental to verbal reasoning and communication, it is also its *origin*. It is, therefore, not a primitive form of appreciation at all; it is the primary source of all awareness.

Words can describe shapes and colours but they cannot possibly convey strong feelings such as fear, pain, hope, frustration and happiness—but imagery can. Romantic love, for example, is characterized perfectly by the shape of a heart. No phrase, however sentimental, can compare or compete with this image and the message it conveys.

Imagery, therefore, is not only the language of dreams, but of the unconscious as well. In dreams, however, the imagery is often representational and symbolic, meaning that people and scenes represent someone or something else. Mothers, for instance, frequently feature in dreams, but more often than not they symbolize compassionate, feminine principles and not the dreamer's mother. Another example is a recognizable friend who behaves out of character in a dream; most likely this person is acting as a stand-in for someone else. Similarly, a policeman suggests the question of authority in the dreamer's life.

The following dreams make sense when it is realized that some of the characters are representing principles, not people:

The Dream—'The Uphill Ramble'
I was on a ramble where the going was tough and uphill. It was an effort to keep up with the others who were with me but with effort I managed to do this. All the time I was concerned that my mother would be left behind.

Looking at this scene, the tough struggle can be seen to represent the dreamer's uphill path through life. It also shows she is trying to compete and keep up with her colleagues or friends. The concern for her mother is a warning indicating that she is leaving behind her compassionate principles and feelings in an effort to win in life.

The Dream—'The Friend'
A kind friend I trust and believe in was behaving in an unthinking and unkind manner. Although I wanted to confide in her, I hesitated to do so and felt let-down and disillusioned by her.

This dream highlights the question of friendship and the enormous responsibility one person can place on another. The flawless image the dreamer has of her friend must take some living up to, and it is this that the dream is pointing out. The message, therefore, is that she should accept her friend as she is and not expect so much of her—or of anyone come to that.

The Dream—'The Policeman'
As I drove my car along a road I noticed a policeman looking in my direction. I slowed down but he still seemed to be very interested in what I was doing and where I was going.

Driving a car along a road represents the dreamer's destiny, his way through life. In one respect, his life needs to be 'slowed down' a little or he could run into trouble and attract the attention of an authoritive body of some sort—this is symbolized by the policeman. By relating this warning to real circumstances, around which feelings of guilt apparently already exist, a problem could be averted before it is too late.

Dreams of the past, including those of our childhood homes and previous abodes, can also represent other times and other places. They are never mere sentimental, action-replay dreams, but are used for comparison or to reflect a time when life was uncomplicated and secure. This can be seen in the following dream:

The Dream—'My Childhood Home'
In this happy dream I was back in the house I lived in years ago as a child. Everything was exactly as I remember it to have been—the furniture, garden and my sisters and brother.

Home is a secure, happy place—or at least it should be. Our childhood home is certainly free from all the responsibility that goes with running it, so returning to it in dreams is an escape into the past, to a time when life was more secure. This rekindled memory is meant to increase the dreamer's confidence and give her a little self-assurance. It is also telling her that she should stop living in the past and begin to look ahead towards a more successful future.

Although this language of substitution may seem an unusual way for dreams to communicate, it is, in fact, very similar to the way in which we convey information when awake. Most conversations include figure-of-speech comparisons where one set of values or rules are used to describe another. A good example of this is the verbal picture of a visit to the spring sales, in search of a bargain. Frequently, this physically stressful, yet exciting, event is retold and expressed in terms of it being 'like a rugby scrum'. This description is then readily translated into vivid images by those who hear or read it, and a clear impression of the event is thus successfully transmitted.

In addition to individually chosen word-pictures, collective or common word-pictures in the form of metaphors, idioms and picturesque phrases are also widely used: 'Out of the frying pan and into the fire', 'Place the cart before the horse', 'If pigs could fly', 'All in the same boat' and dozens more are verbal attempts to express feelings and describe situations and circumstances.

Just as puns are used in conversation, so too do dreams sometimes use them to convey meanings and messages. These range from basic body-language punning, forming scenes portraying 'handing over responsibilities', 'heading in the wrong direction', 'head-over-heels in love', to simple verbal puns like 'hoarse and horse', 'a fish and to fish', 'heel and heal', 'poor and paw', and many more.

Rhyming slang, if the dreamer uses it in everyday conversation, will also be found in their dreams. 'A loaf of bread', meaning head, 'apples and pears', meaning stairs, and 'currant bun' for the sun, have made appearances in many a cockney's dream. And in a similar way, idioms like 'blaze a trail' sneak into boys dreams, just as 'crying crocodiles'—crocodile tears—find their way into the more romantic dreams of girls.

Looked at in this way, the transformation of circumstances and situations into metaphorical, punning or idiomatic dreams is not remarkable at all. In addition, when it is realized that our unconscious is far more resourceful than its conscious counterpart, in that it can draw on the entire universe for its stand-in characters and its symbolic settings, dreams no longer seem to be such a mystery.

The Exercise

When interpreting a dream, its metaphorical meaning and the play upon words are important features to look for. Words themselves are symbols, and the art of reading and understanding what is written depends on knowing exactly what each word-symbol represents. C-A-T, for example, conjures up an image of a cat; H-O-U-S-E a house, T-R-E-E a tree, and so on. When interpreting dreams, the reverse of this process is necessary. The dream is already full of signs, symbols and images, so it is these that have to be converted into a message which can be understood verbally.

The question to be asked of every dream is 'What is it saying?' The language your dreams use will be unique because only you know the origin of your own metaphorical dream images. In your secret language of sleep, you use names with personal associations and places linked with particular experiences to pass on messages. Only *you* know what these represent. These names and places, with their various associations, form a rich store of dream props in the wings of your memory, waiting to be used symbolically at the appropriate time.

Once you know that your past experiences in the form of memory and personal associations are used to create metaphorical scenes, and that substitution is the name of the dream game, you will soon recognize the clues which reveal the meaning and message.

Exercise 7—The Language of Dreams

The purpose of this exercise is to become familiar with the language of your dreams. Begin by selecting a recent dream and try to translate its signs, symbols and images into a verbal picture, and then into a practical meaning.

Make a list of any words, phrases or conversations found in this dream and note any puns, double-meanings or metaphors.

Make a list of the people, animals and objects which appear in this dream, including yourself.

Now analyse your feelings in relation to these. Ask yourself if you are inspired, frightened, worried, envious or happy at the thought of any of them.

Make a list of any problems, failures, aims or achievements that may be associated with any of the people, animals or objects in the dream.

Ask yourself if any of these are similar to your own problems, failures, aims or successes.

Look at the whole dream as a metaphorical message and then try to apply this message to a personal situation or circumstance.

Summary

Dreams   — have their own language.
- communicate through visual imagery.
- reflect past scenes in order to represent situations and circumstances.
- use word pictures, puns and idioms.
- are metaphors.
- substitute one person for another.
- use a character to represent a principle.
- need to be translated before they can be interpreted.
- convey feelings and emotions through their language.

8.

Recognition of Dreams

It is impossible to categorize dreams strictly into types because each dream is different and therefore unique in its own right. They can, however, be recognized as basically literal, symbolic or a mixture of literal and symbolic imagery. Once this is discovered, the dream can then be seen as a warning dream, an encouraging dream, a prophetic dream, a psychic dream, a healing dream or a nightmare, depending on the reason for its creation in the first place.

Life is made up of one experience after another and these experiences often give rise to problems which need solving, accepting or facing. We can do this in two different ways—through intelligent reasoning with our head, or intuitively with our heart. Sometimes we make decisions with our heart, sometimes with our head, but the best solutions are those reached when our head and our heart agree.

Usually, it is our head with its logic that rules during the day, and our heart with its instinct that rules at night. 'Sleep on it' is good advice, for that is when our hearts have their chance to contribute, so listening to our dreams with their message is vital.

Literal Dreams

Literal dreams are of the head, and reflect life as it is—*literally*. An example of this is an action-replay dream. This re-enacts an event exactly as it occurred at the time. The setting is identical, the characters play the same role, and say and do the same things. These dreams reflect the outer world where troubles—and the solutions to them—are practical, so to look for deeper, mysterious meanings in such dreams is a waste of time: they simply do not exist.

These dreams are more mirror-images of events than metaphors, giving the dreamer the opportunity to analyse and experience once again events they did not fully appreciate or understand at the time it happened. The unconscious notices and registers so much more than the conscious self, so when necessary it can reproduce past actions in a dream for a second appraisal. As well as recreating the scene, these dreams also appear to be scrupulously fair and objective, never discriminating against an opponent, nor colouring evidence in favour of the dreamer.

The following dream from a businessman who was at the peak of his career is an example of a typical literal action-replay dream:

The Dream—'The Disagreement'
I was in my office waiting for a colleague and when he arrived we had a serious disagreement over policy. In particular, we seemed to dislike each other and it became a personal slanging match instead of an objective business meeting. We must have made it up because at the end of the dream this colleague and I were in a pub, having a drink together.

The dreamer volunteered the information that the previous day he and his colleague had disagreed in much the same way his dream reflected. The only difference was that the dream ended amicably with a drink in a pub, whereas in reality a very unpleasant atmosphere had developed between them.

By going over his dream it is hoped that the dreamer will realize that the present situation is most unsatisfactory and that an alternative and better outcome is offered by his dream. Since this better outcome was in his dream, and since he himself created that dream, it follows that the idea was already in his mind. Pride, no doubt, is the inhibiting factor, but the message *from* the dreamer *to* the dreamer is quite clear: Make it up!

When a literal dream is intended as a warning it uses realistic scenes in a representational and metaphorical way. The next dream from a housewife is a literal dream of this nature:

The Dream—'The Kitchen'
The dream took place in my kitchen. Everything was as it really is, including my plants on the window sill. The plants particularly attracted my attention because they had wilted and looked as if they were dying. There was also an odd smell which I could not identify.

The kitchen and the domestic scene in this dream form the backcloth, the theme, and the plants represent energy, vitality and health. Seeing these were not looking too healthy warns of a loss or sapping of energy suggesting a possible health problem. The strange smell adds a note of suspicion, so the message from this scene is that any signs of physical wilting or feelings of ill-health should be investigated immediately. This could apply to the dreamer, or to someone in her family, including any pets she may have, but as with all dreams this will have to be related to relevant circumstances known only to the dreamer, before the message is understood fully.

Symbolic Dreams

Symbolic dreams reflect more the inner world, the world of the heart, inhabited by emotions and feelings. Since there is no verbal or literal equivalent for these feelings, they are projected into dreams as signs and symbols. These signs and symbols are to the heart what words are to the head.

Our inner world of images and imagination is far less familiar territory to us than the outer world. In many respects we are prevented from wandering too far into this realm at a very early age, when we are told 'not to imagine things'. This comes as a warning suggesting that anything that goes on inside our head is definitely suspect, if not fictitious nonsense, so when it comes to dreams, especially the more symbolic and imaginative ones, many feel suspicious and do not wish to consider them at all, let alone work with them.

It is the translation of symbolic imagery into an acceptable sense of logic that often presents difficulties, but once the two different worlds of the head and the heart are recognized, each with its different language and ways of processing and presenting information, the task is simplified considerably.

Since symbolic dreams reflect feelings, it is not surprising that many dreams are concerned with emotional problems, relationships, worries and fears; but they also reflect profound emotions, hopes, inspirations and brilliant new ideas and inventions. In the following symbolic dream, signs, symbols, stand-in characters and its metaphorical message can easily be discovered, and even though the dream relates to the most ordinary of experiences, it is still symbolic:

The Dream—'The Bus Ride'
I was hurrying to a bus stop but just missed a bus. I then waited for what seemed to be ages, and eventually another came along. It was already full-up but I managed to board it, along with people whom I did not know. The conductor ordered us about and I awoke before arriving at my destination, not liking being bossed by this man.

Hurrying—as the dreamer did—shows she is trying to attain or reach her goal but nearly always misses it. Waiting for a bus tells her she tends to wait and do nothing, hoping another opportunity will come along, and when it does it is not really as she hoped it would be. The conductor symbolizes none other than her animus, her practical more dominant self which is trying to conduct some positive drive and direction into her life.

In practical terms, the symbology reflects lack of direction, aim and positive drive. The obvious solution is to make an aim, however small initially, and then be determined, metaphorically speaking, not to miss the bus.

The next symbolic dream concerns, quite simply, the question of choice:

The Dream—'The Snails'
There were two snails in a bowl and I had to choose only one of them. They both looked very similar and I could not decide which one to pick.

Snails, in every language, symbolize slow but sure progress. Having to choose just one indicates that the dreamer will have to make a difficult decision relating to two approaches, aspects, or even people in his life. According to his dream this is not going to be easy because there is not much to choose between them. On the other hand, it may also be saying that the issue is not very important anyway so he should not waste time on the problem: he will get there eventually, one way or another.

Literal-Symbolic Dreams

Literal-symbolic dreams are a mixture of real events, with recognizable people and places, and symbolism. The majority of dreams are of this nature, showing that both the head *and* the heart, the intellect *and* intuition, contribute to the creation of the dream.

During the day we are on the move most of the time. We walk, ride, drive, catch buses, trains, boats and aeroplanes in order to reach other places. Encounters on this endless journeying during the day are frequently used in literal-symbolic dreams to convey messages which relate not only to practical things in life, but to personal emotions and feelings as well.

The following dream is an example of combined literal and symbolic imagery, from a dreamer who says she is an experienced horsewoman:

The Dream—'The Hunter'
There was my 16-hand grey hunter ready for me to mount. Once in the saddle he began to move forward, even before I could reach for the reins properly. Soon, he was galloping out of control and I knew I could not stop him.

From a literal point of view this dream is a clear warning telling the dreamer she should take every care when she goes riding. Symbolically, however, the horse is the dreamer's 'horsepower', her driving force and the energy she puts into life. For this to run away with her warns that she must always endeavour to be in full control of any plans, projects, ideas or ambitions she has for the future. In other words, she should make sure she is holding the reins firmly or a dangerous runaway situation could develop.

Buildings, in particular houses, appear in dreams (especially literal-symbolic dreams) more frequently than any other single object or article. Often they are recognized as the dreamer's home or they are a composite of past and present homes, yet always with a subtle difference. These are no ordinary houses—they are mansions of the soul, places a dreamer returns to and inhabits during sleep, night after night.

Inside this mansion are many rooms; some may be full of rubbish, while others are locked and unexplored. Attics crammed with interesting objects, dark mysterious cellars, long corridors, flights of steps and haunted rooms all representing virtues, characteristics and hidden talents waiting to be discovered.

Noting and understanding the significance of literal and symbolic imagery in our dreams helps us to see ourselves as others see us, and it allows us to get to know ourselves better. Translating the imagery into metaphorical sense, the things we fear, regret, dislike and hope for, can all be discovered and viewed from a new standpoint.

The Exercise

It is important to recognize literal and symbolic imagery in your dreams because this will give you a clue concerning the origin and reason for your having created the dream in the first place.

Literal action-replay dreams usually occur soon after the real event has taken place, although occasionally a misunderstanding from years previously is re-enacted in this way, making it appear as if it were yesterday. Whether of recent events or not, these action-replay dreams are all created from conscious, realistic memories.

Whenever a situation in your life develops where you are unable to see eye-to-eye with a person through lack of communication, or when business or other transactions deteriorate, a literal dream reflecting exactly what took place is likely to present itself to you. Often these are spontaneous, especially if you are already working with your dreams, but to be sure of re-experiencing an event in order to better understand it, incubate the dream so that you can do just this.

Symbolic dreams arise from the unconscious for the purpose of expressing openly to the conscious self inner feelings concerning a problem, relationship, hope or fear. Since the language of the unconscious is vastly different from that of consciousness, a symbolic dream, even when described in words, will by its very nature appear completely foreign, and sometimes even nonsensical.

If you remember that feelings and emotions are not objects that can be described in words, and that these have to be translated into logical meanings before they make sense, even the most symbolic dream can be understood. In translating signs and symbols it helps to remember that these—as frightening, mysterious, ugly or bizzare as they may be—were conjured up by you and your unconscious self, so 'Know thyself' is perhaps an appropriate reminder here.

Literal-symbolic dreams will include both real *and* abstract imagery. In addition to the messages these dreams offer, they also illustrate the inventiveness of your combined conscious and unconscious resources.

Exercise 8—The Recognition of Dreams

This exercise will help you to recognize the difference between dreams originating from events in the outer world and those arising from inner feelings and emotions. With this in mind, they can be seen as literal dreams, symbolic dreams, or a combination of both.

Recognition of Literal Dreams
Go over recent events and write down any confrontations, uncomfortable encounters with other people, or circumstances which you do not fully understand.

Look for any long-term practical problem that is not resolved and is causing you to worry.

Now examine the dreams recorded in your Dream Diary and seek out any literal, realistic action which may relate to these clashes or unresolved events.

Compare the real event with the literal dream version and see if this offers additional information which may help you to understand the situation, circumstances or relationship.

Recognition of Symbolic Dreams
Write down any inner secret worry, fear, hope or ambition.

Examine recent dreams in your Dream Diary and seek out any symbolism in the form of individual symbols, signs and abstract scenes.

Translate symbols and abstract scenes into feelings and emotional circumstances, if you can.

Compare and relate your personal feelings with the translated symbology, and hopefully gain insight and guidance.

Summary

Dreams
— can be recognized as literal, symbolic or a combination of literal and symbolic imagery.
— which are literal relate to events in the outer world.
— frequently reflect past events as literal action replays in order to highlight the event.
— of a symbolic nature reflect inner feelings and emotions.
— paint abstract pictures to represent the language of the heart.
— are created by the head and the intellect, and with the heart and intuition.
— whether literal or symbolic, have the power to warn, instruct, encourage, compensate, comfort and heal.

9.

The Source and Power of Dreams

Dreams have always intrigued humanity and in attempts to explain them many different causes and sources have been suggested. The answer to the question 'who or what initiates a dream?' is probably 'ourselves', but having said that there is evidence to show that external influences—from the noise of a telephone ringing, a dog barking in the distance, a car door banging—to telepathic communication, can also initiate a dream, or be incorporated into one.

Ancient civilizations throughout the world believed dreams were messages from the gods or angelic hosts, and even from God Himself, and one of the richest and most informative sources of dreams from the past is found in the Bible. In the Old and New Testaments there are at least 28 well-documented accounts of dreams, varying from the straightforward literal dream, offering a message which needs no interpretation, to the complicated symbolic dream, requiring a dream interpreter to decipher its meaning. These dreams, literal and symbolic, were believed to be not only divinely inspired, but transmitted telepathically to dreamers as they slept.

Old Testament Dreams

The first dream recorded in the Old Testament appears to be an example of direct communication with God. Its literal message is abundantly clear, and requires no interpretation beyond the dreamer's recognition of his own self-guilt: 'God came to Abimelech in a dream by night and said to him ''Behold! thou art but a dead man for the woman thou hast taken is another man's wife''.' (Genesis 28.3)

In contrast to this literal dream are the well-known symbolic and prophetic dreams experienced by the Pharaoh, and recorded in Genesis 41.1–7: 'Behold, I stood on the river bank and there came up out of the river seven fat kine; they fed in a meadow. And behold seven other kine followed them, poor and very ill-favoured and lean-fleshed, much as I have never seen in Egypt. And the ill-favoured did eat up the fat kine.' The Pharaoh then awoke but returned to sleep and, as often happens, continued with the dream: 'He slept and dreamed a second time and suddenly seven heads of grain came up on one stalk, plump and good. Then, behold, seven thin heads blighted by the east wind, sprang up after them. And the seven thin heads devoured the seven plump and full heads. So Pharaoh awoke and indeed it was a dream.'

Joseph's interpretation is well known—seven years of plenty followed by seven years of famine. This interpretation applies to both dreams for although their symbolic imagery is entirely different, their meanings are identical.

In retrospect, the influence these dreams had, not only on the Pharaoh and Egypt at that time but on millions of individuals since, can now be clearly seen, showing the power of dreams to be a subtle force capable of setting in motion a chain of events that can continue virtually for ever.

This chain of action and reaction began some time before the Pharaoh had his famous dreams. When Joseph was a prisoner along with the Pharaoh's baker and butler, he correctly interpreted their dreams by telling the baker that he would be sentenced to death, and the butler that he would soon return to serve the Pharaoh. Two years later, when the Pharaoh dreamed of the cattle and the corn, his reinstated butler remembered Joseph, the dream interpreter with whom he had once shared a prison cell. Remembering too that Joseph had correctly interpreted his dream, and that of the baker, he persuaded the Pharaoh to send for Joseph immediately in order that he might interpret his dreams.

Conjectural though it is, it would certainly appear that if the Pharaoh had not dreamed those dreams, Joseph would not have interpreted them, and so that incredible causal chain could not have started. Joseph, in all probability, would have perished in gaol. As it was, he was released, correctly interpreted the Pharaoh's dreams, and supervised the storing of grain in Egypt during the seven plentiful years. It was during the seven years of famine that followed that he met up with his 11 brothers and his father, Jacob, later renamed Israel. Without this reunion, there would have been no founding of the Twelve Tribes of Israel, therefore no Exodus, no settling in the Promised Land, no line of David, and no birth of Jesus. History and life today would be very different indeed had it not been for these important milestones down the ages.

Prophetic as these dreams were in the short-term, their shadow has undoubtedly cast long-term effects, far in excess of the 14-year period covered by the dreams of the cattle and the corn.

Nebuchadnezzar and Daniel

Dreams in the Old Testament are, like the Pharaoh's dream, mainly symbolic and prophetic. Another example of this is King Nebuchadnezzar's famous dream. Daniel, described in the Bible as 'a captive of Judah with an understanding of all visions and dreams', was called before the king to interpret one of his dreams which troubled him greatly. Apart from interpreting the symbology in this, Daniel was also expected to re-dream the dream because the king had forgotten most of it. This is described in Daniel 2.5: 'This thing is gone from me. If ye will not make known to me the dream, with the interpretation thereof, ye shall be cut in pieces and your houses shall be made into dunghills.'

Daniel 2.25–45 relates how Daniel re-dreamed and interpreted the dream: 'O king thy thoughts that came unto thee upon they bed were these. Thou sawest a great image whose brightness was terrible. The image's head was made of gold, his breast and his arms of silver, his belly and his thighs of brass. His legs of iron, his feet part of iron and part of clay. A stone, cut without hands, smote thy image upon his feet. Then the iron, the clay, the brass, the silver and the gold broke into pieces and became as chaff on the summer threshing floor.'

Although this dream is generally known as Nebuchadnezzar's dream, it appears to be more Daniel's than his. In essence, it is Daniel's imagery, and it reflects the king's strengths and weaknesses. The interpretation he gave to the king, ending with the assurance that 'kingdoms may come and kingdoms may go, but yours will go on forever', seems to have glossed over the 'feet of clay' aspect. Perhaps Daniel wished to placate the tyrant-king and save the lives of himself and his fellow-prisoners, but the symbolism of 'feet of clay', a cliché inherited from this dream hardly suggests stability, not in any age.

New Testament Dreams

There are fewer dreams in the New Testament than in the Old Testament and most of these are literal, uncomplicated dreams offering advice in the form of clear, practical instructions. For example, the angel who appeared in Joseph's dream told him quite distinctly in the following message that he was to marry Mary: 'Joseph, thou art son of David, fear not to take unto thee Mary for thy wife for that which is conceived in her is of the Holy Ghost.' (Matthew 1.20)

Later on in this biblical story, after the three wise men had presented their gifts of gold, frankincense and myrrh to Mary's new-born child, they too received explicit instructions in this way: 'And being warned in a dream that they should not return to Herod, they departed into their country another way.' (Matthew 2.12)

Just as symbolic dreams in the Old Testament set in motion a chain of events that affected the history of the world, so too did literal dreams in the New Testament. One in particular was Joseph's second dream described in Matthew 2.13: 'And when they, the wise men, were departed, behold, the angel of the Lord appeared to Joseph in a dream saying ''Arise, and take the young child and his mother and flee into Egypt and stay there until I bring thee word, for Herod will seek the young child to destroy him.'

If Joseph had not dreamed this and furthermore *acted* confidently upon its instructions, it is doubtful if Jesus would have escaped the Massacre of the Innocents perpetrated by Herod. To consider how history would have shaped if this had happened is, again, pure conjecture, but it can safely be assumed that it would have been very different indeed had it not been for this dream.

Psychological Beliefs

The early Christians regarded dreams as both divine messages and reflections from the individual's spirit or inner self. Gregory of Nyssar in AD 4, for example, saw them as mirrors of the soul which reflected the personality of the dreamer. In his work *On Making Man* he wrote that from dream-visions it was possible to understand one's true nature and values. St Augustine, in order to communicate with his own spirit and supernatural forces, incubated his dreams, and Thomas Aquinas, a seer and dreamer, wrote extensively about the prophetic and divine nature of dreams. He also suggested 'a single cause of both the dream and the event', a belief that was to emerge again 700 years later in the form of C.G. Jung's concept 'synchronicity'.

Interest in dreams from a purely psychological point of view began around the 19th century. In 1861 Scherner introduced 'decentricity in sleep', a state whereby thoughts were transformed into something else. Examples he gave of this were that feelings and objects in dreams became symbols. The body, he said, became a house, the lungs became windmills, the penis a flute and the vagina a cave. Dogmatic though his symbolism was, the principle is one that is now generally accepted.

Strupell, in 1877, authoritively stated that all dreamers were escapists and that stimuli from fears awakened in them thoughts which materialized visually in dreams. These, he said, then progressed along a chain of ideas called the Law of Association or, as Freud was to call it later, the Association of Ideas.

Other psychologists of that time taught that dreams 'should be compared with bodily functions, such as the bowels and bladder', thus showing that they saw them as a physical process, whereby useless thoughts were eliminated as were other waste products of the body. Maury, Stricker, Delage and Radestock, prominent psychologists at the turn of the century, described dreams variously as signs of wish fulfilments, fears, guilt, sexual desires, disappointments, substitutions, and symbols for objects and feelings. All this undoubtedly paved the way for Sigmund Freud who united these beliefs to form his own psychological school of thought.

Freud came to the conclusion that dreams were scenes from an unconscious state underlying conscious awareness. Originally he believed they were reflections relating to conscious experiences only but later recognized symptoms of hysteria and other emotional disturbances which were projected symbolically. By encouraging his patients to talk at length about their dreams and the off-theme thoughts they provoked, Freud perfected his chain-reaction technique known as Free Association of Ideas. This was an extension, in many ways, of the Law of Association described by Strupell a few years previously.

'The Viennese Sexologist' was a name often given to Freud. This was because he believed and taught that emotional psychic energy, or libido as he called it, was the driving force and that this driving force was basically sexual in nature. Symbols in dreams—even those not remotely connected with sex—were nevertheless, according to him, projections of sexual feelings associated with frustrations and guilt. In the light of the present-day view on sex, such beliefs seem ridiculous, but looking back at nineteenth-century European society, with its false modesty and superficial puritanical façade, dreams probably *did* reflect the things Freud saw in them.

It took Carl Gustav Jung, a disciple of Freud, to sort the wheat from the chaff and show that the ancients, the biblical religious believers, the early psychologists, Freud, and twentieth-century scientists—with their various mystical, philosophical, religious, psychological and scientific concepts concerning dreams—were *all* right, from their different standpoints.

Today it is accepted that a dream, like the many different facets of an individual's psychological make-up, is a product of the total person. It reflects their memories, hopes and their belief-system. If a dreamer is religious, then their dreams will be full of heavenly images and angelic hosts. On the other hand, the dreamer who has a scientific background and is also a believer in a divine source, may see that source—Him, Her or It—as a form of pure energy and light. This is an identical concept to that of the metaphysical and philosophical believers who also talk about the Light. Only the imagery is different. The religious, the philosophical and the scientific dreamer all project the God-image, an image found in the human psyche from the beginning of time, but in each individual this image will be special, different and unique.

The Exercise

Your dreams are created by you and it is your beliefs as well as your experiences in life that help create the scenes and imagery found in them. Discovering the meaning of a dream is the object of the exercise, and to discover this it helps to recognize the source of the imagery your dreaming mind has used. Sometimes this arises from a recent memory, a past memory or even from the collective unconscious. This exercise will help you to identify the various sources, and in so doing something of your conscious and unconscious belief-system will be revealed as well.

You will begin to recognize the genius within. By discovering your unconscious belief system, which is very different from its conscious counterpart, you will be able to understand *why* and *when* you dreamed what you did, and probably the reason you chose that particular imagery.

Exercise 9 — The Source and Power of Dreams

In this exercise you will discover that all dreams are, at least in principle, similar to those found in the Old and New Testaments. They are either uncomplicated literal dreams or highly symbolic dreams. In addition to these, seek out other dreams which have also altered the course of history—those of Hitler, Caesar, Joan of Arc and many other famous and infamous people.

Read the literal dream in the Old Testament found in Genesis 28.3.

Read the dreams described in Genesis 41.1 and note their symbolic nature.

Discover the many other dreams in the Old Testament.

Read the literal dreams found in the New Testament.

Select three of your own dreams experienced over the past month and view them in the same way you did the biblical dreams.

Decide which of your dreams are literal and which are symbolic.

Try to recognize the underlying, unconscious standpoint from which your dreams were created.

Ask yourself if any of your dreams have altered the course of your life.

Summary

Dreams
- come from many sources—some from within, some from without.
- have interested, intrigued and informed mankind from earliest times.
- were particularly important to our ancestors and have been recorded for centuries.
- have the power to create history and to steer individual and collective destinies.
- depend on the dreamer's conscious and unconscious awareness, their experience in life and their beliefs.
- found in the Bible are excellent examples of literal dreams and symbolic dreams, and of the long-term effects they can have.
- reflect the dreamer's religious beliefs as well as their psychological nature and their intellectual qualities.
- are rich sources of self-illumination.

10.

Dream Signs, Symbols and Archetypes

Dreams, as we have seen, re-enact events from the outer world against a literal backcloth of reality, and they also reflect inner dimensions, composed of symbols. Since the language used by literal dreams is that of consciousness itself, their interpretation is relatively straightforward and depends mainly on recognizing the action-replay and its relevance to a particular event. Symbolic dreams, on the other hand, have to be translated from the language of the unconscious into that of consciousness before they can be interpreted.

Dreams use the language of the unconscious and this language uses signs, symbols and archetypes to communicate and deliver messages.

Signs

The definition of a 'sign', whether in a dream or elsewhere, is a mark or shape by which someone or something is recognized or represented. It is always *less* than that which it represents and it relates to the everyday world in which we live, even though it may appear in a dream. A personal signature and a trademark are signs, and the British Rail logo is an excellent example which can be found in the world of advertising. This world knows exactly how to use the language of the unconscious—to profitable advantage.

In the following dream a sign leads the dreamer to safety and, as in reality, this sign is less than that which it signifies. In other words, the sign 'exit' in the dream is not quite the escape door it indicates:

The Dream—'A Way Out'
I seemed to be lost and began to feel panic-stricken. None of the streets looked familiar and there was no one about to ask for help. On a wall some letters were written which I took to be the word EXIT. By this word was a small door, which was not locked. I went in and to my great relief found myself back in my own home.

Symbols

A 'symbol' represents and calls to mind something else and it always stands for more than its obvious or immediate meaning. It is a code for that which cannot be expressed in words, although a word—when it implies something beyond its obvious meaning—can become a symbol. When an image of a symbol is explored it can lead to ideas beyond the grasp of reason and even logic. Houses in dreams, for example, often become symbols in order to represent the Mansion of the Soul, the body and spirit of the dreamer. Trees also play symbolic roles, standing for the family tree with its roots and various branches.

An ocean wave is the main symbol in the following dream. A wall of water like this is frequently used to express feelings and overwhelming emotions and its symbolic value is seen by the way it represents and suggests something other than itself, namely a wave of emotion which could engulf and endanger the dreamer:

The Dream—'The Huge Wave'
I am on a cliff-top with the sea stretching before me. In the distance I can see a wave a little larger than most and as I watch it, it begins to move towards the shore, growing in height as it draws nearer. At last it reaches the cliff and breaks a few feet below where I am standing. I feel others must have been engulfed, but I am alright.

Archetypes

An 'archetype' (from 'arche', an origin or cause, and 'type', implying a copy) is the model from which copies are made. It is a unique idea or principle from a primordial source, made manifest by symbols which form an image in the eye or ear of the beholder. God the Creator is the Archetypal Light, so in the strictest sense of the word there can be only one archetype, namely God, from which all else stems.

With Carl Gustav Jung's concept of archetypes there is the psychological definition of an archetype. This finds its origin within a collective psyche or collective unconscious as an archaic remnant which is inherited as an ancestral memory. Just as physical characteristics reaching back to primitive, biological life-forms are inherited, so too is this memory inherited in the form of primordial, archetypal images.

Archetypal dreams are rare, unbelievable, and unforgettable. Since they are a symbolic formula without a conscious equivalent, they are often those dreams which convince the dreamer, at least at the time of the dream, that they are being shown mysterious secrets of the universe. Alas, on waking these secrets escape recollection, let alone definition, but the esoteric impression none the less remains.

The archetype in the next dream has different meanings on different levels, depending on the beliefs, experiences and understanding of the individual dreamer. As a primordial image, the mythological dragon symbolizes the dreamer's power and energy, as well as natural resources of the planet:

The Dream—'The Dragon'
The sky was glowing as if alive with a strange force of nature. Then, on the horizon, I saw a large flying creature, rather like a dragon, which landed near me. I was not afraid, in fact quite the reverse. I felt stronger than I had for some time.

Rich symbolic imagery used by the language of the unconscious underlies every word, thought, deed and action we take, but, since this imagery is grossly overshadowed during the awake hours with conversation and verbal forms of communication, it passes unnoticed. The power of images and symbols is, therefore, at best only superficially understood. Apart from the media and advertising agencies who know that certain designs, slogans, keywords and types of music attract even unwilling attention, the majority of symbols surrounding us remain silent. In fact, advertising campaigns may well have desensitized us unwittingly to much of the symbolism around us at the conscious level.

Although inner and deeper meanings are revealed through archetypal symbology it operates on exoteric levels as well as esoteric. It also appears to conceal as well as reveal, but a dream which seemingly hides something in symbolism is actually offering that which the dreamer already knows *un*consciously, but refuses to accept, believe, recognize or realize.

The Exercise

The influence signs, symbols and archetypes have on you often passes unnoticed. From road signs to sales slogans in the real world, to the subtler symbols and archetypes in dreams, their effect both consciously and unconsciously is undeniable. To discover such signs around you during the day is as important, interesting and valuable as understanding and discovering them when they appear in dreams, so part of Exercise 10 is of a practical nature.

Life is full of everything, except perhaps meaning, and it could well be that many answers are to be found in symbolism. To understand symbolism—whether in dreams or in the everyday world—is to help understand yourself and others, for symbolism—the language of the unconscious—is also an international and intercultural language. The cross, the circle, the tree, the king, the queen, and mythological creatures all appeared in earlier, remote civilizations just as they do in contemporary society.

A symbol is not static, nor is it permanently fixed in its meaning. It can evolve and mean one thing in one culture but have an entirely different connotation in another. The serpent, for example, is usually accepted as a symbol of energy and wisdom in Eastern (and indeed it once did in earlier Western) cultures, but in Western Christendom today it depicts evil.

By examining superstitions, it will be discovered that they arise from ancient symbols now bereft of their original spiritual significance. The Father Christmas story is one example. As a child you were probably told that Father Christmas flies through the sky and comes down the chimney with presents and any request for these must be made directly to him via the chimney. Traditionally and symbolically, the chimney was the opening up to heaven by which the spirit of man could ascend from Earth to Heaven, and down which the Father above could descend and bestow heavenly, not earthly, gifts upon His children.

Once you remember that the purpose of a symbol and an archetype is to reveal and represent something greater than its apparent and immediate image suggests, the search for the greater meaning will be as rewarding and as exciting as King Arthur and his knights' quest for the Holy Grail. What were their experiences if not encounters with their own symbols and archetypes within the region of their own, individual, unconscious worlds?

Exercise 10—Signs, Symbols and Archetypes

The purpose of this exercise is to help you to distinguish between signs, symbols and archetypes in the world around you. They do not belong exclusively to dreams; they are to be found in legends, in advertising, in the town, in the country, in the past, and in the present.

In the next newspaper or magazine you read note how many signs there are.

Discover what these signs are saying and recognize that they are less than the object they signify.

Look for symbols in the everyday world. Apart from fairy stories, myths and legends, symbols can be found in science, religion, mathematics, architecture, and in all fields of human activity.

Discover the deepest symbolic meaning and message you can from the symbols you find.

Decide if any of the symbols you have discovered are 'archetypal'.

Note that all archetypes are symbols but not all symbols are archetypes.

Summary

Dreams — communicate literally and verbally as well as abstractly and symbolically.
— use imagery, the language of the unconscious.
— use signs which are less than that which they represent.
— use symbols which always represent something more than their obvious meaning.
— use archetypes which are universal primordial principles.

11.

Dream Themes, Scenes and Messages

Dream interpreters throughout the ages have always focused their attention on the dream, not on the circumstances of the dreamer nor his or her state of mind. There was no need for Joseph to take into account the Pharaoh's mood when he interpreted his dreams, of the seven fat and seven lean kine and the seven full and the seven empty ears of corn, as indicating seven years of plenty followed by seven years of famine. And Daniel, when obliged to reveal what Nebuchadnezzar's dream of the grotesque figure with the feet of clay meant, did not have to resort to analysing the power-hungry king's mental condition in order to explain it.

As a dream interpreter you are a dream analyst, not a psychoanalyst. A dream analyst is interested in the dream, whereas a psychoanalyst is interested in an individual's state of mind and uses a person's dreams to understand their reactions, phobias and fears. Many would-be dream interpreters make the mistake of interpreting dreams from the standpoint of the dreamer and not from that of their dream. This means they take into account their circumstances and their psychological nature before examining the dream and its contents, thus developing preconceived ideas which mislead and distort the true message.

When the dream has been thoroughly explored from every angle and a symbolic meaning discovered, it can then be applied to the dreamer's circumstances and, if necessary, their state of mind. The meaning of the dream will then be transformed into a personal message.

C.G. Jung taught and believed that to understand a dream, the dream itself must always remain central to the investigation. He also suggested that the question 'What is the dream saying?' should be asked over and over again. In the final analysis, only the dreamer can be sure of answering this question correctly since it was he or she who fabricated the dream in the first place. But by concentrating on the dream in this way, rather than trying to see reflections in it that do not exist, its theme, signs and symbols will soon emerge.

Themes and Scenes

The theme of a dream reveals the subject under investigation. Travelling in a train, waiting at a station, meeting people and then arriving in a strange unknown place, symbolically reflects the dreamer making his or her way through life, so the theme of such a dream would be their destiny. Similarly, a large tree, a forest or wood shows the theme to be associated with family matters because the traditional symbolic meaning of tree is that of the family—the family tree. A hospital, with nurses and doctors, indicates that the dreamer needs help and hospitality, so the theme is help, in one form or another, and so on.

As well as the symbolic or metaphorical theme there is the overall atmosphere or feeling running through a dream. Sometimes this is all that remains after a night's dreaming, but nevertheless this feeling is powerful and important enough to produce a mood that colours the following day. When someone says 'I woke up feeling depressed and knew it would be a bad day', you can be sure this is because of what took place in their forgotten dreams. This atmosphere or feeling also sets the scene or forms the backcloth to a dream, rather like a stage setting, and it is before this that all the events and action take place.

Viewing a dream as if it were a play is one way to understand what it is all about. Objects on the stage make up the props, and the characters, archetypal figures and animals are the actors and actresses. Remembering conversations is important for although actions speak louder than words, especially in dreams, a continuation of this dialogue with the characters is possible later on in an in-depth analysis of the dream. This is known as 'progressing your dream'.

The Artist Within

In addition to being a theatrical stage producer, the dream-producing aspect of the unconscious is also a great artist. This artist uses shades of dark and light and colours to denote the moods of dreams. Dismal, dark scenes portray unhappy, misunderstood circumstances, whereas sunny views throw considerable light on situations and offer bright new hopes for the future. Although many dreamers believe they dream only in black and white, it is now thought that everyone dreams in colour but this, like dreams themselves, fades quickly from memory, leaving only the basic images, apparently devoid of colour.

As well as representing moods, colours convey more specific messages by symbolizing different facets or levels of energy put into life. Red, for example, symbolizes energies associated with physical effort, hard labour, sporting activities and sexual drive. From the health point of view physical complaints associated with conditions of the blood, including high blood pressure, are sometimes discovered through a dream where red is particularly dominant. On the other hand, depending on the circumstances in the dream, red may be reflecting anger, as in the 'red rag to a bull' experience.

The meaning and association of colours in dreams arise from the collective unconscious and apply not only to dream symbolism but to traditional symbolism throughout the world. When the blue/indigo/violet end of the colour spectrum appears in dreams, altruistic, intuitive and spiritual concepts are under consideration. Green and its associated meaning is another example. (At one time this colour was instinctively recognized as an emotionally stabilizing colour, with a result that hospitals and classrooms were, until fairly recently, painted throughout in a rich grass-green.) Not surprisingly, the dreaming mind with its strong links with the collective unconscious, recognizes the significance of colours and uses them as part of its symbolism.

Knowing that dreams conjure up puns and play on words when the occasion arises, an interesting association between colour and words almost escaped detection in the following dream:

The Dream—'The Accident'
I looked out of my bedroom window at the road outside my house and thought there must have been an accident because it was covered in blood. There was no evidence of an actual car crash, nor were there any injured people about.

Apart from the obvious conclusion that this dream was a literal, warning dream, urging the dreamer to take extra care when driving a car or walking on the streets, further light was thrown on its meaning when the address of the dreamer was taken into account. This was 'Redpath Road'. The dreamer later admitted that he disliked the name of his road but he had not realized why—until the name-image link in his dream colourfully pointed it out to him.

Every dream should, of course, first be interpreted in a literal way, to discover any practical warnings or advice, before seeking the more symbolic implications. Some dreams, as already pointed out, are entirely literal and relate to mundane matters, whereas others are symbolic and bear little resemblance to the outer world. There are, too, those which are a blend of both, and even those with literal and symbolic messages.

One way to distinguish between literal outer reality and symbolic inner fantasy in a dream is to view the scene as if it were a painting. On visiting a picture gallery literal paintings are easily recognized—they leave nothing to the imagination. A literal painting of the 'The Houses of Parliament', for example, shows every detail of the building and is often so realistic that it is difficult to distinguish it from a photograph. Such a painting may be a masterpiece but it is also clear to see that originality and symbology played no part whatsoever in its creation. A picture of this nature could be said to have been intelligently painted, metaphorically speaking, by the head and not by the heart.

Consider, on the other hand, an abstract or symbolic painting of 'The Houses of Parliament'. By combining its architecture, tradition, power, party-politics, and nationalism, a colourful image of the place can be transferred onto canvas conveying not only the structure, but ideals and action as well. The impact, impression and message transmitted by a picture of this nature is far greater than a true-to-life likeness of the place could ever be. And so it is with literal and symbolic dreams.

A further advantage of viewing dreams as if they were pictures is that the dreamer, like the painter, can stand back and look objectively at his or her own work of art and give it a title. There is a difference between giving a dream a title and giving one to a picture. In the case of a dream, this can only be done in retrospect, *after* the unconscious has painted the scene.

The Exercise

Understanding your dreams is a progressive experience. The more dreams you interpret the more practised you become, and the more practised you are, the more your dreams will respond by conveying more and more information. This is just one reward from working with your dreams.

Discovering the theme tells you the subject of the dream. Occasionally there are two or even three themes running through the same dream, but these will be found to represent circumstances which are interrelated.

The feeling or mood of a dream acts as the backcloth to the events, and sometimes there is little else to a dream but scene and mood. When this is the case, the dream-message will probably be found encapsulated within. Colours noted in dreams are important and can represent the atmosphere and mood, thus helping to reveal the theme. The discovery of the mood, feeling, atmosphere and theme are important aspects of the interpretation, and once these are discovered the framework of the dream is complete.

Exercise 11—Dream Themes, Scenes and Messages.

Seeking the theme of a dream, with the help of its overall feeling, is the first step towards its interpretation. A title for the dream can usually be found from this.

Discover the theme of a dream by reading and re-reading its account written in your Dream Diary.

Look for the feeling, mood or atmosphere produced or left by the dream. It is vital you discover this, so if it is not at first apparent, ask yourself how you feel about it. Does the dream make you feel happy, sad, worried, excited, etc.?

Note if the dream-setting was day or night and if there were shades of dark or light. Colours should be considered in the light of their relationship to moods or feelings.

Look for metaphorical references to colours indicating, perhaps, a blue mood, the pink of health, green with envy, or just a jaundiced view generally.

Give an appropriate title to the dream.

Consider the dream as if it were a play or a scene from a play. Write the plot or story it tells.

View the dream as a whole as if it were a painting, and decide if it is a literal or symbolic painting, or a mixture of both. Describe the subject it portrays.

Summary

Dreams
— should always remain at the centre of the investigation.
— are analysed by investigating their content, not the content of the dreamer's mind.
— have themes which reflect the subject under investigation and consideration.
— leave distinct feelings behind which act as their backcloth. This sets the mood of the dream.
— often use colours, coloured objects and scenes to represent moods.
— can be viewed as if they are plays, acted upon the stage of life.
— can also be viewed as if they are paintings. This reveals their literal and symbolic content.

12.

Dream Figures

Dreams are like fantastic stage and screen productions. In them, everything is possible. But who is the versatile genius capable not only of writing original scripts and dialogue, but of designing unique settings, controlling the action, acting out the role of each character and every creature, and then—in addition to all this—sitting in the audience to watch his or her own dream-performance? It is, of course, none other than the apparently modest dreamer.

If ever we doubt our own tremendous potential, we have only to remember our dreams. Since we have the ability to create incredible imagery in our sleep without the slightest mental effort and hours of research essential to write comparable sagas when awake, we have proof of our inner resources and originality. Understanding what they mean, or—put another way—understanding what we are trying to tell ourselves through our elaborate dreams, is another matter.

Dreams tell us what we need to know and they do this through directing attention, literally and symbolically, towards those areas in life which are forgotten, ignored, neglected or rejected. If our outlook becomes rigid or limited, a dream is likely to occur which gives the other side of the picture, and if we are afraid of something, this could well be revealed in a nightmare. It is in this way that we show ourselves our true nature and our fears.

When difficult circumstances are analysed, problems arising from them are often found to be of our own making due to our reactions and responses to them. Both the problem and the solution, in this sense, lie within so it is not surprising that a dream, in its attempt to highlight those circumstances, is projected from what may appear to be a negative standpoint. In an attempt to restore the balance, it is necessary that tension, frustrations and fears are expressed and this *can* be disturbing, but it is not the intention of dreams to distress the dreamer. By reflecting the truth they are trying to discover a solution or help the dreamer to accept a situation, but sometimes the truth can be very painful. And when it is, it is reflected as a bad—but honest—dream.

In a dream, a problem, fear or hope may take on the image of a certain character and so become personified. Each of us possesses many different inner selves and these too are portrayed as various figures and characters. They include members of our family, friends, enemies, celebrities, unknown figures, animals and archetypal images. It is the *appearance* of all these characters—some symbolizing feelings, others characteristics, in realistic and unrealistic dream-settings—that seems to cause all the problems when it comes to making an interpretation.

Characters We Know

Characters known to us such as members of our family, friends, enemies and acquaintances who play themselves in a dream, may do so in order to highlight a particular quality or deficiency within the dreamer's character. As an example, take a dream about a colleague who has an annoying habit or behaves badly in the eyes of the dreamer. An analogy is being drawn between this person's behaviour and that of the dreamer, so by looking at the dream as a personal mirror-image the dreamer may be able to prevent developing a similar bad trait or habit. The chances are the potential to do so is already latent and it is for this reason that a dream points out the possibility.

This principle of self-reflection, where the dreamer is urged to look for imperfection and negativity within by recognizing the tell-tale signs in others, is shown in the following symbolically warning dream:

The Dream—'The Difficult Aunt'
The dream took place in the office where I work. An aunt of mine was also employed there, although in reality she has been dead for some years. She was a great source of embarrassment to me in the dream because she criticized the girls behind their backs and was nasty to their faces as well. My friends in the office were treating me badly too and I was beginning to feel lonely and left out in the cold, even though it was not my fault.

The dreamer explained that her aunt had always been a very difficult, frustrated person, with the result that most people avoided her. Later in life she found herself without friends and was a lonely person, so in this dream she was re-enacting the role she normally played each day. The warning this gives to the dreamer is quite clear: 'Don't grow like your aunt'.

Fictitious People and Celebrities

Dreams concerning fictitious characters from plays or novels reflect an artificial approach to life which, for some reason, attracts the dreamer. Maybe they do not want to face reality, but integrating these characters and their colourful experiences into their personality makes up for their own deficiencies and helps to increase their self-confidence. Similarly, dreaming of actors and actresses, pop stars, and other famous people, and of being famous ourselves, can compensate for the lack of applause and appreciation received in life. This would certainly seem to be the case in the following dream:

The Dream—'Star For A Night'
Elvis Presley was just about to go through the stage door of a large theatre when he saw me. Immediately, he called out 'Hi! Come over here, hurry up you can make it'. I

then found myself behind huge curtains, apparently on a stage and as the curtains parted a sea of faces stared at me. Elvis by now was singing and dancing about, so I joined in with him. It was fantastic and the applause at the end was wonderful. I felt it was for me as much as it was for Elvis and awoke feeling absolutely marvellous!

Royalty

Royalty frequently feature in dreams, which is not surprising when we realize how often they appear in most living-rooms, albeit on the TV. Apart from the archetypal symbolism of kings, queens, princes and princesses, royal dreams are usually set in homely surroundings, at horseshows, garden fêtes and flowershows, so have meanings more of a domestic and mundane nature than of fairy-tale mystique.

Personal identification with regal figures, feelings of social superiority, and simply a hedge against the humdrum monotony of life, have all been suggested as reasons for these dreams, but whichever is right, the one activity which predominates in most of them is that British habit of tea-drinking. The Queen Mother is a great favourite in these dreams and she drops in for a cup of tea and homemade cake up and down the country every night. Recently, as seen in the next dream, she has been joined by the Princess of Wales.

The Dream—'The Queen Mother and Princess Diana'
The Queen Mother called unexpectedly at my parents' home in Leeds. She stood at the front door, glanced at a large car parked by the kerb and asked if it was alright if Diana came in for a cup of tea as well. My mother was fussing about and I wished she would calm down. The Queen Mother noticed the agitation she and Diana were causing and politely suggested that when we were in London next, we should all call at Buckingham Palace, and have tea with her.

Animals

Animals, like people, play many roles in dreams. A literal dream of your cat or dog may symbolize their needs relating perhaps to their health or their comfort. On the other hand, they may symbolize characteristics of yourself which reflect a struggle with the so-called animal or baser instincts in humanity.

The 'animal' in man is popularly taken to mean the bestial nature and the sub-human impulses and activities of certain human beings. Not surprisingly this comparison frequently finds its way into dreams, but to compare people with animals in this way is not only inaccurate—it is an insult to the creatures used to represent such abysmal human behaviour. It does, however, show the power of the word-picture, irrespective of the fact that the comparisons are based on a false premise in both dreams and speech.

Examples of this metaphorical misuse are cats being used to describe spiteful women, chauvinistic men likened to pigs, and crafty crooks cast as rats. Neither cats, pigs or rats have these human characteristics yet through verbal inheritance and wrongly associated beliefs they now commonly symbolize inferior traits.

Not all animal-symbolism is based on these misconceptions. Ancient civilizations and the discerning person today recognize the symbolism found in the collective unconscious. This reflects each creature's traditional image. The image of the lion, for example, symbolizes pride, courage, strength and power, a bear symbolizes the Great Mother, a cow the goddess of healing, and so on.

Talking, awe-inspiring and sacred-looking creatures, found not only in dreams but in legends and fairy tales too, represent wise inner counsellors. They symbolize self-help stirrings of awareness in the unconscious, so it is important to understand exactly what these animals are trying to convey. It is at the other end of this animal-scale that the miscast creatures are found, but—to those dreamers who believe men are pigs, women are cats and every competitor a snake-in-the-grass—they none the less mean exactly what the dreamers themselves believe them to mean.

Energy-drives are often symbolized by various fast-moving animals, in particular horses. The use of equine figures to represent this is not really surprising since we hear and read so much about horsepower with every new model of car that comes onto the market. Similarly, tigers have taken on an image of strength and power, due largely to advertising campaigns. Understandably, both these animals feature in dreams when the question of personal drive, strength and energy is under consideration.

How we treat animals in our dreams gives vital clues to the message the dream is trying to convey, as well as revealing certain things about ourselves. Managing to control a creature is far better than symbolically killing it, while eating one shows a greediness for power. The age of the creature is important as well; young animals such as lambs, kittens, puppies and runts probably symbolize the dreamer's inability to grow up. Alternatively, they may represent a child or children. In the following dream the kitten is the dreamer clearly showing the role she is playing in relation to her boyfriend. If she understands the message, she will try to alter her kittenish ways which obviously annoy him, or find a more compatible boyfriend:

The Dream—'The Playful Kitten'
There was this pretty, playful kitten romping around the sitting-room. It noticed my boyfriend and, after climbing up onto his shoulder, began to play with his hair. I expected him to respond in a friendly, playful way but instead he looked annoyed.

Archetypal Figures

The Self is an archetype. It is a figure holding out hope for things to come and in it lies the potential of the individual. Initially, in the search for greater self-discovery, this figure will be the same sex as the dreamer. Later, when we have travelled a little further along that path of self-discovery, the figures will be both male and female, representing in Jungian terms the *anima* and *animus*.

Archetypal figures appear in many guises, from a shadowy figure to a character or creature we do not recognize. Since we have so many different inner qualities, moods and faces—which range from the neglected or worst side of our nature to the unfulfilled genius waiting to be expressed—there are just as many different figures to symbolize all of these.

When the need arises to reveal the darker side of our nature, we call upon the image of a person who, from personal experience, best represents the negative traits we need to acknowledge and understand in ourselves. Everyone is a Dr Jekyll and a Mr Hyde to some degree—and the encounter with our own Mr Hyde usually comes as something of a shock.

Anima and Animus

In addition to the good and bad characteristics, we also possess a counterpart figure. In every man there is a feminine aspect, and in every woman there is a masculine aspect. When a man searches for his dream-woman, he is looking for someone who fits the identikit image he has of his own feminine counterpart, his *anima*. And every woman, in her search for her dream-man, uses her masculine counterpart as her model. Falling in love and having obsessional crushes on one particular person is the result of projecting the archetypal image (of the *anima* in the case of a man or the *animus* in the case of a woman) onto a likely face.

The archetype of our ideal partner often appears as a god or goddess, prince or princess, hero or heroine. The unconscious image of this partner is so closely linked with our own *anima* or *animus* that in some dreams it is difficult to know whether we see our counterpart self or the ideal partner we hope to meet one day. In the story of *Sleeping Beauty*, where the prince awakens the princess, the princess represents both the dreamer's image of his perfect partner *and* at the same time symbolizes the awakening of his other half, his *anima*. If, however, you identify with the princess, then the prince symbolizes your dream-man or the awakening of your male counterpart within, your *animus*.

The Exercise

There is no better way to 'know yourself' than through your dreams. This is accomplished by understanding the motives and behaviour of the characters found in your dreams. Since it was you who created these characters, for the express purpose of telling yourself something about yourself, only you can relate what their message is saying.

In this exercise the different figures who have appeared in your dreams to portray personal characteristics have to be identified, so you will be looking for people you know, fictitious characters, celebrities, animals, archetypal figures, and your own *anima* or *animus*. Once having recognized these, you will then be in a position to analyse each character and try to understand their motives and reasons for behaving in the way they did.

These discoveries then have to be related to personal knowledge, circumstances, situations, experiences, worries, hopes and fears.

Exercise 12—Dream Figures

By listing and then analysing the figures found in your dreams, you will be able to recognize many self-reflections and truths.

Make a list of all the figures featured in the dreams you have recorded in your Dream Diary over the past month.

Identify and classify these as people you know, fictitious characters, actors, actresses, celebrities including members of the Royal family, and archetypal figures.

Make a list of any animals, fish, birds or other creatures.

Try to understand how these figures feel by placing yourself in their position. Note, in particular, their mood if you can. Are they happy? Sad? Frightened?

If you discover a shadowy or unrecognized person, concentrate on every detail associated with him, her or it that you can remember. This might be your Mr Hyde or it may be your genius.

Should a dream include your mother or father, see them first as playing out their own role as the person you know them to be. Then see them as archetypal principles, with the mother-figure representing compassion and femininity, and the father-figure representing authority and masculinity.

Archetypal figures in the form of angelic or elevated beings discovered in your dreams will be associated in some way with your high ideals, religious beliefs, aspirations, and future potential.

Discover how the characteristics and moods of all the figures relate to you, your ideals and your present circumstances.

Summary

Dreams   — know no bounds.
            — are created by you, showing you have attributes as great as any inventor, author, scriptwriter and film producer.
            — inform literally and symbolically through the use of many different characters.
            — use people you know, fictitious characters and archetypal figures to reflect personal traits and individual potential in order to help you to 'know yourself'.

— introduce royalty, actors, actresses, policemen, nurses, doctors, animals, birds and fish in attempts to point out the dreamer's role in life.

— compensate.

— introduce the dreamer to his or her counterpart Self, the *anima* or *animus*.

13.

Collective Dreams—Individual Messages

There are certain actions, places, characters, animals and scenes which appear time and time again in our dreams. In principle these have the same meanings, and it is only when these meanings are applied to different personal circumstances known only to the dreamer that they become an individual, meaningful message.

One example of this is the dream of being lost in an unknown town and walking alone along unfamiliar streets. Symbolically it means the dreamer has lost his or her way in life and does not know 'where they are'. Many experience this dream when they have lost their sense of direction through having no aim or hope for the future. This happens to most of us at some time or another but usually we pick up the trail and continue on our way: if we do not, then a dream of this nature is likely to occur to point out our exact position.

Travel and movement, in one form or another, are always present in dreams, for this symbolizes our destiny. Few dreams, if any, are totally motionless scenes. Depending on the movement or mode of transport, much can be discovered about the effort a dreamer is putting into life, the nature and urgency of a problem, and the time-scale involved. Jet travel obviously suggests high-flying ambitions and speed, cycling indicates that plenty of personal energy is being used to drive ahead, whereas boarding a crowded bus tells the dreamer they are going with the crowd and so perhaps need to become more independent and self-reliant.

Making our way through life brings us into contact with others and with our surroundings, so it is our home, relationships, feelings, health and our hopes for the future, all contributing to our destiny, that are closest to our heart. It is not, therefore, surprising that collectively, dreaming minds incorporate these facets of life into dreams which have similar meanings, yet at the same time become personal messages when applied to individual circumstances.

Travelling, houses, dreams of various characters and people, water, animals, hills and mountains, all provide basic themes for dreams which are experienced by everyone if and when the need arises. Understanding their symbolism is simple, for it is based on our surroundings and our everyday language, so they reveal not only the meaning of the dream but show that both words and dreams produce images from the same source in exactly the same way.

Although it is seldom realized, our everyday conversation is full of double-meaning and symbology. From the casual remark 'watch your step' to discussions using more intellectual metaphors, word-pictures are chosen for their ability to produce powerful, message-conveying images. Dreams also choose and create word-pictures for the impact they make. Examples of this linguistic link between dreams, everyday events and conversation can be seen in the following dreams:

Journeys

Walking, running, jogging, skipping, cycling, travelling by car, bus, train, boat or aeroplane—all represent the different ways in which dreamers make their way along life's highway, their destinational path. Stopping at crossroads, bus stops, railway stations or airports often occurs in dreams, showing that a stage has been reached in life where the dreamer should pause, in order to decide in which direction to travel next.

The Dream—'The Train Journey'
I was sitting in a train, looking out of the window enjoying the countryside flash by. There were other people in the compartment but I did not notice them particularly. The train stopped at a station, I got out, and the train moved on. I then realized I had made the mistake of getting out at the wrong station, and was stranded. When I woke up, I was in a very worried state.

The Collective Meaning: The worried feeling left by this dream shows it to be a warning dream. Travelling on that train reflects the dreamer's placid attitude as she makes her way through life. She is not particularly interested in, or bothered by, other people, nor is she paying much attention to where she is going. To alight at the wrong station and then realize this points out that the dreamer should consider the future more carefully in order to avoid a situation arising from disinterest or neglect.

The Individual Message: Only the dreamer, a lady whose family had grown up and left home (and who had, in fact, lost interest in life), was able to identify the circumstances symbolized by this dream. By applying the complacency shown with the warning given, she was able to begin taking an interest in life again, so hopefully she will avoid a predicament which could lie ahead.

Buildings

Buildings, especially houses, feature in dreams more than any other single object or character. Unless the dreamer is house-hunting, in which case a house will literally reflect the property they are looking for, dream-buildings symbolize the whole self. They are the Mansion of the Soul. Sometimes dreamers return to their dream house night after night and know it almost as well as they do their real home. Since this house represents them, body and soul, and since they do not know themselves totally, it is not surprising that in this house there are often locked rooms, secret staircases, corridors, attics full of treasure, and cellars, where they dare not set foot.

When a dream house is viewed from the outside, the condition of the paint, the state of the brickwork and the foundations are important features to note because these give the dreamer a symbolic view of how he appears to others. It represents their appearance—if this is dilapidated, they can smarten up their outer-image.

The Dream—'The Terraced House'
Visiting this house is a regular nocturnal habit and I know it well. It is one of a terrace and it has a few steps leading up to the front door. From the outside it looks small and narrow but once inside it is rambling and enormous. In fact, there are so many rooms, I have not yet fully explored all of them. There are several living-rooms which are spacious but it perplexed me to discover that some of them are occupied by odd-looking tenants. There is a cellar which is cold and dark and when I venture to the top of the stairs leading down to it, I have a haunted feeling. The rest of the house is warm and friendly and usually I love going there.

The Collective Meaning: This house is a typical Mansion of the Soul. For the outer appearance to be small and narrow suggests that this is how the dreamer thinks he or she appears to others, but the dreamer also knows this is a false impression. Inside, they know there is a wealth of space and potential which may not yet have been expressed, so there is much more to them than others realize. The tenants in some of the rooms represent roles the dreamer plays when in certain circumstances and the haunted feeling in the cellar is a hidden fear which sooner or later will materialize, when it will have to be faced.

The Individual Message: Dreamers who visit the Mansion of their Soul do so in order to view and take stock of themselves in the light of recent experiences. Again, only the individual dreamer will be able to apply the meaning of the symbolic scene to circumstances they alone know, and so derive the personal message. If the dreamer is honest, he will discover that he has developed certain characteristics, symbolized by the dubious tenants in the mansion of their soul, which are not attractive and should be evicted from their personality.

Water

Water plays a vital role in life. We are dependent on it physically and we rely on it psychologically to create the images which symbolize our deepest feelings and emotions. This symbolic use is reflected in our everyday language as well as in dreams, with descriptive word-pictures in the form of such expressions as 'floods of tears', 'still waters run deep', 'getting into hot water', 'sink or swim', and many more.

As the symbol representing the mysterious realm of the feminine-unconscious, water becomes a source of spiritual energy, baptizing the emotions in the primeval waters of life, and so bringing about a rebirth and new hope for the future. And as the 'fluid' side of the personality, it ebbs and flows as moods, taking on the shape best fitting the circumstances. On its darker side, there are the tides of tumultuous emotions. These can inundate, engulf, and drown emotionally, just as effectively as in reality, for we are not only dependent upon water to survive—we are at its mercy too.

The symbolism associated with water is reflected in dreams of the sea, lakes, rivers, streams, pools, ponds, springs and fountains, and also in activities associated with water. Swimming, diving, water-skiing, rowing, and boating are all used metaphorically. These activities relate to emotional reactions and encounters in life and, although each dream is special to the dreamer, there is that underlying commonalty with its collective meaning, which becomes personalized only when individual circumstances are applied to it.

The Dream—'The River'
Looking over hills into the distance I could see a river winding its way through a valley. I made my way towards it and stood on the bank watching the clear water run by. Something on the opposite bank attracted my attention but there was no way I could swim across that river, even though I wanted to.

The Collective Meaning: This dreamer is both looking ahead and at her present situation and sees quite clearly that life, symbolized by that river with its twists and turns, is passing her by. Seeing it in a valley shows that the emotional side of her life is narrowed-down and is running low, but something desirable on the opposite bank indicates she does have an objective, even though she believes it to be unobtainable.

The Individual Message: By recognizing the circumstances symbolized by this dream and its implied meanings, it should be possible for the dreamer to get into the swim of things a little more and so not allow life to drift by. The danger of attaining her objective should be weighed against a boring, frustrated existence, especially as there are more ways to bridge that river than swimming across it.

This dreamer revealed she has been in the same job for some years and has not received the promotion she feels she deserves. Her love-life is non-existent at present, too. All this is shown in the dream, and so too is a remedy. 'Take a chance' is the overall message telling her 'nothing ventured, nothing gained', so it is hoped she will take this advice and jump in.

Another common dream involving water shows a view of the ocean from a cliff-top. In the distance a huge tidal wave approaches the beach where there are many people. This wall of water moves nearer and nearer to the shore, sweeps up it, drowning everyone in its path, and rises up to within a few inches of the cliff-top where the dreamer is standing. The dreamer is always safe but watches in horror at the inundation around her.

Translating the symbology in this dream reveals that from time-to-time tides of enormous emotion do sweep up on individuals—usually when they are least expecting it—and metaphorically drown them. Those who have this dream are observers, noting it happen to other people while they themselves feel they are slightly above all that. Such a dream serves as a reminder to say that no one is really safe, if they possess any feelings at all.

The Exercise

Collective, basic dreams with similar symbols and scenes account for almost one quarter of our dreams. As well as travelling dreams, those of houses and those of water, there are other basic dreams which have similar meanings yet reveal individual messages when applied personally. These are events which are watched by the dreamer and, although they do not participate, the action relates directly to them.

Watching an aeroplane in the sky, which sometimes lands safely and sometimes crashes, is one such example. Occasionally, this dream proves to be prophetic but more often than not it is symbolic, showing that the high-flying aims or ambitions of the dreamer need to be brought down to earth urgently. This particular dream is experienced when problems from the outside world weigh heavily upon the dreamer.

In this exercise you will discover that many dreams are of the shared, basic type and you will be able to discover which of your own dreams are of this nature. You will probably find, too, that when you begin to take an interest in them, they will respond by appearing in your dreams, just to illustrate and prove their existence.

Exercise 13—Collective Dreams—Individual Messages

In this exercise you will be looking for collective, basic dreams which in essence all dreamers have from time-to-time. These have similar meanings but become individual, personal messages when applied to your own circumstances. It helps to identify these themes if you ask other people about their dreams of this nature.

Seek out from the dreams already recorded in your Dream Diary any which involve travelling, describing houses or reflecting water.

Pay special attention to your present dreams for these may well produce excellent examples of the dreams you are seeking.

If possible, compare your own collective, basic dreams with those of other dreamers.

Note in which of your dreams you are participating and in which you are the observer.

Summary

Dreams — can be collective but become personal when their meanings are applied to individual circumstances.

— always include movement.
— involving travel represent the dreamer's road through life, their destiny.
— in which houses are featured symbolize the dreamer as a whole. They are the Mansion of the Soul.
— of each dream-house are, like the dreamer, unique.
— reflecting water symbolize deep feelings and emotions.

14.

The Psychology of Dreams

Freud tells us dreams represent our repressed desires and that they are conceptual visions of the unconscious imagination contaminated by the conscious. Jung, on the other hand, sees dreams as experiences of the collective unconscious of mankind, where encounters take place with those inherited primordial principles in the form of cultural archetypes. Some contemporary psychiatrists, using the computer as their model, see them simply as ways of ridding the brain of unwanted behaviour patterns and outmoded information. They say dreams are 'a multi-modal perceptual simulation'.

Philosophers believe that in dreams we try to resolve our problems, and theologians suggest dreams are divinely inspired, while conversely there are those who claim such messages are dictated by the Devil. The sci-fi author pretends dreams come from influences outside the galaxy—and some psychics believe it.

We could carry on and on with these definitions and, although they are all probably correct from the standpoint from which they were launched, they contain an element of conjecture. Conjecture is one thing, *proof* is another. Science has helped us to understand when and how we dream by discovering REMs (Rapid Eye Movements occurring during sleep associated with visual dreaming) and mental circuitry, but this does not tell us why or what we dream.

The question 'why do we dream?' is as profound as 'Why are we here?', so really the question is as unanswerable as it is unaskable. What we dream is another matter. Many great thinkers from the Bible and from Homer onwards have offered their reasons for this, but the truth is that no one really knows anything on the subject at all because of that sharp division between the dreamt dream and the narrated dream. Someone once said that death does not exist because the only people qualified to verify its existence are unable to do so. A similar paradox is true of dreams.

It is true, however, that we know everything about dreams as told or written down, but this is how they appear to us retrospectively in the wide-awake world. In this sense we do not even know our own dreams since these too are recollections which, using the autonomous circuits of memory, force us to modify and adapt to conventional, conscious standards. It is, therefore, the narrated dream we are always discussing, not the dream itself.

Body Awareness

'The eye of man hath not heard, the ear of man hath not seen, man's hand is not able to taste, his tongue to conceive, not his heart to report what my dream was' says Bottom in *A Midsummer Night's Dream*. Sight, hearing, taste, smell and touch normally find expression through eyes, ears, tongue, nose and skin, but in dreams interior communication with its links are different. From the standpoint of a dream the five senses are often controverted into a combined sixth sense which turns the world inside out.

From the outside we see some people and objects as beautiful or attractive. Dreaming of these through altered vision shows us the same people and objects microscopically from the inside. Imagine, for example, the face of a person you love. Invert your vision and see that face from the *interior*, from a dream's point of view. The air as it is sucked into the mouth and down the trachea is gale-force, water for drinking becomes a raging torrent, and the superb meal eaten by romantic candlelight is nothing more than a disgusting pulp, not too far removed from the contents which finally emerge after a journey through the alimentary canal.

Traditionally, canals symbolize the birth canal showing that a descent into the unconscious is also a descent into matter where the body, as a metaphor, becomes an active hive of industry. From this standpoint the mouth is a vast cavern, the gullet a drop into the depths of the Earth, arteries and veins vital conduits, the nervous system an electrical circuit, and so on. Similarly, the Mansion of the Soul, the dream-house, is of course none other than a view from the interior.

If the dreamer has a physical or emotional problem this is likely to be expressed in dreams with an industrial theme, as a disruption or a stoppage in the production line. If the theme is a dream-house and the problem is deeply emotional, the symbol of this will probably be found lurking down in the cellar. Physical conditions on the other hand tend to be discovered more on the ground and first floors where broken furniture, cracks in the walls and creaking stairs warn of relative pathological conditions. Looking at worries and health in this way highlights the difference between 'having a body' and 'being aware of having a body'. This perception is sometimes referred to as 'body consciousness'.

Cosmic Awareness

Hippocrates, the father of medicine, believed in body-energies and focused attention on these rather than on the body's physiological workings. The exploration of psychosomatic medicine today follows much the same path, thus making medicine aware of the vitality and spirit within the body. It is the spirit, psyche, subtle body, dream-body, or dreaming mind, names for an unknown or unknowable phenomenon collectively regarded as the unconscious, that speaks to us through dreams. And when this does speak to us from the inside, it often appears as a god, a goddess, a mysterious being, a hermit, a man, a woman, or even a monster—one of the ever-present archetypes.

The unconscious, in contrast with consciousness, cannot be discussed as a phenomenon belonging to the present because it, like dreams, can only be discovered through retrospective reflection as a memory. Yet we know it exists as the creator of dreams and of certain psychic and physical signals. The unconscious also has to be thought of in terms of the personal and collective unconscious, the individual pool and the shared ocean of experience.

In a dream, conscious awareness is united with the unconscious because a dream has roots in both consciousness and unconsciousness. It is a bridge over which images from the inner world travel to the outer, and impressions from the outer world travel to the inner. On the occasions when preoccupation with the personal unconscious is diverted or overcome, a symbolic rise from the depths can launch us high into the spacious dream world of the collective unconscious, among the universal archetypes. Here we have an independent existence, another life entirely, where the dream dreams the dreamer.

'People do not dream, they are dreamt. We undergo our dreams,' wrote Jung, who tended to see dreams from the collective unconscious standpoint for most of the time. It is interesting to note that the Germans clearly make the distinction between 'I dream'—'*ich Traume*', and 'the dream dreams me'—'*es traumt mir*'. This is seen in the first of 11 verses of the poem called 'The Inverted World', from the collection *Die innere Welt, der ausseren Welt, der inneren Welt* by the Austrian writer, Peter Handke:

I wake up asleep:
I don't look at objects, and the objects look at me;
I don't move, and the ground moves under my feet;
I don't see myself in the mirror, and I in the mirror see myself;
I don't pronounce words, and words pronounce me;
I go to the window and I am opened.

To be catapulted out of one life into a second, where the only semblance between the two is that the second—like the first—is the dreamer's own experience, a fantastic journey to a place that can only be called the Land of Dreams. The person we are most likely to meet there will be ourselves, although rarely can we accept this when we bring the memory of strange encounters back to reality. The king, the queen, a god or goddess, a shadow—can these figures truly be ghosts of ourselves? Freed from the limits of reality, our inner selves—the archetypal selves—will be discovered out there in our personal dreamscape. The quality of these inner beings is energy, so each dream figure will represent different aspects of vital forces at the individual's disposal. These vital forces manifest as principles, so not surprisingly they can take on every form imaginable.

The shadowy figure who frequents the land of dreams is probably the neglected potential or frustrated side of the dreamer's nature. Everyone has a shadow-figure and, because this is nearly always one of their worst sides, it tends to remain in the background, unnoticed.

The encounter with the shadow can be frightening but once it is accepted that it is part of us, fear vanishes, for how can we be afraid of ourselves? Sometimes our own shadow has shades of another, reminding us of someone we greatly dislike. This is because that person has become our mirror and in this we see our own reflection.

Great Mother Earth

Every woman is a realm of incarnate feminine energy, embodying feeling, instinct, intuition, compassion and unconscious awareness. She is the Great Mother Earth representing wholeness, and this wholeness is found in four main archetypal figures—the Mother, the Princess, the Amazonian and the Priestess, and their negative counterparts:

The Mother is recognized by the protective, maternal spirit with an ability to nourish, shelter, love and make a home. She also has an opposite side to her face—the **Terrible Mother**. This mother is possessive, devouring, smothering and destructive. She is the angry green-eyed goddess who jealously enslaves her lover and husband, as well as her children.

The Princess is the child within the woman, the eternally youthful girl and the flirt. She has the power to attract as well as being attractive. Her other face, the **Fatal Siren**, is not so pretty. She is the wrecker of marriages and is the image of erotic fantasy.

The Amazonian is the intellectual qualities in a woman. When this aspect of herself is developed she will be a successful career woman well able to compete with men. The counterpart to this image is the **Huntress**. She is the career woman who hounds and despises men either because her ambitions have never been fulfilled or because she has failed to develop or recognize her own animus.

The Priestess resides in the inner sanctum of woman, the heart, and is full of intuition and instinct. Society disparages these qualities so there is no visible place for her in the real world. None the less she exists, secretly, and if she does emerge she is often wrongfully recognized by most as her darker counterpart, the **Witch** or **Sorceress**. The Witch or Sorceress is a primitive form of female intuition that cuts a woman off from life and the spiritual sphere. She becomes trapped in her own world and, as an archetypal figure appearing in dreams, symbolizes all the negative aspects of womanhood.

The Wise Old Man

The Wise Old Man complements the Great Mother Earth. Every man is the embodiment of the intellect, enthusiasm, determination and conscious appreciation. Together, these represent logical reasoning and are found in the four main archetypal figures—the Father, the Prince, the Warrior and the Priest, and their negative counterparts:

The Father is recognized as a figure of authority, law, order, social convention, the provider, and masculine protectiveness. His negative counterpart is the **Ogre**. Here is the oppressive, cruel father who threatens with rigid discipline and over-conformity.

The Prince is the youth containing the seed of potential growth for the future. He is also the seeker. The distinction between the seeker and his darker side, the **Wanderer**, is slight. This vital force shuns responsibility and commitment, thus producing the eternal 'Peter Pan'.

The Warrior is the daring, successful individual embodying ambition and drive. When this aspect of the self is developed, tycoon qualities are manifest. The opposite side of this coin is the **Dictator**. This aspect, with its aggressive egotism, becomes dominant when the emotions are suppressed and neglected.

The Priest is the knowledgeable manipulator of forces and energies, the extrovert mouthpiece for inner thoughts. His counterpart is none other than the **Black Magician**, a figure who often appears to be helpful initially but is then revealed as a trickster.

The four aspects of womanhood and the four aspects of manhood, each with its shadowy counterpart, form the basic archetypal pattern within the individual. Rarely does one archetypal figure dominate the whole self, but when it does the results are disastrous. A balance between the four positive aspects is what should be strived for, plus the recognition of the four negative aspects, knowing that under certain circumstances, they too may emerge.

These archetypal figures may themselves be symbolized. For example, a spider, with its husband-devouring nature, can symbolize the feminine figure of the Terrible Mother. Sometimes, this is how a mother appears in an offspring's nightmare. Other examples are policemen to represent the Father-figure, Sleeping Beauty to represent the Princess or romantic girl, the mermaid to represent the Fatal Siren, and so on.

In addition to all this, every woman possesses within herself the figure of a man who is, in Jungian terms, her animus, and every man possesses within himself the figure of a woman, who, again in Jungian terms, is his anima. These figures are the proverbial 'dream man' and 'dream woman' and their images are the key to understanding the opposite sex, and to helping us reconcile our head with our heart, our emotions with our intellect.

The Exercise

Dreams view life from many different standpoints. Sometimes they see it from a telescopic standpoint, sometimes from a microscopic standpoint. These stances, not surprisingly, introduce strange dreamscapes and into these are cast various archetypal figures.

If you can accept that you possess within you basic archetypal figures, each representing a different characteristic, you will then be able to understand what it is you are trying to tell yourself through your dreams. Watching other people act out their roles during the day enables you to recognize the Wanderer, the Siren, the Warrior, the Mother or the Dictator around you—but remember you also play many parts, although these are not as easy to recognize in yourself as they are in others.

This exercise involves observation during the day as well as noting in retrospect figures in your dreams. Recognizing your own characteristics in the cloaked, archetypal figures is important and you will find that once you begin to concentrate on this aspect, your dreaming mind will respond by providing you with plenty of excellent examples. And once you do recognize these characteristics, you will be able to watch yourself switch roles or moods to suit the occasion or encounter. This is clearly visible in dreams but it is not so obvious to you when you do it during the day.

Exercise 14—The Psychology of Dreams

In this exercise, using yourself as the model, try to take the standpoint of the creative aspect of yourself responsible for altering your image and moods when awake, and producing your dreams in sleep.

Watch yourself for character-changes during the day when awake.

If a shadowy or unrecognizable figure has appeared in any of your dreams, try to discover which of your eight archetypal images it represents.

Note any archetypal figures which reflect your developed or dominant characteristics.

Note any archetypal figures which reflect your underdeveloped or undesirable characteristics.

Try to distinguish between your archetypal figures and the figure of your animus or anima.

If animals, creatures or objects are found in a dream, discover if these are symbolic stand-ins for any of your eight archetypal figures. Is a spider, for example, another way of expressing an overbearing female, archetypically the Terrible Mother?

Summary

Dreams — are memories, therefore it is always the narrated dream we talk about and analyse.
— can take a telescopic view of life, seeing it from a global standpoint.

— sometimes take a microscopic view of the body, from the interior.
— allow the spirit, psyche, subtle-body, dream-body, dreaming mind, all names for the unconscious, to express itself.
— show us our different characteristics as archetypal figures.
— introduce to us our four main archetypal figures and their darker counterparts, representing qualities, characteristics and moods.
— sometimes use symbology to represent these archetypal figures which, in turn, represent a particular characteristic.

15.

Dreams and Death

Belief in an afterlife arises mainly from religious teachings, evidence from spiritualists, death-bed visions, and from those who have experienced temporary clinical death. There is, however, another source which for the most part is ignored yet night after night offers us glimpses of another dimension with which we are more familiar than we probably realize. This source is our dreams.

There are many unanswered questions concerning life itself so evidence to support an existence after death poses even greater questions. One reason for this dilemma seems to be that we are looking at life and death from the wrong standpoint—the three-dimensional field. From here, we cannot but help identify ourselves with our physical body and the so-called real world about us. Not surprisingly, this makes it almost impossible to believe that the motivating force within us can possibly exist without a physical body. Coming to terms with death and belief in a continued existence is, therefore, very difficult indeed.

The grief at not seeing a loved one around as before is real and terrible for us, the beholders. But if we could take a stretched-out time view and see that we, as a spirit, inhabit a body—seen as the Mansion of the Soul in our dreams—for a limited tenancy only, we can perhaps begin to understand and accept that we all have to vacate it sooner or later. 'In my father's house their are many mansions'—John 14:2. In this we see that the tenant moves on from temporary accommodation into a more permanent abode.

Fortunately, the logical, conscious standpoint is not the only one from which to investigate such a vital question as this. The unconscious assesses both life and death in a very different way, from an entirely different standpoint, expressing its findings through feelings, inspiration, instinct and intuition in dreams in the form of powerful symbolic imagery. This aspect in each of us knows, without doubt, that there is life after death; furthermore it pays little attention to what seems like an abrupt end to physical life. It regards life as one long continuum.

The following dream, from a very sick woman who died shortly after telling me her dream, is one example of the way in which the unconscious reflects this message. In its simplicity it shows death to be a panacea and at the same time assures the dreamer that awareness or life goes on.

The Dream—'Death'

I was standing by my hospital bed feeling very well and strong. The doctor came along and said I was cured and could go home. I felt exhilarated but when I looked at the bed I saw myself lying there, dead. I still felt exhilarated.

The sceptic may think this is merely a wish-fulfilment dream, in the hope of a complete cure, but ending in death it can hardly be that.

This next dream also expresses solace and hope, but in contrast to the literal imagery offered in the previous dream it uses a sequence of collective archetypal and symbolic imagery. The dreamer was to undergo radical surgery soon after experiencing this dream.

The Dream—'Deep Mid-Winter'

I was floating through a forest in mid-winter. A woodcutter was felling trees which crashed onto frozen ground that showed signs of having been previously ravished by fire. Suddenly, it was as if it were springtime and new, green blades of grass and vegetation were pushing their way up through the charred yet fertile ground. I awoke feeling happier and certainly more confident than I had for many months.

Some dreams have more than one meaning and this is one such dream. One interpretation is that it offers the dreamer a message of hope foretelling recovery from the forthcoming operation. But it also symbolizes death, not as an end but as an event in a seasonal round of birth, life, death and resurrection.

In the first instance the woodcutter who saws away the dead wood can be seen to represent the surgeon who cuts away the diseased tissue, making way for a growth of healthy, new tissue. In the second instance the woodcutter is recognized as the archetypal figure of the Reaper of Death. The forest in the dead of winter symbolizes physical quiescence, or the apparent death of all life. But spring surely follows winter and in the charred fertile earth new life is stirring and will soon emerge.

Maybe the dreamer will survive the operation, maybe he will not; either way the dream can be seen as a sign of hope in both the short term and the long term, for overall it gives a profound glimpse of the everlasting cycle of life.

Archetypal and collective symbols projected into a dream of this nature can, if understood in the alchemical and not the chemical sense, assure and reassure the dreamer—and those who hear the dream—of transformation and continued survival. To understand it in this way, all that is necessary is to adopt the other standpoint, that of the unconscious, the view the alchemists and mystics take. In this context, sleep is seen as the prime state of awareness and the awake state as secondary.

Some evidence to support this is found in the fact that babies dream long *before* they are born. Logically, scientists believe this to be impossible because babies have not had any experience in the real world, therefore they have nothing to dream about. Nevertheless, experiments show that they do, and continue to do so when born. For the first few days of their life they sleep for

95 per cent of the time and according to their brain-wave patterns they are having extremely active dreams. But as they experience more and more in the outer world, through their five physical senses, they stay awake longer and longer until eventually, as adults, they sleep and return to that greater field of existence for only one third of each day.

The Mystery of Sleep

Before we can dream, we have to sleep, and in the mystery of sleep lies a profound clue relating not only to the phenomenon of dreaming, but to death and to our very existence. Little is known—other than a few physiological facts—about this state, and if we were not so familiar with sleep it could be frightening, yet it is not. When we are tired (a feeling indicating the need to escape from outer reality and make contact with that inner sublime source) we long to close our eyes and slip off into that strange unconscious state.

How close the state of sleep is to the state of death we do not know, but we do know that descriptions of heaven, the firmament or paradise offered by religious texts, spiritualists and those who have apparently experienced death and returned to life, are identical to scenes described in dreams. Shakespeare, as mentioned earlier, certainly saw the similarity when he wrote 'to sleep, perchance to dream—ay there's the rub; for in that sleep of death what dreams may come when we have shuffled off this mortal coil?'

Further evidence to support the belief that the sleep-state and the state of death have much in common is to be found in every churchyard. There you will discover the inscription 'fell asleep' or words to that effect, on virtually every tombstone. In this lies the promise of resurrection and rebirth, for sleep—whether nocturnal or the sleep of death—is not a permanent state but one of transformation.

Visions and Dreams

In wide-awake visions and in dreams, dead relatives, partners and friends often appear to a dying person. Sometimes they act as messengers, telling them of their impending departure from life, sometimes they come to accompany them on the journey from here to eternity. But the dead also appear to others who are close to a person who is soon to die. In one dream a woman saw her sister who had died when very young. She stood by her bedside, smiling, and holding a white wreath in her hands. She said 'I have come for mother'. Their mother was in perfect health at that time but a month later she died suddenly from a heart attack.

Reports from both those who have experienced death and survived, and those who have glimpsed death in a dream and died soon after, frequently describe an identical bright, illuminating light, or 'a being of light' who appears to be an angel from heaven or some great spiritual master. From a man who had been certified as clinically dead, yet lived again, comes this description: 'I floated right up into a pure, crystal-clear light. It is not the kind of light you see on earth. I did not see a person yet this light had a special identity. It is the light of perfect understanding and perfect love. I now know no fear of death whatsoever.'

Comparing this with the following dream related by a man who died a week later, similarities cannot be ignored: 'It was just a ball of light, almost a globe about 12 to 15 inches across. As it appeared a feeling came over me of complete peace and relaxation. I could see a hand reach down from the light and it said ''come with me. I want to show you something''. I reached up and took the hand and as I did so I felt I was being drawn up out of my body. I looked back and saw my body lying there on the bed. As I left it I took on the same form of light, almost like white smoke but it had colours, too.'

The Exercise

By understanding sleep, not from the physiological point of view, but from that of the spirit, dreams can be seen as excursions into another dimension. For one-third of each day, and indeed for one-third of our life, our attention is withdrawn from the outer world and focused on inner space, where we *experience* in a prime unfettered way. This region is where we were before we were born, where we go to in dreams and where we return to when we die.

Returning to the source each night keeps us in touch with our origin and our spiritual home. The realization that this is so suggests a very different concept of life and death compared with the inadequate explanations offered by logic and science. It is the outer, material world that is seen to be the limited, transient world, and the inner world with its limitless horizons that is recognized as the real, everlasting state of being.

As an exercise, try to see life from this point of view. See sleep not as an intruder wedged into wakefulness, but as a source of strength. During sleep you receive physical healing of the body as well as emotional and spiritual sustenance, so acknowledging this as the divine source that it is, just before going to sleep, helps to strengthen the link.

Exercise 15—Dreams and Death

Recognizing that the land of dreams is also that of eternity, dreams can prepare you for death by showing you that there is nothing to fear. We are already familiar with sleep and visit that other realm, the source, each night.

Search your dreams for evidence of survival after death.

Note if any departed relatives, partners, friends or animals have tried to contact you through your dreams.

If you wish to become more familiar with your own inner realm of the spirit, look for dreams rich in archetypal and symbolic imagery.

Invite other people to tell you of their experiences and dreams involving other dimensions and the dead.

Incubate your own dream of eternity, heaven or the life-hereafter if you feel it would help you to understand life, death and their meaning.

Summary

Dreams
    — of death provide answers to life.
    — offer evidence of survival after death.
    — remove the fear of death.
    — show sleep to be the prime state of awareness and existence.
    — experienced by the dying bring comfort, peace, relaxation and reassurance.
    — and visions both reveal that there is another dimension beyond the limited three-dimensional field—the Source.

PART TWO

The Interpretation of Dreams

16.

Confronting your Dreams

The origin of dreams, literal or symbolic, lies in the unfathomable depth of consciousness. For want of a better descriptive term this unknown background is called the *unconscious*. Although its nature remains a mystery in many respects, certain qualities and effects have been observed; from these, conclusions regarding the unconscious have been made. And since dreams are the most common expression of the unconscious, they provide most of the material for its investigation.

Few dreams are literal action-replays of past events, to be taken at their face-value. Most are not, therefore, in accord with what we call logical reasoning but instead show substitution and deviation, strongly suggesting that as well as using its language of symbols, stand-ins and representations, the unconscious also has an independent function. Dreams of this nature not only fail to obey our instructions, but oppose all conscious belief and intention.

If the conscious attitude to life is dogmatic and one-sided, a dream often takes the opposite view, as if to redress the balance. If, on the other hand, the conscious attitude is that of the middle of the road, a dream will emphasize this either to applaud stability or perhaps to show the dreamer that his or her approach to life is too narrow and lacking in the spirit of adventure.

The attitude of the unconscious is important for it is a psychological statement revealing a hitherto unknown, suppressed characteristic, or a potential gift. Only the dreamer truly knows what this statement is saying because the truth, if revealed to someone else, may violate their self-respect. The dreamer who has disgusting dreams, cruel dreams or unspeakably awful dreams may ask: 'Why do I have such lurid dreams?', but the majority who experience these never pass them on to third parties, for fear of being misunderstood and misjudged.

The Interpreter

'A skilful dream interpreter is he who has the facility to observe resemblances,' said Aristotle. Since the majority of dreams are metaphorical or symbolic, recognizing this is the first step towards understanding them. Discovering what or whom they resemble or represent is the second.

Since dreams are private messages from yourself to yourself, obviously the best person—in fact the only person—to interpret them is *you*: you created them for specific reasons, using your own unique set of references. Although dreams have a collective, symbolic language they also use everyday words, phrases and puns as verbal resemblences and many of these have a relevance to the dreamer only. This is because they arise from experiences, events and ideas in life which form a personal network of associations.

When interpreting your dreams, begin by reminding yourself that you created them in the first place, therefore everything in them, bizarre though some scenes may seem, relates to, or means something to you. Maybe your unconscious dredged up past half-forgotten memories, used snippets from television, reflected incidents which were not registered consciously, or even was totally original in its bid to pass on its message. Whichever it is, telling yourself that your dreams are your own unique productions places you in more or less the same state of mind you were in when you created them. Interpreting them from this standpoint is, therefore, a great advantage.

The more complicated the dream, the more steps it takes before its message is revealed. To understand a literal action-replay dream, little more is necessary than taking it at its face value and recognizing the situation to which it relates. But a symbolic or metaphorical dream has first to be translated from the unconscious language of dreams into the more literal language of the real world, and then applied to a situation or circumstances, before its message emerges.

Finally understanding what it is you were trying to tell yourself is not always the end of the story. The importance of any message is that it progresses, alters, illuminates or tempers life in some way. Dream messages are no exception so if they contain advice and solutions, as they often do, try to act upon them. The classic example to remember in this respect is the Pharaoh who took such positive, practical action when he heard Joseph's interpretation of his dreams.

The following selection of dreams includes collective and personal dreams, simplistic, literal action-replay dreams, symbolic and archetypal dreams, and grotesque nightmares. Read through 'The Dream' and interpret it yourself before comparing it with what I have suggested. Look at every dream from the practical, literal standpoint first, not the mysterious, for they are mainly concerned with this life and everyday matters. Only when this has been explored, albeit briefly in the case of some dreams, should you move on to the metaphorical, psychological, psychic, symbolic and archetypal approaches.

17.

Literal Dreams

Literal dreams seem to be less complicated than symbolic dreams because they use scenes and characters known to the dreamer. To some extent dreams reflect the way the dreamer thinks. If he or she tends to use logic and reason in the face of trouble, to solve problems and to run their life generally, then their dreams will have practical everyday themes and include familiar settings, objects and recognizable people.

The meaning and message of a literal dream are usually of a practical nature. These are easily discovered but they can have a symbolic meaning as well. Very often, both apply to the dreamer but the practical meaning, especially if it is a warning, is the most important because, if acted upon, it could avert danger or avoid serious trouble, so always look for this first.

'The Doctor's Surgery'
I was in the doctor's surgery, just as I had been the previous day when the doctor told me that my blood pressure was too high. The doctor in the dream told me this too, but she added if I learned to relax, I would be alright.

This is an action replay of an event from the previous day. Its purpose is to reinforce the warning about having high blood pressure, but in addition to this it offers the dreamer a way of helping herself by suggesting she learns to relax, a practice well-known for its tension-reducing ability.

'The Accident'
The only part of the dream I can remember was driving my red sports car along a straight road. Suddenly, the road took a sharp curve to the left and I put my foot on the footbrake but nothing happened and I found I had hit a brick wall. I awoke feeling the dream might come true.

This literal dream is warning the dreamer to be extremely careful when driving his red sports car. It also tells him to make sure the car is well maintained, and in particular he should pay special attention to the state of the brakes. If he does not take action on the advice of this dream, it may well become prophetic.

From the symbolic standpoint the dream shows the dreamer has a driving ambition which he needs to control and handle carefully. If he does not, then he could be stopped in his tracks by coming up against that proverbial brick wall.

'The Past'

This same dream repeats itself time and time again. It takes me right back to my childhood and then, like a film, shows me events that have taken place over the years. It does not make me feel sad nor particularly happy, I just watch it.

This dream will probably continue to repeat itself until the dreamer understands what it is she is trying to tell herself in this way. As a re-run of her life she should look at the events, not as part of a dream, but as experiences from which she can learn something. They probably relate in some way to her present situation, so once she sees the link between them the dream will recur no more.

'Shoplifting Nightmare'

I was in a large department store, by the cosmetic counter. I stole a lipstick and put it into a large holdall but before I could walk away from the counter a store detective came up and arrested me. When I woke up I realized the dream had gone over something that really did happen to me last year. I want to forget it but now this dream has brought it all back to me.

One aspect of this dreamer wants to forget all about that shoplifting spree, but another aspect cannot, so relives the experience to remind herself how awful it was to be arrested in public. Going over it in this realistic way is meant to act as a future deterrent and not simply to stir up feelings of guilt.

'Loss of a Neighbour'

My next door neighbour was very sad because her husband had died. She was crying and I tried to comfort her but found myself feeling as bad about it as she did. It is over two years since he died and his widow has recovered from the shock and is no longer sad, so why should I dream this now?

In this dream the dreamer placed herself in her neighbour's shoes. She was feeling all the pain and emotion her neighbour felt when she lost her husband two years ago. The fear has probably crossed the dreamer's mind that she may have to face similar circumstances one day. To experience these feelings in a dream can emotionally innoculate against them, should they ever be brought on by a bereavement.

'The Future'

This was such a happy dream I was very sorry when it ended and I woke up. It was about a wonderful holiday that I have been hoping for one day. Everything about it was perfect. The beach, the sea, the hotel, the food and the people were all a delight.

Life, it is said, is how we make it so the message from this dream is that if the dreamer makes careful plans and then makes up her mind that everything is going to go exactly as she wants it to go, she can really have that dream holiday. It is not impossible to make a dream like this come true, especially when a little positive programming is practised during the day, to help put into practice the good ideas and feelings hatched during the night.

'Ex-Boyfriend'
I spoke on the telephone to my ex-boyfriend and he asked me to meet him in a cafe. When I arrived there I found him with several of his friends who play together in a musical group. He went on playing the drums and ignored me completely.

The telephone conversation between the dreamer and her ex-boyfriend shows there is still a connection between them and in some ways they are still on the same wavelength. Seeing he ignored her in the cafe, and continued to play his drums, however, shows him beating out a message of independence. In other words, this dream is telling the dreamer that the relationship, from a romantic point of view, is over.

'Uphill Struggle'
Soon after I retired I dreamed that the road outside my house, which is rough and steep, went on and on. I usually manage to walk up it easily, but in the dream it was a terrible effort. I am a fit person so I know it does not reflect my health.

Walking with difficulty up this rough road shows the dreamer's path through life seems to be an unrewarding, uphill struggle. He probably feels there is no point in carrying on now he has retired but this is where he is wrong. The dream clearly shows him the situation he is in. If he does not do anything about it, life will drag aimlessly on and on, so he should begin to make new tracks leading to a new goal. He knows his health is good, so there is no excuse for him not to do this.

'The Lesson'
The classroom, other pupils and master were so real that when I woke up I could not believe it was a dream. The one person in the class I do not get along with was the entire centre of the dream because she had been singled out for ridicule by the master. Normally, I would have been delighted, but in this dream I actually felt very sorry for her.

The obvious lesson to be learned from this dream is that of compassion for others, even those whom we do not like. Maybe the dreamer can become better acquainted with the girl she thinks she dislikes by understanding how she feels. From the dream it appears this girl is often singled out for unfair ridicule but no one seems to notice, or even care. Both the dreamer and the other girl could benefit from this dream, if some friendly steps are taken.

18.

Symbolic Dreams

Symbolic dreams reflect feelings, deep emotions, intuition, insight and inspiration in relation to the dreamer's destiny. Sometimes they use substitution, with one character standing in for another, sometimes they incorporate past incidents to represent more immediate circumstances. Most dreams of this nature are on a personal level reflecting everyday symbolism and representation, while others are further removed from conscious awareness and use collective and archetypal symbolism. Only after careful consideration do these become meaningful because the source from which they arise, the collective unconscious, does not form part of the dreamer's personal network of associations.

In our dreams, we are likely to meet dragons alongside familiar objects, yet their presence seems as normal as that of a cat or dog in the home. The wise old man, the wishing tree, the magical walled-garden and the hidden treasure are there too, as part of our undiscovered world, supplying us with that which is lacking in our life and helping us to achieve our heart's desire. If, as it would appear from this and other evidence, the unconscious is really so superior to that of consciousness, why bother with the real world at all? The answer, perhaps, is that while incarnated and incarcerated in a physical body, in a dimension appreciated only through conscious awareness, the way to understand, survive harmoniously and to evolve in these circumstances is to take and make the best of both worlds, the conscious and the unconscious.

Through the symbology of dreams we encounter far-reaching ideals, and it is by bringing these back to reality and putting them into practice that we can understand and assist ourselves and others. Carefully consider the following destinational, self-analytical, warning and hopeful extracts from dreams, and then compare your understanding of them with the suggested interpretations. Only when the dreamer applies the extracted meaning to his or her own personal situation and circumstances can the complete meaning and message be discovered, but analysing a dream from the collective standpoint contributes considerably towards this discovery.

Top Ten Dream Themes

Certain dream themes are used by most dreamers at some time or another to convey messages symbolically. The ten most commonly used are as follows:

1. Journeys (= destiny)

Dreams featuring a journey, travelling or moving in some way from one place to another represent the dreamer's destiny, their way through life. It is not, therefore, surprising that these are by far the most common of all dreams. The dreamer may be walking, driving a car, travelling on public transport, riding a horse or roller-skating. Depending on the driving force and taking into account any delays and encounters on the way, much is revealed about the dreamer's destiny and their path through life.

2. Houses (= the dreamer)

The second most common dream concentrates on a house, the Mansion of the Soul. This represents the dreamer as a whole—body, mind and spirit. Different characteristics are to be found in each room, with ideals discovered in the attic or even a tower attached to the house. But fears may be lurking in the dark basement and the dreamer's outlook on life can be seen through various windows. The garden surrounding the house is the dreamer's personal Garden of Eden, symbolizing his or her environment.

3. Water (= feelings, emotions and circumstances)

Dreams of water are almost as common as those of a house and again this is not surprising since they reflect deep feelings and emotions. Water also provides excellent metaphorical scenes which sometimes turbulently convey a message and at other times calmly state the truth. If the still waters that run deep mean anything when awake, their image in a dream, depending on whether the water is clear or murky, means even more.

4. Falling (= a fear of falling from grace)

The feeling of falling through space or jumping off a cliff is experienced by most dreamers several times a year. This is believed to be more an experience in light sleep than a dream, occurring soon after 'falling asleep', but nevertheless this feeling is often incorporated into a dream. When it is, it warns that the dreamer has lost control of a particular situation or perhaps they feel they have fallen from grace or lost status. They may even have fallen in love.

5. Flying (= a psychic ability)

Over half of all dreamers can fly in their dreams. By flapping their arms, jumping into the air and sometimes peddling as well, they find they can levitate and travel weightlessly several feet above the ground. This is known as astral travel or astral projection, a state whereby the soul is thought to temporarily leave the body. On occasions the astral traveller has journeyed to faraway places and returned with information as evidence showing that they indeed made such a journey. Symbolically it means they can rise above worldly problems.

6. To be chased (= problems are not faced)

To be chased by a monster or an unknown person strongly warns the dreamer that life is catching up on them. Maybe they are trying to run away from (or even get away with) something, but whatever it is the pursuer is usually an aspect of the dreamer's own self. Sometimes the dreamer is naked or is running down the street wearing only a very short vest. This means they are vulnerable, especially to criticism, or it could be that they feel their cover is down and they do not wish to reveal their true emotions.

7. Loose teeth (= changes are to be expected)

When it feels as if teeth are loose or if one or two fall out, it means the dreamer is going through a state of change. These dreams usually occur during adolescence and before the middle years at times of uncertainty and upheavals. The transition from school to work, changing from one job to another, getting married or moving house are when they are most likely to occur. The symbology used to represent this state is the transition from babyhood to childhood, and from old age to very old age, times when teeth really do fall out.

8. Snakes (= energy drives)

Snakes lend themselves perfectly to symbolic expression. From the religious serpent to the snake in the grass, the viper in the bosom to the phallic symbol, they have the power to convey human energies in more than a dozen different forms. Sexual drive, jealous ambition, wisdom, cunning, good, evil, healing, envy and souls of the dead may all be represented by a snake. Which of these it represents is discovered by investigating the context in which the snake appears.

9. Royalty (= the inner realm)

More dreamers dream of members of royalty than care to admit it. Apart from a one-way familiarity on the part of the dreamer, due to the sovereign and her family's frequent appearances on television, which brings them into the dreamer's living room, the symbology of kings and queens, princes and princesses is much more personal. It relates to the inner kingdom of the individual dreamer, where the king and queen may represent the dreamer's parents or, depending on the context in which they appear, they may even represent self-importance and ideas of grandeur.

10. Death (= a new beginning)

Seeing oneself lying dead in a coffin is most alarming but symbolically it has a positive message indicating the end of one phase in life and the beginning of the next. It is an 'off with the old and on with the new' message, encouraging the dreamer to look forward to a rebirth and second chance in life. To see someone else dead is rarely prophetic; it may be pointing out that they too are beginning a new phase in life or it could reflect the dreamer's hostile thoughts directed towards that person whom they wish, metaphorically, were dead.

19.

Life's Journey

Dreams About Travel

Life is a journey from the cradle to the grave and this journey is our destiny. Metaphorically, it is sometimes an uphill struggle and at other times the going is smooth, but whichever it is, every step along the way can be reflected symbolically in a dream. Train journeys, skipping, and even marking-time represent part of that journey and since we are continually on the move, if only through time, Destinational Dreams, involving travel and movement, are by far the most common.

'Travelling Man'
Many of my dreams show me travelling from one place to another in search of I know not what. My wife is never with me but what I am looking for has nothing to do with her.

Travelling and seeking in this way tells the dreamer that he does not know what he truly wants from life. 'Seek and you will find' is one way of looking at the problem, but his dreams show he has done enough of this. It is time he set himself a specific aim, albeit small, and go for that as the first step in the right direction.

'Feet'
Both my feet were injured and walking was a problem, yet my feet are really in excellent form, so why should I have this dream?

Dreams focusing on the feet warn the dreamer to be extremely careful how he treads, and difficulty in walking means he should consider every step he takes. If this metaphorical meaning is applied to circumstances known to the dreamer and he acts upon this advice, he should at least avoid 'putting his foot in it'.

'Good Friends'
A good friend and I were on a coach trip, travelling at speed. We were chatting and laughing at the world flying by and I woke up feeling as if I had been on holiday.

This happy journey shows two friends with a shared destiny—at least it is shared for part of the way. They have probably experienced similar things in their lives, so they have much in common. Each will help, support and encourage the other and so make life more meaningful and certainly much happier.

'Missing the Bus'
Having waited for what seemed hours I turned my back for a moment and during that time I missed the bus I was hoping to catch. I watched it drive away with the most awful feeling inside, and when I awoke this feeling was still there.

Having waited a long time for that bus indicates that the dreamer has already waited some time for a certain opportunity to turn up. Missing the bus as she did warns her that she must be prepared to be vigilant and jump to it, whatever 'it' represents, directly she spots it. Wait, watch and be ready to hop aboard.

'Towns and Cities'
Most nights I dream I am driving through cities and towns in search of an elusive something. I do not have to travel in my work, nor do I visit many places, let alone towns and cities.

Dreams reflect the person so here is seen someone whose ambition drives him to great lengths to discover something that will lead him nearer to his goal. Maybe this goal is nearer to him than he realizes so he should begin to look within himself and not at those distant towns and cities, themselves symbolizing rather remote communities which the dreamer does not seem to be part of.

'The Bike Ride'
I was riding my bike along a road which led to the top of a hill, then sloped away steeply. I was very careful not to get too near the edge. I cycled on and came to a narrow lane leading away from the danger zone and ended up in some fields but unfortunately woke up before reaching anywhere in particular.

This dream represents a situation which the dreamer will recognize once the signs and symbols are translated. The road is her destinational path along which she has elevated herself to a point where a potential danger lies ahead. This will be averted but the narrow lane suggests certain limitations are to be expected. Riding a bicycle shows that personal effort has been put into life and it is this same personal effort that will take her on to fresher fields.

'On Top of the World'
Having walked for miles I arrived on top of a mountain with a beautiful clear view all round. I was alone but did not mind this a bit.

Walking alone means progress and satisfaction in life for this dreamer has been due to her own physical effort. Soon a peak is to be reached when she will feel on top of the world. She will then be able to see exactly what her position is and where she is going next.

'The Brick Wall'
While walking with my fiancé across a field we came to a brick wall, but instead of climbing it we both seemed to float up and over it.

Walking together in a field represents a shared destiny with things going well, at least for a time. The brick wall warns of an obstacle facing both of them but together they will rise above it without much trouble.

'Running Downhill'
Something very nasty was chasing me down a hill and at the bottom was a narrow brook that I jumped over quickly and easily.

To run downhill away from hostility tells the dreamer that she is running away and not facing the brutal truth. Doing this will not solve anything. The narrow brook represents a feeling or emotion which will be easily and quickly overcome; whatever it is this dreamer fears, it is not as bad as she thinks.

'Blue Skies'
Standing on a hillside overlooking a valley with a far-reaching view before me, I felt the warmth of the sun, as it shone from a lovely blue sky. This dream could not possibly relate to my life as it is at present. Rain and storms would be more appropriate.

Dreams do not reflect warmth and sunshine just for the sake of it so it must mean that this dreamer is soon to emerge from dark and dismal days. Her dream is telling her that she will then be able to view her situation objectively and feel satisfaction at the way she passed through that valley and rose above her troubles. Blue skies really are around the corner, so she must not lose hope now.

'The Wrong Track'
A zig-zagging road lay ahead of me. I came to a T-junction and after deliberation took the left-hand road which turned out to be a dead end. I went back to the junction and tried the other road which soon turned into a steep hill. I never did reach the top.

The zig-zagging road symbolizes the dreamer's destiny, showing that although she puts a lot of effort into life she does not seem to get anywhere. Taking the direction initially and ending in that cul-de-sac was not really a wasted journey but more an experience from which she could learn something. The steep hill indicates that she is beginning to rise above problems around her, but it will not be easy. She should, however, try to keep on the same track she is now on.

'Survival Course'
Along with a friend I was on a sort of survival course. We both succeeded in doing fantastically dangerous things, things we could never have done in real life.

Life is, among other things, a survival course and a dangerous one at that. The successes in this dream symbolize possible triumphs which could be achieved in life, if they were seen from a more adventurous standpoint. The dream is meant to give confidence to the dreamer, who can then inspire his friend.

'Enforced Journey'
A man persuaded me to get into his car and against my better judgement I did. It was an horrific experience and ended with me being lost in a place I did not recognize.

First, there is the clear literal warning saying that the dreamer must not be persuaded or forced into a car against her will. Secondly, the symbolic meaning tells her that she must not allow herself to be taken for a ride by someone she does not like or trust. If she does she will end up in very unfamiliar circumstances and feel she has lost her way in life.

'The Ski-Lift'
I was waiting for a ski lift to take me up to the top of the mountain. The person in front of me fell and hurt herself and so did several others. This made me nervous and I awoke before I was transported to the top of the ski slope.

If the dreamer was going on a skiing holiday soon after this dream, it should have served as a practical warning. From the symbolic point of view, waiting means anticipation, and the mountains represent the dreamer's high ideals and pinnacles of hope. To see others fall before reaching the top may undermine her confidence but it does not mean she is necessarily going to do likewise. Her path is different from theirs so she must go ahead irrespective of their failures. She can, however, learn something from their stumbling blocks.

'The Trick Cyclist'
Looking up at someone standing on a tall building I was amazed to see them get onto a bicycle and ride it on a high wire between two buildings. This person only reached half-way across and I woke up!

Someone, and maybe it is the dreamer, is treading a very precarious path at present. The message is 'keep calm' and do not deviate too far one way or the other. To reach halfway means the person in question is at least halfway there.

'The Turning Wheel'
A great wheel, with teeth around the edge, was turning slowly.

The wheel was a symbol of the alchemists representing 'the circulating progress', destiny. The individual is always at the centre. A tooth-edged wheel tells the dreamer she should be sure to fit into the pattern of life, like a cog in a wheel, if she wants her life to run smoothly.

'The Quay'
I was on a ship which sailed across an ocean, possibly the Atlantic. The sea was very rough for part of the way then it calmed down. We reached a quayside and when I stepped on shore I vowed I would never go on a ship again.

It seems this dreamer's voyage through life has taken him through a few storms but he has now reached a stage where he has disembarked from the turmoil. His vow never to sail in the future means he does not intend to put himself in a position where similar situations could ever develop again.

'The Narrow Path'

I was walking up a narrow lane which was getting steeper and steeper. Ahead of me I could see a large tree and one of its branches had fallen across my path. There did not seem to be a way round it because the sides of the lane were too high for me to climb.

This dream reflects the increasing uphill struggle the dreamer is having at present and it warns of an obstacle ahead, in the shape of that branch. This probably symbolizes someone in her family who is standing very firmly in her way so she has to decide whether to confront him or her, or retreat. The narrowness of the lane shows there is little escape, nor much choice but to do one of these things.

'The Motorway'

While driving happily around country lanes I suddenly found myself heading for the motorway. There was no turning back but once I was actually on it I was not as afraid as I thought I would be.

The peace and quiet of the present is soon to be broken for this dreamer. He can expect the pace of life to increase considerably and although it may seem dangerous and high-powered to begin with, he will soon find it is not as bad as he expected. In fact, it could be quite exciting.

'Speeding'

I was riding a fast motorbike and speeding in forbidden places, although there were no restrictive signs. A policeman caught up with me and ticked me off. I do not own a motorbike or even a car.

This dream is a warning, telling the dreamer that speed is not the name of the game and that observing life's unwritten rules makes sense. The policeman is the authoritive aspect of himself who really knows what is right and what is wrong, so he should try to listen to this more often.

'The Red Fire-Engine'

A red fire-engine was racing along and making an awful noise. That is all there was to the dream, but I somehow associated it with the news next day that my friend had tried to commit suicide.

Red is for danger so here is a warning sign to begin with. And fire means energy, life-energy. Maybe this *was* a telepathic message from a friend in need telling the dreamer of his desperate plight. Help and support from the dreamer would, it seems, be most welcome.

'A Friend in Need'

I was walking in a wood with a friend I have not seen for many years. Both of us felt miserable and we were discussing our family problems. There was a very anxious atmosphere among the trees and I awoke feeling quite concerned about this friend.

The dreamer and her friend have a close link from the past and both seem to have family problems. Trees symbolize families and the anxious feeling probably relates to these. The dreamer should try to contact her friend to see if she could talk to her about her problems, and vice versa.

'Lost in the Back Streets'

I got off a train before it had stopped and then found I was lost in the back streets of an unfamiliar town.

Alighting from a moving train warns the dreamer not to opt out of a situation before he has achieved that which he set out to achieve. If he does, he will find himself in a far worse position than before and not know where he is or where he is going.

'A School-Girl's Dream'

This is a recurrent dream where I find myself on top of a bus going to school with my friends. I am shocked to find I have no clothes on and I desperately try to hide myself with my schoolbag. I am very worried at the thought of having to get off the bus, naked.

Travelling on top of a bus shows this schoolgirl is heading towards a goal, probably school and learning. Finding herself naked means she is afraid of revealing her true self to others and tends to cover up her feelings. In young people, the shedding of clothes in a dream is a sign of shyness and it also symbolizes the discarding of inhibitions, usually sexual.

'Back Seat Driver'

I was sitting in the middle of the back seat of my husband's car, and from this difficult position I was actually driving the car. To make matters worse, my husband was in the front seat telling me what to do.

This seems to be a case of the back seat driver taking over. Although the dreamer is, metaphorically, probably used to taking a back seat in her marriage, she may not have realized until this dream pointed it out to her that it is she who is the driving force in the relationship. Her husband expects a lot from her and even expects the impossible, but her dream tells her quite definitely she is in control.

'The Sports Car Driver'

A long straight road lay ahead and I was driving a lovely sports car with a long, low bonnet. I felt like a real racing driver and passed almost everyone else on the road. It was marvellous to have so much power under my control.

It is right to assume this dreamer is an ambitious young man, although Freud would almost certainly see in his dream strong sexual expressions as well. The straight road, the long, low bonnet, and the competition could all symbolize his urges in this direction, but it can also be seen to reflect his career and the desire to succeed. From this standpoint his future looks good, as he overtakes others also trying to reach the end of the road first.

'Cross-Country Race'

I was running in a cross-country event and among the competitors was my old games master from my school days. Somewhere along the way fighting broke out, but I was not involved in this.

This cross-country race represents the dreamer as he takes part in the daily rat-race of life. He probably has a sporting outlook, seeing he used this theme to convey his message, but he also feels he can teach those who think they are superior (symbolized as teachers) a thing or two. Seeing he did not take part in that fight tells him he should continue not to enter the battle of wits which often rages around him.

'The Foreign Airport'

I was stranded at an overseas airport. There was a steep flight of steps to the exit and the passport office but I was too frightened to move.

Foreign places mean foreign experiences are to be expected. To be stranded at an airport shows this dreamer is between two phases in her life and is afraid to take the next step forward. It will take energy and courage to do this, but first she should try to establish her own identity. 'What sort of person do I really want to be in the future?' is the question she has to ask herself.

'Walks of Life'

My grown-up daughters and their husbands were walking ahead of me. I tried to catch up with them but they walked faster and faster and took short cuts, so in the end I gave up and was alone, miles behind them.

It is a fact of life that one's children do their own thing and often get ahead of their parents. This dreamer is disappointed that her offspring have not taken her along with them, but as the dream is trying to point out, their path is not the same as hers, and they are in the fast lane, anyway. If she could accept this she would know it was impossible to ever catch up with them. This does not mean she has to be lonely, but rather that she should not look to her family as the only source of company and support.

20.

Self-Discovery Through Dreams

The language of dreams is a psychological text and often it is saying something very different from what we would expect. Many problems in life are psychological, in that they involve feelings which cannot be put into words. In fact, some can *only* be expressed in dreams for here they are safe from prying eyes and the judgement of others.

Understanding our feelings when they are represented symbolically presents difficulties only when we try to apply logic to them with words and conscious meaning. The language of dreams and the unconscious cannot be learned as if it were a foreign tongue because it is not a language of words but images, and these images can have more than one meaning. In addition to this, they mean different things to different people

The collective dream language with its traditional images usually forms the main part of a dream. This uses different characters and objects as symbols to represent someone or something else, so it is this disguise that has to be recognized. For example, a house and water traditionally represent dreamers and their emotions. The house becomes the Mansion of their Soul, and a pond becomes the pool of unconscious feeling welling up inside.

Houses and Buildings

In our dream house and in the garden or on the streets around it, we often meet friends, foes, and those we do not know. If these characters are playing themselves, they probably symbolize personal characteristics and traits which we have ignored or perhaps not recognized.

In the following dreams each part of a dream house can be seen to represent one of these characteristics or an aspect of the dreamer. The outside is the dreamer's appearance as well as the face or personality he or she presents to the world. Doors are opportunities which open up onto new understanding, windows are 'the windows of the soul' (the all-seeing eye of awareness), a cellar is the unconscious, and so on.

'A Shack'
I was living in a shack at the bottom of my garden but I went into the house to cook my food, wash and to go to the loo. In the dream the appearance of the house from the outside was far grander than it really is.

This dreamer seems to be downgrading herself. The grander version of her house is showing her that she has qualities and potential she has not yet recognized, so she should begin to build up a much better and truer image of herself, beginning with her outer appearance. There is no better way to gain self-confidence than by looking good.

'The Gift'
I went up lots of stairs and eventually reached the top. I knew I had to look for something that contained a gift. There seemed to be many doors up there which opened easily. I found a box in one of the rooms and knew it contained the thing I was supposed to be looking for but unfortunately I woke up before opening it.

Ascending stairs shows the dreamer is probably rising above a problem and is seeking in an intuitive and enlightened way. All those doors which opened easily tell her that she has plenty of opportunities to discover what that gift is. Probably it is a talent as yet undiscovered, but seeing it in a box points to the fact that the dreamer already knows something about this 'gift'. The box is the clue so it is this which needs to be identified. If 'the box' cannot be transformed into logic, a further dream on the subject should be incubated.

'Two Houses'
There were two houses, side by side. One was much larger than the other and I was living in the smaller one. From it I could see right into the larger one and I found myself walking about in there but I did not feel at home or comfortable.

The smaller house represents the dreamer as she is at present. The larger house may be a glimpse of what she could become, but from the feeling she had when she visited the house, she is telling herself that she does not really want to be that sort of person at all. On the other hand, the larger house could be someone else whom she admires but does not wish to copy or resemble in any way. Which of these meanings applies to the dreamer, only she can say.

'The Classroom'
In a classroom full of children I watched several very naughty boys and girls but the teacher seemed to ignore what they were doing. The odd thing was that the ones who were behaving themselves were singled out and disciplined by this teacher.

This classroom symbolizes the school of life where the dreamer sees many adults behaving badly, like naughty children, and getting away with it. It also shows she has a sense of fair play but she should, on the strength of this dream, ask herself if she is that teacher, and perhaps castigates those around her who do not really deserve harsh treatment.

'The Hedge'
There was a non-descript looking house surrounded by a hedge. What worried me about this hedge was that it completely encircled the house. There was no opening in it anywhere.

This non-descript house sadly suggests to the dreamer that she is a nondescript person. Additionally, her dream points out that she has created a protective barrier around herself to such an extent that this has now virtually imprisoned her. The message is 'break out' of this self-imposed prison, before the hedge grows too high, when it will be too late to escape.

'Looking Back'
I was coming downstairs to the ground level in a house but kept looking back. At the bottom there was someone, a man, waiting for me but I did not recognize him.

For some reason this dreamer is coming down to earth after living too much upstairs in her dreams. Looking back as she did shows she is hankering after the past, going over memories which prevent her from living in the present and enjoying the company of someone who is obviously waiting for her. It is time to look ahead and think about the future, possibly with a view to meeting someone who has their feet firmly on the ground.

'Missing Floorboards'
I was in the top room of a big house. Several floorboards were missing and I nearly stepped into one of the gaps. Although I felt confident and even a little excited, I also felt rather frightened when I realized I could have hurt myself.

Although only the dreamer knows the circumstances or situation to which his dream relates, it none the less reveals something about him as a person. It would appear he has reached a fairly high position in life, he is still ambitious and he is sensitive enough to realize that he could put his foot in it and spoil things. His dream also shows something is already amiss so he needs to tread very carefully and try to repair any damage in order to restore the status quo.

'A Strange House'
In this dream I was walking along a road and found it blocked by a strange yet familiar house. There was no way round it so I am afraid I had no choice but to break in, go right through the house and out at the back. Here I found I was back again on the road and I felt really pleased with myself, but at the same time, I also felt a bit guilty.

A rather bold person is apparently standing directly in the path of this dreamer. Having pointed this out to herself in this way, she also symbolizes a solution. This looks like a face-to-face confrontation which will somehow involve the invasion of this person's privacy. It will probably not be as difficult as the dreamer fears and once she has done it, she will no doubt experience feelings of satisfaction, plus a touch of guilt.

'And the House Was Bare'
I had been out enjoying myself with others who had been good company but when I returned home I found the place desolate. All the furniture had disappeared but I did not feel it had been stolen or that I had been burgled.

This house can be seen as the Mansion of this dreamer's Soul. Unfortunately, it is not so much a question of 'put your house in order' but 'put something in it'. This means furnishing it with treasured memories, aims, hopes and the things that go towards filling all the empty spaces in one's life. Enjoying herself with others tells her that this is a good thing to do, but it does not compensate for that which is lacking within herself.

'Down the Garden'

In this dream I went down to the bottom of my garden and on looking back towards the house, I saw a lovely rabbit hopping on the lawn. It nibbled a blade of grass here and there. I tried to catch it but could not.

This dreamer's garden is her Garden of Eden, her immediate environment. Seeing she went to the bottom of it shows her taking an objective view of herself, and her place and role in life. A rabbit in a dream indicates timidity, and hopping about as they do, nibbling here and there, implies lack of concentration and direction. This tells the dreamer she should be bolder in her approach, and make a few firm aims which she then achieves. Trying to catch the rabbit shows she is already trying to control the habit of 'rabbitting about' but finds it difficult.

'Soul-Searching'

I entered a dark building and tried to switch on the light but nothing happened. This dream has repeated itself many times now and I do not have a clue as to its meaning.

Entering a dark building symbolizes a soul-searching exercise questing the truth or an answer to something. Being unable to switch on the light indicates that no light has been thrown on the scene so far, and the repetition of this dream means the dreamer has not yet understood what it is he is trying to tell himself. When he does, the dream will stop because it has fulfilled its purpose. By incubating the right dream, more clues could be brought to light.

'The Old Home'

I often return in my dreams to my childhood home. My father is there and so are all my friends from the old days. They are always happy dreams.

Returning to our childhood home in dreams shows a need to return to past memories to escape from present commitments. Childhood is comparatively safe, enjoyable and exiciting and so images of this can be used to compensate when things in later life are not so rosy. The father-figure in this dream introduces authority and strength, meaning these qualities may be lacking in the dreamer at present. Above all, dreams of this nature are intended to give a boost of self-confidence.

'Moving House'

We were moving into another house and the thought of the upheaval was worrying me, especially as I did not recognize the house we were supposed to be going to.

Personal insecurity is reflected by this dream. It could be associated with the family as a whole, where changes are about to take place which the dreamer cannot face. The future could be rather different from the present but it is better for the dreamer to be aware of this in advance than have it thrust upon her without warning.

'Down in the Dumps'
I was in the basement of a house which was in pitch darkness. I was trying to cross over to where the stairs should be but I could not find them. I woke up feeling very depressed.

This dream was not the cause of the depression; the dream and the depression share a common cause. Whatever this is lies deep within the dreamer's unconscious, and only he knows what it is. Seeking the stairs shows there is a possible way out of this down-in-the-dumps situation but at present it is not obvious. The dreamer should, however, continue to look for this.

'Painting and Papering'
After finishing painting and papering a room I went out then returned to admire my handiwork, only to discover that the paper had slipped right down the wall, showing all the old, dirty paper underneath.

A room in a dream symbolizes a particular characteristic or facet of the dreamer's personality, so re-decorating it shows the dreamer is trying to clean up or improve this aspect of himself in some way. The dream warns that feelings of exasperation are to be expected due to wasted efforts so extra care should be taken to ensure that everything is in order from the start. Papering over the cracks never was a good idea.

'An Unfinished Building'
There was a strange, unfinished building with a flight of stairs that led to the top. There did not appear to be much else inside except these, but I remember thinking that when it was completed it would be quite a spectacular place. Although I knew it would be dangerous, I began to go up the stairs but woke up before getting very far.

This building shows the dreamer how far she has progressed towards attaining her goal and becoming the person she really wants to be. The stairs mean she has plenty of ambition and has high ideals but the lack of anything else in the house warns that she needs something more than ambition and ideals. It would be dangerous to attempt to negotiate the heights at this stage, but as she saw from her dream, she cannot get very far as things are. Much hard work is necessary to complete that building.

'The Burning House'
My house was on fire and I watched it slowly being destroyed. When the flames died down all that was left was charred rubble, but among this I found an egg.

The burning down of this house warns of the total destruction of the dreamer's image. He must be prepared for an enormous change but the good news lies in the shape of that egg. This symbolizes the embryo of his new personality, his new image, which will arise like the phoenix, from the ashes of his past experiences.

'View From the Kitchen'
I was standing in a large kitchen looking through a picture-window at the garden. I

could see several people lounging about in deckchairs, relaxing and thoroughly enjoying themselves, but I could not bring myself to go out there and join them even though I knew I would have been welcomed.

It is clear to see that this dreamer is rather anchored to her kitchen sink and is almost a slave to hot stoves. She has reached a stage where her whole life revolves round domesticity but through her dream she is telling herself that she should try to take time off and be like some of her friends who manage to enjoy themselves, their gardens and their homes.

'My Grandmother's House'

I was walking about in my grandmother's house, back in the West Indies. Everything was the same as when I was a child, except for a new carpet which I particularly noticed.

This dream shows the dreamer is thinking a lot about her origin with its cultural background. Ancestors, including grandparents, are traditionally guardians of behaviour and they are signs of protection too. The new carpet represents her new life where nothing has changed so far as the family is concerned, but it also means she is 'walked upon' by others. With such a stable, supportive background, the message is that this dreamer has nothing to fear from the present so should walk with every confidence in herself.

'The Candlelit Dorm'

When a child I went to a boarding school so it is not really surprising that I dreamed of the dormitory. In the dream it was candlelit and I was eating fish.

A dormitory-scene indicates that the dreamer is trying to discipline himself in some way during his sleep. Candlelight reflects high ideals and throws light on spiritual matters and understanding, and eating fish means replenishment for the soul. Maybe there is a pun in soul/sole, too. Food for thought is offered here, which should sustain the dreamer in his seeking.

'Through the Mill'

It was raining and I was looking at an old, disused mill. I went inside where it was dark and dusty but when I came out the rain had stopped and the sun was beginning to shine.

This dreamer, it would seem, has recently 'been through the mill'. The experience, which would seem to have involved some form of physical effort, is over, and as a memory can now be added to life's rich pattern. The future, symbolized by the sunshine, is good so he should stop looking back to those days of the dark satanic mill.

'At the Bar'

I was in a house that was more a club than a home. I went to the bar and ordered drinks but when it came to paying for them I did not have enough money. The barman was cross and pushed me, but all I could find were a few coins which were nowhere near enough.

Several warnings are given through this scene, not least that the dreamer treats his home like a club or a pub. He also spends too much time trying to escape from the truth and in so doing probably overspends and finds himself in trouble. Acting as the barman, he did well in pointing this out. In a literal sense this could reflect financial trouble but he may be in debt in other ways through taking more out of life than he is prepared to put in.

'A Windowless Room'

I was in a windowless room. The feeling was terrible and I felt panic at the thought of not being able to escape.

Apart from being in the dark over something, this dreamer also feels trapped. There is no clue as to the nature of the problem, but until she removes herself from that room the problem and the panic will remain. Taking up an entirely new approach would have the effect of moving into another room with a view, and from there things will not seem as impossible as they do at present.

'Up in the Gods'

There were swing doors leading to the foyer of a theatre. I went through them and found people were waiting for the performance to begin. I then went up a steep flight of stairs to a seat high above the stage but unfortunately woke up before seeing the play.

Passing through those swing doors shows the dreamer moving from conscious awareness to his unconscious world. The people in the foyer were aspects of himself, all waiting to see what was to be presented in that personal theatre and on its stage. Past, present and even future events would be enacted and where better to see all this than from that elevated position in the gods?

This dream could become the first in a series of dreams which unfold the dreamer's tale, so he should consider incubating the next instalment.

'An Office'

I found myself in an office full of official-looking documents and files and all the while I was expecting someone to come in but no one did. If they had I knew I was going to be questioned in an authoritive way and I felt most uncomfortable at the prospect of this. I do not, incidentally, work in an office and have little to do with paperwork.

An office symbolizes officialdom in some form or another. The feeling and the look of those documents warns of a problem relating to mistakes made in calculating, perhaps. Since no one came into the room, an aspect or nature of the problem, it appears it is early days so far as investigations are concerned. The dreamer probably feels a little guilty over something, so if he is honest with himself, he will be able to recognize what this is all about, and also discover that it may not be too late to put the record straight.

'An Old-Fashioned House'

I am in this old-fashioned house which I know would be fabulous if it were modernized. The fireplace attracts my attention and standing by this is an old woman with a kettle in her hand, about to make tea.

The message here is that the dreamer needs to modernize herself. By dropping old ideas and creating new aims, she could be as fabulous as she wants to be. Focusing on the fireplace tells her that her life revolves around the hearth, the family, and the little lady making the tea is none other than her domestic image, showing that tea-making is virtually her only role at present. But all this can be changed!

'The Tower'

I was staying in a building which had a watch-tower. From this tower, where I was, I could see for miles and miles in all directions.

Towers symbolize strength—a tower of strength, as well as towering ambitions. A watch-tower suggests the dreamer is keeping a wary eye on her situation and is in an excellent position to do so. She should, therefore, know well in advance of any trouble heading her way and be able to do something about it before it causes too much of a problem.

'Outer Appearances'

My house was leaning over at an unsafe angle and there were cracks in the walls. The chimney pots were damaged and the paintwork could do with replacing. All in all, I was shocked by what I saw in this dream.

The external state of this house represents the appearance of the dreamer and the shock this gave her should prompt her into doing something about it. The passing years take their toll so it is not simply a case of decorating superficially. Rejuvenation, through exercise and diet, could be just as important as a modern hairstyle and new clothes.

'The Haunted House'

I visit this same house time and time again in my dreams and I know it is haunted right at the top, under the eaves. I am afraid to venture up there but I have done so once or twice, and experienced a terrible feeling that I cannot begin to describe.

This house, symbolizing the dreamer, contains at least one mystery that has yet to be understood. It cannot be expressed other than by that feeling of fear, but since this is located in the upper part of the house and not in the cellar it could be associated with the dreamer's own powers. It will, however, remain as a haunting feeling until it is challenged.

If the dreamer dreams lucidly, she could arrange a confrontation, remembering all the while that it is she who created the dream and everything in it, including the haunting feeling.

Water

'Water, water everywhere nor any drop to drink' was intended to describe the ocean but it could equally well be applied to water in dreams. Used symbolically, water appears frequently in dreams to reflect emotions, feelings and spiritual revelations, from metaphorical situations where the dreamer has found himself 'getting into deep water' to spiritually rejuvenating experiences beneath sparkling waterfalls.

Water in dreams has the power to convey energy as well as messages and meanings. It can have a calming effect, or conversely it can produce turbulent feelings which badly affect events the next day. Swimming in crystal clear water has been known to heal aches and pains but, on the other hand, a dream where the dreamer was wading through breaking waves caused her to wet the bed. But which came first? The full bladder, or the dream?

Water has countless images, many of which have personal associations for the dreamer only. The following selection of dreams, however, are of a more collective nature and are experienced by most dreamers at some time or another.

'The Tidal Wave'

I was on the beach and saw a huge wave coming towards me. There were others on the beach and we all ran for safety. I was above the water-line when the dream ended so I survived but I do not know what happened to the others.

This is probably the most common dream of water there is. Since most people have to face emotional pressure at sometime in their life, it is not surprising that they symbolize the situation in the same way, and use on-rushing water as the engulfing force. No one except the dreamer knows what the personal circumstances are, but whatever they are the dreamer is warning himself or herself of approaching trouble. This dream also shows that others are often in the same boat but this does not really concern the dreamer, although it may have been introduced as a note of comfort to know others have suffered similarly. Almost without exception, dreamers survive this dream, so from a prophetic or reassuring point of view the message is that this dreamer will safely overcome the experience.

'The Girl and the Waterfall'

While standing by a waterfall, a lovely lively girl slowly approached and stood beside me. We both watched the water, then she seemed to melt away. On waking I felt very happy and much better than I had for years.

Waterfalls in dreams have the power to wash away fears and problems. They also bring healing energy for they are the waters of life itself. The lovely, lively girl is the spirit of the dreamer, with an eternally youthful image. No wonder the dreamer felt rejuvenated, and probably years younger too, after this dream.

'Rocking the Boat'

I was in a small boat on a fairly calm sea. I decided to stand up and everyone else shouted at me in a very rude and rough way, saying that if I did not sit down they would throw me into the water. I got rather agitated by this and woke up in a state.

The metaphorical message to this dreamer seems to be pretty clear: 'Stop rocking the boat'. If this is applied to a situation that involves the safety or security of others, in a physical or business sense, then the dreamer would do well to try not to make things worse. If he does not heed the warning and act on the advice he has given himself in this dream, then he could find himself in deep water.

'Distant Horizons'
I was standing on the shore feeling I wanted to get into the water and have a swim, but I could not bring myself to do this. On the horizon I could see large ocean-going ships.

The desire to swim shows the dreamer's desire to literally get into the swim of things. The ships symbolize her various aims sailing away, so unless she is prepared to get into the water, she will have to wait a long time for her ship to come home.

'The River Flowing with Milk'
There was an ordinary river running between banks. It had a very chalky look about it and when I looked more closely I was certain it was not water, but milk.

This dreamer's life is passing her by quietly but nevertheless fairly quickly so she needs to make the most of every moment. The chalky appearance of the water that turned out to be milk is a promise of sustenance and good health in the future. It also shows the milk of human kindness is flowing through her veins so she most likely is a great comfort and help to others, and is probably a healer, too.

'A Foreign Port'
I was in a foreign port watching ships and smaller boats bobbing up and down in the water. It was a very peaceful scene which made me feel unusually calm and contented.

Foreign parts in dreams mean foreign or unusual experiences are to be expected. Ports are havens or harbours from the storms of life so whatever the future holds (remembering that this may be the calm before a storm) the dreamer can rest assured that she will be protected from the worst.

'Rock Bottom'
I still am not sure if I was on some rocks at the bottom of a pool of clear water, or if I was in some sort of a deep pit, but there was light above me. To reach this I had to jump, fly or swim up to the surface but I knew I would have to learn how to do this.

It would appear that this dreamer has reached an all-time low in life and is at rock-bottom at present. At least things can only improve from here. Even so, tremendous personal effort will have to be made before he can rise above whatever is causing the problem. The signs to encourage him are the light above and the fact that the water or atmosphere is clear and not murky. He can at least see where his aim lies.

'The Bridge'
Something was chasing me and I made for a bridge over a swift-flowing river. I

stopped half-way and was frightened to go on or to go back.

Something is catching up with the dreamer but only she will know what this is. The bridge is a connection between two sets of circumstances, but it serves only as a temporary haven while she decides which way to go. The swift-flowing river shows things are happening quickly and time is running out so she will have to make a firm decision one way or the other very soon.

'The Paddling Pool'
It seemed like a good idea to paddle in an inviting-looking pool. All of a sudden I took a step and found myself in really deep water.

Paddling in shallow water means the dreamer is tentatively feeling her way into an emotional situation. The dream warns her that unless she is extremely careful she will find herself deeply involved right up to her neck. Having realized the risk she is taking she now has to decide if she really wants to get even her feet wet.

'Oil on Troubled Waters?'
Someone delivered vast quantities of cooking oil to my doorstep. I had not ordered it and certainly did not want it.

This dream warns of personal intrusion, followed by an argument that has little to do with the dreamer. Maybe she will find that she will have to pour oil on troubled waters, in which case she will be pleased she is properly equipped to do so.

'Incoming Tide'
This is a recurrent dream, varying a little, but the theme is always that of the tide coming in steadily and relentlessly. It is not a happy dream but it is not frightening either.

The feeling left by this dream seems to be one of foreboding and the action in it indicates inevitability. Time and tide wait for no man . . . Repeating the message through recurring dreams means the dreamer has not yet accepted what it is that is going to happen. When she does, the dreams will stop.

'The Canal'
I was walking along a canal and I came to a lock. The sides were built up with steel and bricks and a canal-boat was having difficulty in squeezing through.

The traditional meaning of canals is that of the birth canal, the vagina; the water is the embryonic fluid. If this dreamer is expecting a baby, the dream relates to this; if not, then someone she knows is probably having a baby, so she can expect to hear details of the safe but arduous delivery.

'The Flood and the Mountain'
I was walking along a road and on each side there was flood water. In the distance were mountains, bathed in swirling mist.

This dreamer's life is awash with emotions of some kind at present so he will have to tread very carefully indeed in order not to put his foot in it. If he continues on the same path and does not deviate too much, he should eventually reach safer ground and by keeping an eye on the future he will attain the goal that lies ahead—even though it is a rather hazy idea at present.

'The Square Pond'
There was a square pond, still and deep, surrounded by a low wall. There were no fish in it but I kept looking and hoping that I would find some. It was a forlorn hope.

The pond with its deep, still water focuses on a deep emotional feeling or problem. Seeing it is square symbolizes the self, and the wall around it suggests a secret and isolated problem known only to the dreamer. The absence of fish indicates an inner emptiness and the longing for a deeper understanding, but looking and hoping for this is not enough. The dreamer should not give up hope but continue to look for those fish and, if necessary, go out and catch a few for herself.

21.

Encouraging, Warning, Helpful and Revealing Dreams

Since dreams reflect life with its encounters, relationships and problems, it is not surprising that when these are expressed in the language of dreams, their symbolism is as varied and surprising as life itself.

Dream-narratives and the objects found in them do not have just one meaning but many. A table, for example, means different things to different people. It is the centre of family life and much of what goes on in a family occurs round a table. Family discussions, family rows, family happiness and family sadness are expressed here. Sitting at a table the dreamer's father may, in the past, have disciplined him and rapped his knuckles more than once. This 'table', therefore, becomes a humiliating landmark in the dreamer's life, an example justifying the traditional interpretation of a table, which is that it is a sign of self-sacrifice.

To another dreamer, however, a table may be associated with a wonderful feast, happy Christmas dinners and wedding breakfasts, so in no way is their dream-table seen as the sacrificial altar of life.

Extracts from the following dreams include events and objects which reflect everyday life and although they have collective meanings they also have personal meanings as well. When the dreamer applies the general meaning to their own circumstances and takes into account their feelings concerning the particular sign or symbol, the message conveyed through this symbolic dream-image should then be recognized.

Babies

A baby in a dream usually symbolizes a new idea for the future. It is the dreamer's brainchild. To hold someone else's baby shows the dreamer is getting hold of someone else's brainchild or idea and using it as their own. This is not necessarily plagiarism. When a friend has or does something original and someone does likewise, it is not stealing; for the dreamer to give their baby to someone else shows they are 'getting rid of' their responsibilities.

There are many other dream babies as well, as shown by the following selection of dreams centred on this theme.

'Thriving Baby'
I was carrying a baby in my arms and as I walked it actually grew. This surprised me but I felt quite pleased that it was thriving so well.

If this dreamer wants to have a baby, but has so far not been able to, then this could be a compensation dream. It could even be prophetic, telling her that one day her dream will come true, but only time will prove this. Most probably it is a symbolic dream indicating that the dreamer has produced an original idea, associated perhaps with a new business venture. It appears she has already begun this, although it is still in its infancy and she is not sure if it will survive. This is represented by the baby. The feeling of pleasure and that it is thriving so well show that not only will it survive, but if the dreamer continues to carry it for a while longer, it will grow rapidly.

'Many Children'
Many children were around me trying to attract my attention. Some were painting things, others making clothes, and all seemed to be occupied with some task or other. However, one child did not seem to know what to do and pestered me to help him.

Unless the dreamer is a schoolteacher, in which case this dream is an action-replay of her waking hours, these children symbolize ideas she has but cannot decide which one to concentrate on. The child who does not know what to do, yet is surrounded with opportunities, is the dreamer. It is a matter of deciding which task or hobby is the most fulfilling, and a clue toward discovering this is found in the fact that the child who was pestering was a boy. This suggests that the dreamer should look for a practical, even mechanical way of expressing her talent.

'Left Holding the Baby'
I was holding a baby, but since my family are all grown up and I have no intention of having any more, this puzzled me completely.

This baby represents a situation or circumstances which are really the responsibility of someone other than the dreamer. It is a warning dream concerning liability and imposition.

'Pregnant'
I discovered I was pregnant. The realization came as I was walking along a road, approaching a crossroads. As I thought about it I noticed I was holding an old piece of wood that looked like driftwood found on a beach.

This dreamer is approaching a juncture in her life which means she will have to make up her mind which way to go. Discovering she is pregnant may be a literal message but since this is usually a conscious realization it is not likely the unconscious would bother to point it out, too. This pregnancy most probably represents expectancy for the future which is 'pregnant' with new ideas and embryonic hopes. The driftwood could warn of family commitments and attachments, and the problem of breaking or drifting away from these.

'Whose Baby?'
I had been landed with someone else's baby but I felt very responsible for it. Sometimes I couldn't find it and then got in a panic. Once I dropped it but it did not

seem to mind and I picked it up again and wondered how could I be so unthinking. All this gave me a guilty feeling.

This dreamer has been landed with someone else's brainchild. She is the custodian of an idea or project started by another and for some reason she is expected to adopt it and bring it to maturity. She has tried dropping the idea but her conscience will not allow her to do this so there is nothing for it but to get to grips with it and give it a chance.

Animals

Basic human behaviour and nature is often reflected as an animal in a dream. Sometimes an untamed desire manifests as a powerful tiger, or a fear becomes a little mouse peeping round a corner, but whatever the creature its symbolic meaning derives mainly from its verbal use and abuse found in everyday language.

A snake in the grass, naughty monkeys, sheepish grins, as well as the wolf in sheep's clothing, all go to make up the symbology necessary to pass on an important message.

'The Jungle'
I seemed to be in a clearing in a jungle and from where I was hiding I could see the village and the primitive way the people lived. Then some wild animals entered the scene and terrorized the inhabitants.

Most Europeans have been brainwashed into consciously believing that primitive existence is exactly as this dream describes it. But the unconscious dreaming mind of this dreamer knows better than this so is using it symbolically to reflect not tropical turmoil but suburban unrest in the concrete jungle, where he himself lives. The wild animals are the untamed beasts who roam the streets and the villagers are the majority of innocent dwellers, minding their own business.

'A Cat and Dog Life'
A dog was chasing a cat and I felt very worried for the cat. Suddenly, the tables were turned and the cat stopped, turned round and went after the dog. I was on the cat's side although I love both cats and dogs, but it was the dog who made the first wrong move.

The cat and the dog represent two different approaches to life. The cat is the more feminine and intuitive, and the dog the more masculine and intellectual. As principles, the two are often at loggerheads, so much depends on the dreamer's standpoint to understand the message fully. Perhaps this scene relates to a husband and wife situation or to an inner personal conflict between the dreamer's head and heart.

'The White Rabbit'
A large white rabbit hopped around the house just like a domestic cat. I have never had a pet rabbit and know nothing about them.

Rabbits and hares act as psychic guides through the warrens of our unconscious and our dreams. Like the white rabbit in *Alice in Wonderland* this rabbit was inviting the dreamer to follow its trail and take note. It will probably appear again in future dreams when it will hopefully lead the dreamer to further unknown regions of her inner world.

'Puppies'
A litter of lovely puppies was playing together and I had to choose just one of them. This was difficult to do because one was a little smaller and weaker than the others and my conscience told me that was the one I should choose. A robust puppy would have been the sensible choice but I woke up before having made up my mind.

These puppies represent friends, probably young friends, who need friendship. The weaker one is someone who is going to be an under-dog in life, or so it seems to the dreamer, so she feels he or she needs special attention to make up for any unfairness. If this puppy resembles a particular person she knows, she should give them a little more of her time and if necessary give the support she thinks they need. Who knows, maybe she is wrong.

'A Slug and a Rat'
In a cup from which I was about to drink I noticed a horrible slug. It crawled up the side and turned into a rat which scampered away.

The slug is a slippery customer whom the dreamer does not seem to recognize. Seeing it turn into a rat means it (or he or she) will soon perform another low-down trick, and this time its identity will be revealed. The dreamer himself has to be considered as the culprit so he must be very honest with himself, remembering that his unconscious self is unbiased and independent.

'Black Cat'
There was a lovely black cat sitting at the side of the road and I hoped it would walk across in front of me, for luck, but it didn't move.

The road this dreamer wishes the black cat would cross is her own path of destiny. A black cat traditionally means good fortune so at least this is in the air. Patience is needed plus effort to bring about the desired crossing.

'Sheep and Birds'
While I was looking at a flock of sheep in a large field some large birds flew down out of the sky, casting shadow. Other people who were watching with me ran for cover but I stayed. There was an ethereal feeling about this dream.

Fields in dreams symbolizes 'fields of sport', 'fields of interest', 'fields of activity'. Sheep represent those in life who are followers and the large birds brought a message that could cast a shadow of doubt over beliefs. The reverent feeling suggests the dreamer's field of religion is reflected here and seeing he stayed to watch the descent of the birds shows he has the courage of his own convictions. This dream should fortify his beliefs and help him to remain true to himself.

'Creatures Great and Small'
A lovely little furry creature, like a guinea pig or a rabbit, was in a run in the garden. It suddenly began to grow and grow until it became a small lion.

Progress in life is indicated for this dreamer and with this will come a transformation of character. Gone is the timid rabbit and in its place is a much more powerful personality. This new-found role will need to be played slowly, especially at first, because with it comes release from the safe garden run, and freedom of the jungle. If this metaphorical state is related to personal achievement and promotion it will make sense, both as a warning not to overdo things and to give courage when it will undoubtedly be needed.

'Dogs and the Wilderness'
Wasteland stretched in all directions and I wandered aimlessly on and on. A few wild dogs came near once or twice and would have attacked me, but I hid behind some sort of scrub-bush until they went away.

Clearly, this dreamer is in the wilderness at present, without aim and almost without hope. The desert dogs are bad memories which hound him from time to time, but self-preservation is high on his list of priorities so he intends, even if he does not realize it, to carry on. 'Keep going' is the message and sooner or later something will appear on the horizon.

'Vicious Dogs'
As a dog lover I do not understand why my dream involved several dogs, all of whom were snarling and snapping. One of them nipped my ankle and another actually bit my hand.

This dream has nothing whatsoever to do with dogs as creatures. These dogs are symbolic and represent those people about whom it is said 'Who needs enemies with friends like that?' It is meant to serve as a warning about those around the dreamer who take her for granted, take advantage, and even bite the hand that feeds them. If these folk are seen as top-dogs and dogs-in-the-manger types, their bark will be worse than their bite and so the dreamer need fear them no more.

'The Bear and the Abyss'
I was clinging to the side of a bottomless pit and eventually slipped down and down. When I stopped I was faced with a great brown bear. This terrified me and I woke up in quite a state.

The bottomless pit, the dark night of the soul or the abyss, is a shocking state representing the depth of depression and misery. Life seems to be no longer worth hanging on to, due to the terrible circumstances. The bear is symbolic of the *prima materia*, the overpowering mother figure. This will mean something to the dreamer when her plight is seen in relation to this archetype but only she will know if it is the female within herself—the siren—or if it is the image of an oppressive maternal influence.

'The Soldier on Horseback'
I heard horses' hooves on a road, then a large black war-horse with a soldier on its back appeared. There were mourners following but there was no coffin. They all faded away into the distance.

The horse and the soldier represent war. Many men and horses have been slaughtered in battles, most with no known grave, hence the mourners without a coffin. Memories of the First World War are revived with this dream, along with the message that old soldiers, and horses, never die, 'they only fade away'. From the dreamer's point of view it shows how he feels about war, the futility and waste of life. It may also warn of a war-like situation brewing on his homefront, which he should try to avoid if possible.

'An Egyptian Cat'
An Egyptian type of cat appeared in my house and although I am a cat lover I did not like this one. I was actually frightened of it, probably because it had a human face I did not recognize. I felt I had to get it out of my house.

Cats symbolize intuition and instinct, and an Egyptian cat represents psychic power as well. For this cat to be in the dreamer's house means it is one of her own inner faces, and this needs to be recognized, not ignored or eliminated. By accepting that she has these qualities the dreamer will find life takes on an added dimension, but it is probably the feeling of such power that frightens her. Once she knows it can help her in so many ways, she should be able to come to terms with it.

'The Carthorse'
A carthorse was pulling something—a cart or a plough. It slipped, and as it did so it turned into three smaller horses.

Horses symbolize energy and drive—horsepower at man's disposal; the cart or plough represent a burden in life. For the larger horse to divide into three smaller horses means the dreamer is expected to do the work of three people.

'Animal Faces'
Cats and dogs with human faces were walking on the streets. It was rather like a cartoon come to life.

Two types of people are symbolized by this dream. The cats are the psychic, intuitive types and the dogs are the more down-to-earth, logical people. They also represent cattiness and doggedness which are characteristics found in most humans. This dreamer is viewing his fellow men and women in the same symbolic way cartoonists see them, so if he is an artist all he has to do is to paint his dream.

'The Tiger and the Nun'
This sounds crazy but it was a very real dream. A kindly nun was riding on the back of a strong handsome tiger. Sometimes the tiger snarled but she managed to stay on its back.

The nun probably symbolizes the dreamer who usually shows the world her passive, gentle nature only, but she is trying to come to terms with her more energetic, forceful self, her animus. On the other hand, it may be that she is being taken for a ride by a person, her boyfriend perhaps, whom she finds exciting but ruthless. If neither of these explanations apply, then they should be applied to others who may be in circumstances similar to those created in the dream.

'Baboons'

I was surrounded by horrid, large baboons. They were behaving menacingly towards me and although they did not touch me I felt terrified of them.

Baboons represent primitive instincts and an infantile outlook. These baboons may be a manifestation of the dreamer's own instincts, but since there were so many they could represent the menacing behaviour of certain acquaintances. Whoever they are, the dreamer sees them as uncivilized and uncouth, so the dream warns against having too much to do with them.

'Dead Horse'

I was looking down a narrow lane and saw a man with a dead horse.

That terrible saying 'flogging a dead horse' comes to mind. The man is the dreamer who is rather hemmed in with problems and has no choice but to continue on the same track. The dead horse means he has exhausted something and there is no more life or benefit to be extracted from it. There is no point in his continuing with something he has long hoped would be a success because it is finished, 'dead'. He will make more progress if he moves on without it and begins anew.

'The Dog and the Cockerel'

It was semi-dark and I was looking out of a window watching several dogs running round and barking at a large cockerel.

The semi-darkness means the dreamer is partially 'in the dark'—he does not fully understand a particular situation. There is something he does not consciously realize, but seeing he was looking through a window means he soon will. Knowing that dreams are honest, unbiased and use symbolic imagery, the cockerel and the dogs could well be himself and his friends. If so, then he is telling himself that his friends see him as being too cocksure of himself, and as a result they torment him. All he has to do is to stop being such a crowing cockerel.

'The Squirrel'

I was with my boyfriend and a squirrel ran round the room and then it came up to me and bit my finger.

The traditional meaning of squirrels is that they represent domestic affairs, a storing-up of goodies in life's larder. A bite warns that all is not well on this front and, since the dreamer's boyfriend is involved, the future with him—in the domestic sense—should be very carefully considered indeed. 'Biting the hand that feeds you' may apply, but it is up to the dreamer to relate all this to her own personal feelings and knowledge of her boyfriend's washing-up ability. He may be a good lover but hopeless when it comes to making the bed.

'The Dog, the Fox and the Rabbit'
A dog was chasing a fox, then the fox started to chase a rabbit. They all ran off into the distance without any one of them catching the other.

The Meaning
This threesome represents a chain reaction in the dreamer's life where one mood influences the next, and so on. Each animal symbolizes a different way of handling the situation, in its own characteristic way. The dog has the top-dog attitude, the fox adds a little craftiness, and the rabbit tries intuition. Nothing seems to be resolved in the end but at least things are moving.

Fish and Water Creatures

Fish play their part in symbolizing feelings in dreams. As primitive ancestors in the scale of physical evolution they are often associated with fundamental principles such as birth and rebirth, renewal of life and miracles.

All water creatures have the symbolic potential to reveal treasures of the deep unconscious. The frog, for example, indicates transformation, in essence the changing of the frog-personality into that of the regal prince; the whale is the realm of the female unconscious; the crab has the ability to regenerate; the oyster carries within its shell a pearl of wisdom.

'Circling Fish'
I was looking into a pool of clear water watching two fish swimming in the same circle, but in opposite directions. This is all there was to the dream but it was so real that on waking I could not believe I had not just left this scene.

Fish swimming in opposite directions to each other in a circle represent two approaches to life which negate each other. The circle symbolizes the dreamer's inner being, the self, within the cycle of life. According to Jung, the soul has a round appearance. The fish could represent the dreamer's individual and collective unconscious, or their intellect and instinct—a head versus heart controversy. Bringing the two into harmony is the problem but at least this has been pointed out to the dreamer who should now try to achieve this.

'Fish Supper'
There was a table set for one person so I sat myself down and waited. Someone I did not know or even bother to look at brought me a plate with cooked fish on it, which I ate. Apart from there being no vegetables with the fish, it was not an ordinary meal, yet I cannot say what was different about it.

The spiritual significance of fish is that it has the power of renewal, hence its symbolic appearance in many religions. The Celts venerated the salmon, and in the Christian religion its piscean image symbolizes spiritual rebirth. To eat fish as this dreamer did means she will be able to begin life anew. If she has passed through a difficult time recently she can confidently expect a fresh start, possibly based on her religious beliefs.

'Odd Fish'
On a fishmonger's slab many fish were laid out as if for sale. When I looked closely I discovered that they were not the sort of fish one usually sees but instead they were very odd and many were ugly.

'Odd fish, odd folk,' as the saying goes. These fish probably represent acquaintances and friends known to the dreamer. If he recognizes that these friends are 'odd fish' then maybe he can accept them at their face value and enjoy their company which will at least be different.

'A Frog and a Lizard'
A frog sat by a pond and did not move when I went near so I sat by it and watched with him. Along came a green lizard that slowly changed from green into a muddy brown colour. This did not seem to be afraid of me either, and although I played with the lizard I much preferred the frog.

Both these creatures represent transformation and change. Symbolically, frogs are potential princes and lizards are quick-change artists who can disguise themselves in an instant. If these two reptiles can be equated with two young men known to the dreamer, she will be able to see them for what they are, but she has already decided which one she prefers. The frog may not be as witty or handsome as the lizard but he will turn out to be much more reliable and successful in the end. The lizard, who has a certain charm, is a chameleon character who changes his moods quickly and is a much more elusive fellow altogether.

'A Dead Whale'
Lying in the middle of a field was a whale. All I did in the dream was to stand and look at it trying to decide if it was dead or alive.

The symbols in this dream are a land-bound whale and a field. Whales are archetypal of massive strength and power, dispensed benevolently. They also represent the realm of the mother. The field represents the profession or the dreamer's 'field of interest'. If the dreamer relates all this to his life he will find that, although he is in a position of some power and authority, he has allowed himself to be misled in some way. Somehow, he must get back in the swim of things before it is too late.

Birds

Birds represent high-flying ideals, aims and ambitions, as well as flights of fancy. They are messengers too, of both good and bad news, depending on the species. The context in which a bird appears in a dream usually gives a clue to its message.

A bird with its young is traditionally assumed to be an excellent sign for the future, but a moulting, songless bird denotes merciless and inhuman treatment of outcasts and the poor by those who should know better.

'Bird Song'

I was in a garden, the sky was a beautiful blue and a high-flying bird was singing. I knew it was a lark even though I could not see it properly. A most attractive man joined me and together we watched and listened to the music of this bird.

There is a romantic saying 'let's make sweet music', which means 'let's make love'. From this dream it would seem the dreamer is on the brink of a new romance and everything in the garden is wonderful. Or is it? The dream is also a warning pun posing the question 'Is it the real thing or is it only a lark?' Maybe the dreamer knows the answer already, or maybe only time will tell.

'Magnificent Bird'

A magnificent bird the size of an ostrich struggled out of an egg. It preened itself and almost at once became an adult, mature bird. This dream came after several sleepless nights, caused by worry.

This bird symbolizes a remarkably determined and powerful aim or plan which is about to be hatched by the dreamer. Every confidence can be placed in the future success of this and once actually started it will grow from strength to strength very quickly. All worry concerning this project can be safely dispensed with and the dreamer can now rest assured that all will be well.

'Neglected Birds'

There were two birds, one was a pigeon, the other was a chicken. Both apparently belonged to me, although I never had anything to do with pigeons or chickens in my life. The pigeon was well fed and looked healthy but the chicken was neglected and looked really sad.

Birds can symbolize high-flying ambitions, so from this scene it appears the dreamer has two such ambitions, represented by the pigeon and the chicken. The one represented by the pigeon has already taken off but, unfortunately, however much care she lavishes on the other, it will never get off the ground properly, because chickens cannot fly.

'Circling bird'

A bird circled in the sky above me, then it flew off to the west, returned, and perched on my shoulder. I knew, even in my dream, that it was to the west that it flew because I could see the sun was setting in that direction.

Symbolically, birds are messengers bring both good and bad news as well as advice. When this bird circled above the dreamer it was showing him that in his effort to achieve his ideals or hopes he was 'going in circles', not knowing which direction to take. Consequently, he does not get very far. Flying to the west points to 'lost horizons', telling him that he should make a definite aim towards something which he wishes to achieve, even though it may seem beyond his reach. For the bird to return and perch on the dreamer's shoulder is a most reassuring sign of success, because this means his hopes will eventually come home to roost.

'The Egg and the Eagle'
There was an egg, a little larger than a hen's egg, and from it hatched a rather ugly looking bird. As I watched, I realized it was an eagle and, after a few attempts at flying, it took off.

An egg symbolizes potential life, Easter, cosmos from chaos, or the emergence of new hope. In this context it would appear to mean a new start in life for the eagle, synonymous with the phoenix, the alchemical symbol of winged spirituality and rebirth, represents triumph over adversity. So, from the ashes of this dreamer's past, she will soon be able to rebuild a stable future.

'The Crow and the Giant'
I was out in the fields and in the tree around the edge I noticed a large black crow. Suddenly a giant appeared, grasped the crow, and killed it.

This scene of conflict represents the dreamer's strengths and weaknesses as well as warning him that he should beware of these. A crow symbolizes many things from warnings of death to the spirit of Bran. Giants also mean different things to different people, from ogres in fairytales to the image of authoritive adults who, when the dreamer was a child, really were gigantic in size by comparison. Since the giant and the crow are probably aspects of the dreamer he should try to discover which characteristics they represent and then make sure they do not conflict with each other.

'The Swan'
I watched a large, white swan fly over over some houses. At first I thought it was a stork, but as if to let me know it was not this it came back, and I was in no doubt at all that it was a swan.

In mythology the swan is a bird of the sun and signifies solitude and retreat. A white swan symbolizes beauty, purity, grace and sincerity, so in the Christian religion it is associated with the Virgin Mary. In pre-Christian belief it was the White Goddess, the compassionate aspect of Mother Nature. In her dream the dreamer is reviewing these feminine qualities for a reason known only to herself, but whatever this is, she should try to follow the flight of this bird and so become a living example of these special qualities.

'Pent-up Potential'
There were several fluttering birds caged in a confined space. Normally I would have felt like letting them out but in this dream I looked at them without any feeling whatsoever. It was then I noticed that one bird was pecking and subduing the others.

These birds, representing ideas, hopes and aims, seem to be severely restricted. Although the dreamer will know the reason for this, there is, according to his dream, a dominant factor which has escaped his notice.

Symbolized by that pecking bird, this factor is probably an overpowering stubborn streak he has that does not allow room for any other form of self-expression. This one characteristic is preventing the dreamer from becoming a fulfilled and mature person, so having seen the position symbolized in this way maybe he can, metaphorically speaking, clip the wings of that one bird and so give the others a chance.

Snakes

Irrespective of individual feelings towards snakes, they also have collective unconscious meanings which often manifest in dreams. A person who is horrified by them when awake may find they hold no terror whatsoever in a dream because in this context they are conveying not fear or even necessarily a warning, but a principle.

Snakes symbolize the principle of *energy*, from basic sexual drive to energy capable of bringing about physical curves and emotional healing. In between these two extremes of expression they symbolize all the lesser human traits, making their appearance as anything from the proverbial snake in the grass to the cunning of a jealous competitor.

'Coiled Serpent'
What I took to be a coil of rope suddenly started to move and it was then that I realized it was a live serpent. I am really afraid of snakes yet in this dream it did not have a negative effect on me.

The coiled rope, serpent or snake indicates that the dreamer has become aware of an energy curled up within. This energy, known as kundalini in the East, is beginning to stir and it is important that the dreamer recognizes this awakening and transforms and uses it in a practical way before it begins to use her.

'The Snake and the Lion'
A lion took a snake in its mouth and began to shake it but the snake managed to free itself from the lion's jaws and get away. A feeling of horror and fear came over me as I realized it was lurking nearby in the undergrowth.

The snake and the lion symbolize two of the dreamer's characteristics—an enthusiastic energy-drive and his courage. The energy-drive, the snake, may be that of basic ambition, forging its way through the dangerous competitive jungle of life, or it could be purely physical, in which case it is of a sexual nature. The lion, on the other hand, is the courageous spirit of the dreamer which tries to take control of the dreamer's impulsiveness but unfortunately loose its grip on this. The warning here is that the dreamer should realize that he should take control of his powerful drives, or be prepared for the consequences.

'The Snake, River and Bridge'
I was hanging onto a ledge under a bridge and looked down at a river below where I

could see a snake. I fell into the water right by the snake and very quickly got hold of it just behind its head and then held it high above my head. This gave me a most satisfying feeling.

The bridge shows the dreamer to be between two options, the river suggests her emotional life is underlying these considerations, and the snake is a warning related to all this. The action in the dream shows that once she takes the plunge she will be able to control things far more easily than she anticipates. Only she can possibly know what these options and circumstances are but the message is reassuring in that there is nothing to fear and she will triumph in the end.

'Snake in the Grass'

While walking among some bushes and long grass I came across a snake, but I could only see its head. A voice told me to be careful and not to tread on it but it was too late. I did. It was more a feeling of surprise that came over me, not horror or fear as I would have expected. I think this was because the snake did not rear up or retaliate in any way. It slithered off quickly.

The dreamer is about to encounter a dangerous situation which is at present concealed, although unconsciously that small voice within is well aware of this. As a warning, 'beware of a snake in grass' is appropriate, even though it would seem it is too late to avoid a confrontation with someone or some unseen force. It could represent a ruthless, underhand, ambitious colleague who hopes to take the dreamer by surprise, or it may be part of himself which is trying to be over-assertive, but whatever or whomsoever it is, if the dreamer notes what he is telling himself in his dream, he will know that when things do come to a head, the problem will pass without too much trouble.

'The Snake Under the Sideboard'

The dream was all about a party which seemed to get rather out of hand. One moment I was having a fantastic time, the next I felt uneasy, and the reason for this was that under the sideboard was a nasty-looking brown snake. It came out and accidentally I stepped on it and felt its hard, round body under my foot. It was revolting.

Freud would have had no difficulty in identifying the energy this snake symbolized—sex. Parties in dreams often signify the prelude to sexual encounters and from the impression left by this dream it seems the dreamer was not prepared for what was in the minds of others at the party. Treating this as a warning she may be able to avoid unwanted amorous attention and recognize a situation building up to this before it is too late.

'Hissing Snake'

A nasty looking snake slithered across my path and as it did so it hissed at me. Fortunately there was another path leading away from the one the snake took so I quickly ran down this. The surprising thing was that once on this path, it seemed like a different world, although I cannot say why it was different.

The hissing snake, whether a person or an unconscious warning, is a blessing in disguise. Seeing that it made the dreamer alter course in the dream means she should do likewise in real life, because when she does the whole world will seem very different indeed.

'The Scarf and the Snake'
A man was twisting a scarf round and round in his hands until it looked like a twisted rope. It seemed to come to life, but even worse, it turned into a snake which lunged towards me.

This dream is clearly a warning indicating that things are not quite what they seem. Obviously the snake symbolizes an energy-drive directed at the dreamer by a man who fascinates her, but at the same time scares her. The scarf springing to life as it did is almost certainly a sexual sign reflecting the man's intentions. These could be most unwelcome, so unless the dreamer avoids situations where things could happen she will have to face the consequences. With a dream like this she cannot possibly say she has not been warned.

'Healing Energy'
Although I am petrified of snakes, in this dream I found a snake that produced feelings that made me feel happy, not scared. It was thin and was twining itself around a stick as if trying to attract my attention.

Since healing depends on energy it is not surprising snakes symbolize this as well as other energy drives. Seeing this snake had a good effect on the dreamer and that it twisted itself around a stick, resembling the Caduceus of Mercury—the ancient sign used by healers and the British Medical Association today—health and healing are the theme in this dream. Maybe the dreamer is in the healing profession or perhaps he needs to heal himself through his own inner strengths, but either way his dream tells him that there is considerable energy at his disposal to help both others and himself.

'The Python'
A nasty-looking python was in some murky water which I was paddling in. Other people saw it but only I was frightened by its presence.

Seeing only the dreamer was worried by this python means that whatever is going on beneath the surface of a particular situation concerns him only. Murky water represents unseen trouble, and paddling in this shows that the dreamer has got his feet wet—he is already slightly involved. The fear may relate to his inner state of apprehension which needs to be conquered, or to an actual threat from that situation.

Insects

Most insects symbolize minor, but none the less irritating, problems in life. The exceptions are butterflies, dragonflies and bees, representing freedom of spirit and transformation towards greater understanding. Sometimes the problems which bug the dreamer are innermost fears and thoughts so it is useless to ignore them for they have a nasty habit of infesting even the best kept dream houses.

'The Grasshopper'
Several insects were pestering me and I kept brushing them off, but one of them was a grasshopper. As soon as I knocked it off it hopped back onto my arm.

Insects represent petty annoyances which can be brushed off easily. A grasshopper is also an annoyance but one that has remarkable powers of persistence, returning when least expected. The problem this represents can be solved only by the quickness of the mind, which will place the dreamer one jump ahead. If his is not achieved, the warning is that all could be lost, for the grasshopper is cousin to the all-consuming locust.

'Snail-pace'
I was watching two snails moving very slowly along a path. They were side-by-side and they looked identical.

The two snails represent two people or two similar sets of circumstances, suggesting that the dreamer has either to make a choice or simply to realize that whomsoever or whatsoever they represent, there is not a lot to choose between them. This situation should not be too difficult to recognize, especially when seen in relation to time, for it seems to be an infuriatingly slow affair that does not make much progress. On the other hand, 'slow but sure' progress is better than going in the wrong direction altogether. Which of these is applicable only the dreamer can decide.

'Moths'
I was in a room that was very bright and full of light. I looked across towards the door and there were hundreds of moths coming through it. I said to someone, 'Shut the door and turn off the light—that will stop them coming in'. There then seemed to be an extra-brilliant flash of light and I woke up.

For the room to be so full of light, and in particular that burst of brilliant light just before the dreamer woke up, means she will soon understand something that has been puzzling her for some time. She will see the proverbial light and as a result experience a flash of enlightenment. The moths symbolize inspiring ideas which may, at first, appear to be overpowering, so to close the door and switch off the light as a means of escape in the dream can be taken to mean that the dreamer should take a break from whatever it is all this represents, if and when it becomes too much of a good thing.

'Spiders'
I have had this dream several times now and in it my husband is showing me lots of spiders. There are very tiny ones and larger ones, all moving about making lots of cobwebs around me. This gives me a very nasty feeling.

As 'insects', these spiders represent small annoyances and irritations, but in their own symbolic right they have additional meanings. Seeing there were so many of them in this dream suggests the dreamer is afraid of being caught up in a web that becomes a trap made up of domestic trivialities. Her husband plays an important role in all this but exactly where he fits in, or what the domestic circumstances are, only the dreamer can say. She has shown herself in her dream exactly what her position is more than once but so far has failed to recognize its significant warning. Maybe she can now escape before it is too late.

'The Bee'
While walking down a road a large, fat bee flew into my ear, buzzed and fluttered its wings and flew off. It did not sting me although I was afraid it might.

To be buzzed by a bee warns of 'honeyed gossip' meaning the dreamer should not listen to idle talk about others. If she hears anything of this nature she should not pass it on because if she does it will be at her own peril and come back on her with a vengence.

'The Sting and the Cupboard'
I was in a claustrophobic room with little light and no air. I opened a cupboard and out flew a nasty little flying insect. It made straight for me and gave me a nasty sting.

The room symbolizes a particular situation in the dreamer's life and his reaction to it. Whatever this is, it certainly needs bringing out into the open or he will never understand what it is all about, nor will he be able to see his true position in relation to it. The cupboard he opened is an inner alcove of his mind which is usually closed, but having opened it forgotten thoughts or memories emerged that quite surprised him. Maybe it was his pride that was stung or maybe it was a stinging reminder telling him that he has power within to do something about this rather secretive problem.

'Flies and Food'
Someone handed me a plate laden with food but lots of flies tried to land on it. It took all my time to keep them off and as soon as one flew away another arrived.

The dreamer has been offered plenty of food for thought but it seems she cannot begin to digest this because of petty interferences which somehow spoil the whole thing. Even though she has, metaphorically speaking, been handed this opportunity on a plate, she does not seem to be able to make the most of it.

'The Butterfly'
A butterfly came into the room and landed on my arm. It was so real, I could see every detail on its wings and body.

A butterfly symbolizes the fleeting incarnation of the spirit into the physical body so the appearance of one in a dream may represent the dreamer's own spirit or that of a departed person, depending on the context. It also symbolizes transformation and change of character for the better, but since it is the dreamer's butterfly it is up to her to decide which it is. (The word 'psyche', incidentally, originates from the Greek name for a butterfly.)

'The Big Spider'
All I can remember from this dream was that there was a large, black spider. It gave me a horrid feeling and I was frightened of it as well as thoroughly disliking it.

This spider may represent a feminine figure within the dreamer, who has a possessive and overpowering nature. Some female spiders devour their mates so this dreamer is warned against nagging her husband to death. On the other hand, it may represent an over-dominant mother who restricts the dreamer to such an extent that she feels she is trapped like a fly in a web. Depending on personal circumstances, which spider this is should easily be recognized, and then suitably put out of the window.

22.

Dreams and Life

Dreams are about life and life is about dreams. Together they form a unique partnership, even though their complementary roles sometimes appear to be more in opposition than in harmony. When, however, dreams are seen as dress-rehearsals for the real thing, it is not surprising they seem like this. In life we usually have only one opportunity to achieve something or make an impression but in dreams we can make as many attempts as it takes to perfect such things. Nightly charades often pre-enact anticipated events for the sole purpose of preparing us for the event. By pointing out pitfalls and how not to behave, we can, hopefully, do our best when the opportunity arises.

Mistakes made in life are vitally important, because we learn from these experiences. Past events, therefore, are re-enacted in dreams if they can contribute in this respect. These, plus familiar scenes, objects, fictitious characters and symbolic figures, help us not only to understand the world, but to survive and win in our own private game of life. The scenes and actions in the following dreams reflect this, the fundamental game everyone plays.

Love, Sex, and the Hermaphrodite Symbol

Emotional involvement and disharmony, as well as sexual attraction, activity and encounters, find expression in dreams. Compensatory sexual dreams are thought to be experienced by fewer dreamers now than in Freud's day mainly because sex is no longer a taboo subject. Films, television and magazines provide ways of sublimating this and so have, in effect, taken away much of the need to dream about it.

Dreams of bisexuality, where women dream they are men and men dream they are women, are fairly common but by no means do they necessarily indicate transvestite tendencies. These dreams perhaps hark back to a previous life where the dreamer was then a member of the opposite sex, but usually they indicate a balancing of outlook between the feminine and masculine potentials within the dreamer. It is the anima or animus, as the case may be, demanding attention. Thus this, the hermaphrodite symbol, is a sign of unification, a merging of the two inherent natures into a third, creative whole.

'Lover's Return'
A person with whom I once had a wonderful love affair came back into my life. It was so real I did not want to wake up but I did and found it was only a dream which I hope will come true.

Whether an action-replay or prophetic, this dream shows there is still a link between the dreamer and her lover. If it is an action replay then it is compensatory, but only time will tell if it is prophetic.

'The Man Next Door'

I was having a decidedly close, sexual relationship with the man next door. In reality he is a very staid, good neighbour, but whenever I see him in the garden now I feel terribly embarrassed and can hardly face him.

Without consciously realizing it, the man next door to the dreamer none the less arouses her sexually. Experiencing what sex would be like with him in a dream certainly saves complications, especially as he lives on her doorstep, so it is one of those dreams best forgotten, at least during waking hours!

'Lover's Secrets'

My boyfriend was fully clothed, lying on my bed. He was reading my diary, which made me furious, and I woke up feeling rather cross with him.

The dreamer has a familiar relationship with her boyfriend but seeing he had his clothes on shows he does not reveal much of himself and she really does not know him very well at all. Probably they are both secretive and withhold facts about themselves. For him to read the dreamer's diary means he is prying into her private life hoping to discover a few things about her past. Unconsciously she is aware of the arms-length situation that exists, so if the relationship is to last all will have to be revealed.

'Distant Lover'

A man whom I like very much was standing some way from me and I had to shout to make him understand me. If only he would move nearer, I kept thinking, I would not have to do this.

The distance between this man and the dreamer represents the emotional gap between them. Unless he does take a few steps towards her this will never satisfactorily be bridged and there will be no love affair.

'The Wrong Clothes'

The thing that fascinated me in this dream was that I was wearing the wrong clothes. They were men's, not women's. It must have been a dream of the present because they were up-to-date fashions and everything else was as it is now. Although it did not bother me at the time, when I woke up and thought about it I became quite worried. I do not want to be a man nor do I have any lesbian feelings whatsoever.

In dreams, clothes represent the person others see. It is also the image the dreamer wants to project to the world, as well as to themselves. Seeing this dreamer was wearing men's clothes shows she needs to express her masculine abilities such as practicality, authoritiveness, power and other generally extrovert qualities. When she has done this she will find she has become a different, much more balanced and confident person.

'*A Wonderful Fiancé?*'
It all centred around my fiancé who I am to marry in two months time. The awful thing was that he was not the wonderful, tolerant, kind, understanding person I know him to be when I am awake.

This dreamer has an unconscious fear that her wonderful fiancé is not as perfect as she imagines. Probably she has superimposed his real image with her own image of what she wants her dream-man to be like and, although love is blind, it is not permanently blind. Seeing the truth now will save much heartache in the future, so if it is not too late, she should take another long look at him.

'*Going Bald*'
Although I have plenty of hair on my head at present, my dream scared me because in it I was quite bald. My girlfriend did not seem to mind as much as I did.

Hair symbolizes virility and strength so to lose this in a dream means the dreamer fears losing sexual ability and attractiveness. Seeing his girlfriend did not seem to mind supports the theory that bald-headed men *are* physically attractive to women.

'*Does He Still Love Me?*'
In this dream my husband—who left me years ago—returned. He was really loving at first but then he turned nasty. In real life he has recently asked me to have him back but this dream has made it difficult for me to decide whether I should give him another chance.

Several things are revealed in this dream. First, the dreamer would like to have her husband back despite what he did in the past, and she could forgive him. Secondly, she is telling herself that leopards do not change their spots. If he comes back, he will be loving for a time but will undoubtedly revert to his true self and behave badly sooner or later. The question is, should she have him back or not? Warning or not, if she does not give it a try she will always regret it—at least she will not be under any misapprehension.

'*Dancing Mood*'
I was at a dance as a wallflower, then an attractive boy came over to me and asked me to dance. It was one of those rather old-fashioned, slow dances, a waltz I think, but he began to hold me closer and closer. It was lovely and I was really sorry when I woke up to find it had not really happened.

Dancing in a dream represents a prelude to love-making. This may have been a compensatory dream, but more positively it should be seen as a distinct possibility. By taking it to mean this, the dreamer should adopt the role she would most like to play and so be more likely to attract that dancing partner in her dream.

'*Disintegrating Engagement Ring*'
The stones in my engagement ring became loose and fell out, then the whole ring seemed to disintegrate. I looked at my wedding ring and was relieved to find this was still alright.

The disintegration of this engagement ring means the romantic phase in the relationship with her husband is over—her fairy-tale wedding has been eclipsed by a mundane marriage. No doubt she is disillusioned but the good news is that her wedding ring is still intact, telling her that she has a reliable foundation upon which to build for the future.

'The Wedding'

I was at a lovely wedding among complete strangers and did not even recognize the bride and groom.

A wedding symbolizes the unification of two people, two ideas or two principles. Depending on the dreamer's personal circumstances this wedding could relate to any one of these, but since she did not recognize the couple this suggests it relates to a balance between her extrovert and introvert selves, her head and her heart.

'Two Faces of Eve'

My boyfriend seemed like a child and I found myself mothering him until in the end I didn't know if he was my son or my lover. At first he liked this but soon he became touchy and behaved like a spoilt little boy. I have no children but would like them one day.

This dream warns that, although some men remain boys at heart and like being mothered sometimes, they do not like being smothered by a lover. It also points out two faces of Eve—the broody female and the feminine Venus. The former face should always be kept well veiled.

'Arrows of Desire'

My ex-wife was holding two darts or arrows to her chest. Our daughter came up to her and the two of them seemed so happy I felt like an outsider.

This scene conjures up the past, showing the heart-felt stabs once felt by the dreamer as a result of Cupid's arrows. It also shows him, if he admits it, how he later wounded or broke his wife's heart. Sentiment, regret and envy for the mother-daughter relationship are reflected in this dream but what he does about all this is now up to him.

'Emotional Inoculation'

I was at a party with my boyfriend and he introduced me to a girl by saying 'This is my fiancée. I could not believe it but when I asked him to explain how and when he had met her he refused to discuss it with me. This has unsettled me in my attitude toward him when I go out with him now.

This dreamer is enacting an inner suspicion that her boyfriend is unfaithful. Anticipating him loving someone else is both a warning and an emotional inoculation against a possible let-down in the future. Should it happen it will not come as such a shock, as she has already experienced it in a dream. On the other hand, maybe she is over-sensitive due to her own insecurity and so allows her imagination to run away with her.

'The Kiss'

I was kissing a lady I know but had never been attracted to in this way when awake, until, that is, I had this dream. Since then the lady in real life has given me some rather coy looks and I am beginning to feel growing affinity between us. I must be honest and say that also in the dream I knew my wife was in the background.

Although this dreamer thought he was not attracted by this lady, unconsciously he undoubtedly was. He can take this dream as a warning telling him that if he allows an affair to develop, his wife will always be there in the background, or he can interpret it as a go-ahead signal from the lady in question. Now he knows the situation it is up to him to decide whether or not to progress his dream in his waking hours.

'Biscuits and Cheese'

The day after I had a row with my girlfriend I dreamed we were preparing a meal together. This consisted mainly of cream cracker biscuits and slices of cheese and I was trying to outdo her with the amount of cheese I was putting on the biscuits.

Freud would probably have seen great sexual connotation in this dream, but this would exist in any relationship between lovers. The more important issue is that of sharing life together. Symbolically, a meal is food for thought and cream crackers represent unleavened bread, the sacrifices one has to make in life for happiness and peace of mind. Cheese means success. Trying to outdo his girlfriend by placing more cheese on each biscuit points out to the dreamer that he needs to put more into his share of the relationship than he has in the past if he wants it to continue.

The Family

The childhood relationship we have with our family influences the relationships we form later with others outside our family. These outside relationships begin early on in life, even before nursery, and are followed by encounters at school, at work, in social activities and in romantic liaisons.

The basic pattern formed by our first relationship is triangular—mother, father, child. Some children find their love for the parent of the same sex is tinged with rivalry, others find a more loving affinity with the parent of the same sex, while yet others have an equal love for both parents. Whichever it is, this emotional pattern seems to continue throughout life and it is this that is often reflected in a dream.

The need for self-reliance and independence may also be expressed in a dream. The first bid for this is the breakaway from parents and family and so this event is used again and again to represent further attempts to sever connections later on in life. When a marriage or close partnership is about to come to an end a dream concerning the family is sometimes experienced, but this is rarely seen as a symbolic action-replay of the initial major breakaway situation in life.

When there is extreme difficulty in freeing oneself from another person, especially a partner, a dreamer may actually kill off one or other of the parents in a dream. This is a pictorial scene showing the dreamer destroying not that parent but their attachment and link with a person or partner symbolized by that parent. It has nothing whatsoever to do with matricide or patricide.

The father and mother, and this includes the couple who adopt or foster a child from an early age, provide the image of fatherhood and motherhood, masculinity and femininity, which in time the child assumes. They symbolize too the male and female principles, tendencies and natural forces—good and bad—encountered throughout life. Parents, like the paradox of life itself, give to the child and take from it. In their attempt to make 'a good child' the father is the authoritative figure or principle, and the mother the nurturing figure or principle. In over-reacting the father can become the ogre, totalitarian and oppressive, while the mother can become the terrible mother, over-possessive and destructive.

Other members of the family play archetypal roles as well as the parents. Grandparents, for example, stand in for protective circumstances and a stable background, while sisters and brothers can represent rivalry between the dreamer and a friend or an acquaintance, as well as symbolizing inner strife and conflict with one's own shadow self.

From all this, the family circle can be seen to symbolize the human family as a whole, so if a member of the family appears in a dream he or she invariably represents a corresponding archetype.

'Drunken Father'
My father, who is very correct and puritanical, was actually rolling around, drunk. It was a most surprising dream because I could not believe he was behaving like this.

This dreamer probably has a great respect for his father, so much so that he has made him into a model of male virtue. In this virtuous role he has become slightly destructive in that he has unintentionally made his son feel inferior. To see him drunk shows the dreamer that his father is only human like himself and he should not, therefore, see himself as a lesser being.

'The Heavy Hand'
In this dream something terrified me. I felt as if I was about to be attacked. All I could see was a man in black but I could not see his face. Soon after waking I linked this with my father who had been very heavy-handed, hitting my sisters and myself into submission when we were children.

This dream is probably an action-replay of a past event, warning that someone is at present trying to oppress the dreamer. This person will be recognized by the threatening situation they have created but the dreamer is reminded and reassured of the fact that she is no longer a child so does not now have to submit to anyone.

'Reversing Badly'
My father was trying to reverse his car and was doing it very badly indeed. In the end he backed into a tree and damaged it.

This dreamer's father probably represents her own authoritative nature and driving force, so she is telling herself that she should not retrace her steps, look back too much, or hanker after the past. If she does, she will do more harm than good. The tree, symbolizing the family, will suffer even if the dreamer does not, so the advice from this symbolic scene is that she should try to keep forging ahead.

'View From The Top'

I was going up a spiral staircase, and once at the top I could see for miles into the distance. Then I noticed that someone had put an obstruction, a boat I think, in front of my view. With that, my father appeared and was furious with whoever it was who had caused this obstruction. He then directed me to a different flight of steps so I went down these and discovered another flight going up.

Going up a spiral staircase shows the dreamer rising above a situation and seeing it objectively. The obstruction, a boat indicating destiny, means that she may still be 'up the wrong staircase' and could reach the same conclusions another way. The appearance of her father symbolizes her positive, assertive self which offers an alternative, logical solution.

'Fighting Back Positively'

This dream took me back to my childhood when I used to have friendly fights with my father. Unfortunately, in the dream the fighting was not friendly—it was almost fighting to the death. On waking I was quite disturbed.

This dream is an action-replay of a friendly fight which was, at the same time, a lesson in self-defence. If the dreamer applies the message of self-defence to a present situation, he will understand what he has to do. By taking the dominant role, as his father once did with him, he will be able to control the situation, which is probably a battle of wits, not fists, and not allow it to develop into a dangerous struggle.

'Family Home'

I entered the house I lived in before I left home 20 years ago. My mother and sisters were there, then my father came in and told me my cat had been savaged by a dog and he was going to kill the dog for doing it. Then my father asked several questions but everyone turned to me, expecting me to know the answers.

This dreamer is using her secure childhood to help face up to present insecurity. She is incorporating into this dream the comforting aspects of motherly understanding and at the same time using the more forceful characteristics of the father. For a dog to attack a cat shows there is a fierce battle between her head and heart, intellect and intuition. And for the father to suggest killing the dog warns she should not react hastily but take a balanced view. Seeing others expecting her to answer questions shows she is in a responsible position where she will be expected to know what to do.

'Mother to the Rescue'

My mother, who has been dead for years, was telling me what I should do about an unpleasant situation that has recently developed in my life. She was not domineering, but was helpful in a way that I know she would never have been in real life. We hardly ever conversed, let alone exchanged confidences.

The dreamer is using her mother to represent the principle of the mother who knows exactly how she should behave and react to the present difficult situation. She is her wiser, inner self, so what she has to say should not be ignored. Alternatively, this could be a message from the dreamer's mother bridging the gap between not only the living and the dead, but between mother and daughter.

'A Mother to Others'
I have a family of my own but in this dream I was mother to half the neighbourhood. It was a most enjoyable experience, leaving me with a feeling that I can only describe as warm, yet not maternal.

The feminine qualities of feeling and compassion have been expressed through this dream. Protection of those less fortunate or able is one of the qualities of the mother, so the message from this could be that the dreamer should pursue a path where she can use her own attributes which are similar to the archetypal Mother.

'A Mother's Tears'
My mother was crying, yet when she was alive I do not remember her ever doing this. She was always a happy person so seeing her looking so sad distressed me considerably.

These tears are probably tears shed by the dreamer for herself. Her mother represents compassion within, so she is probably feeling sorry for herself but at the same time she is trying to put on a brave face about something. If the reason for these tears could be identified it would help her to come to terms with the situation.

'The Goddess Within'
This dream distressed me, but having thought about it I am sure it has a powerful message that will help me in my relationship with my wife. In it, I was shouting and raving at my mother, and when I had said all the nasty things I had stored up inside me I felt terribly guilty. I never argue with my mother.

This argument is not with the dreamer's mother, nor his wife, but with the feminine principle as a whole. The physical manifestation of this is his wife so it is she who has to take the brunt of his unbalanced feelings. Something his mother has done in the past may account for a disappointment in his life, but life is full of apparent disappointments and who can say these were not for the best in the long run anyway? To rid himself of guilt all this dreamer needs to do is to turn to his anima, his feminine counterpart within, his goddess, whom he has totally ignored for far too long! He need look no further.

'Powerful Opponent'
My brother seemed to be older than I am but in fact he is really three years younger.

We have always got on very well but in this dream I felt he was a threat to me in some way.

This dreamer's brother most likely represents a male opponent either at work or within his social circle. For some reason he is feeling threatened by a lesser yet more powerful man, a situation similar to one experienced earlier in life. As a child, he may have felt his parents spoiled his brother, and this gave rise to jealousy. If he is honest with himself he may well discover that the threat is none other than his own envy tinged with insecurity.

'My Grandmother's House'
I found myself in my grandmother's house back in the West Indies. It was exactly the same as it was when I was a child, except for modern English furniture, not West Indian. I was amazed to find a new carpet, rather like the one I have myself, on her floor.

This dream shows that the dreamer is thinking a lot about her earlier life and cultural heritage. Grandparents and ancestors represent this. She is realizing that she is exactly the same person who, as a child, visited her grandmother, and over the years only her environment has changed. The new carpet is an encouraging sign meaning she should not fear being trodden on because she has a very secure confidence-giving background.

Monsters and Mythological Creatures

Since the majority of dreams reflect everyday problems it is not surprising they use everyday verbal expressions involving animals, reptiles, birds and fish to symbolically construct their messages. But underlying this mundane superficiality there exists the inherent collective symbolism of the unconscious. Here, a horse represents more than the dreamer's driving, ambitious energy, and a pig is more than a bad-mannered, gluttonous person. These creatures—along with many others—become archetypal principles of evolution, terrifying powers of nature, and dangers to be encountered and overcome, psychically and spiritually.

In this context Pegasus is no mere horse; he offers the possibility of winging from one plane of existence to another, and the mare, sometimes the nightmare, is the earthly bridal partner of the sun. Her shoe is given to brides on their wedding day as an unknown, perhaps unconscious, gesture of remembrance. And in this same context the sow is Adamantine, the goddess of fertility, while the boar is the solar force of solitaries. The Celts venerated him as a sacred animal and wore boar masks and boar tusks on their helmets as signs of divine protection. They sacrificed the boar too, and carried its head on a dish at Yuletide, a custom still enacted to this day, and although consciously the link with the sun is forgotten, unconsciously it is still acknowledged. Why else the ceremony?

Dragons, serpents, centaurs, celestial birds, flying bulls and monsters of the deep, along with their captors and conquerors, also inhabit our inner worlds.

When they appear in a dream they are involved in either a psychological nightmare expressing mental conflict and fear, or they are a controlling influence in a metamorphosizing drama where something that was a danger is transformed into something wonderful and beautiful, as in the tale of Beauty and the Beast.

'The Gryphon'

There was this amazing creature looking out of a cave. It was half bird, half animal, and as far as I could tell it had the head and talons of an eagle but the body of a lion. I felt I should not have seen it and if it saw me looking at it something awful would happen to me.

The appearance of this creature suggests it is a gryphon. Dante said this creature denoted the two natures of Jesus Christ—solar power and wisdom. Christianity as a religious doctrine, however, depicts the gryphon as the devil. Seeing this creature was sheltering in a cave shows its realm to be that of a deep recess within the dreamer's unconscious and, as guardian of this, it has to be negotiated with before the dreamer can gain access and further insight into his own nature. The battle will be one of wits, but now the dreamer knows that the gryphon exists his quest in life will to metamorphose it into an amenable image. This can be done by progressing the dream consciously when awake through controlled visual imagery. Once this is done, access to the cave with its treasures will be possible.

'Celestial Dog'

This was such a fantastic dream that told me so much at the time, yet on waking I remembered so little. It began with a dog in space which could fly as far as the moon, snap at it and take a piece out of it. Somehow I knew it was the cause of all eclipses of the moon—events, incidentally, which drive dogs mad. During this part of the dream I was a terrified onlooker but as the night drew on the dog altered in character and became quite passive. By the time I woke up I had become well acquainted with it and everything it represented in my life. But alas! All I was left with after a few minutes of wakefulness was this and the belief that this dog was the Celestial Dog of heaven.

The dog is usually considered to be a solar animal and so it is, during the daytime when it is on guard against evil, but at night it becomes the companion of the moon goddess, and can then be most destructive. As two dogs, the solar and the lunar, they symbolize the positive and negative forces throughout the universe, as well as the positive and negative forces within the dreamer—in essence his male and female qualities.

There are, in fact, two messages in this dream: the collective macrocosmic and the individual microcosmic. The macrocosmic shows that the balance of nature is essential for survival and that this principle runs throughout the universe, on every level. The microcosmic message tells the dreamer to weigh up his own sun and moon qualities, thus complying with the 'as above, so below' principle.

'The Green Man'

This dream was an awful nightmare. I believed I was awake at the time but now realize I was asleep and it was all part of a bad dream. Standing by my bed was a man not only dressed all in green, but he had a green face, green hair, green hands and green eyes. He was smiling at me, but this did not make me feel any better. He said two words which seem utterly nonsensical but if they mean anything they may hold the clue as to whom this person was. These were *Vertrauen* and *Glück.*

For this dreamer to believe she was awake in this dream means she is soon to 'awaken' to certain facts of life, beginning it would seem with this dream—or nightmare as it appeared to her. The Green Man is a well-known legendary figure. He is Robin Hood, the archetypal spirit of the greenwood, a friendly elemental soul of the earth which could appear frightening if not recognized as this. His message is one of encouragement for the words *vertrauen* and *glück* mean 'faith' and 'happiness'. As with many things in life, when a fear is understood it is no longer a fear.

'The Dragon in the Dungeon'

I was in the dungeon of a castle very like that of Caernarfon Castle, although somehow it was not that place. There was a sound in the distance and someone said it was the dragon. Everyone started to run and I stumbled over the cobble stones. The dragon was catching up with me and I could almost feel its hot breath on my neck. Fortunately I woke up at this point but I was so frightened I had to put on the light.

Seeing the dreamer associated the dungeon in her dream with the dungeon of Caernarfon Castle gives a clue as to the nature of the dragon. It was probably the Red Dragon of Wales. Dungeons are in the bowels of the earth, similar to caves, so in dreams they represent the dreamer's deep unconscious where the earth mysteries, among other treasures, are kept. The dragon symbolizes the geodetic force of nature known as worm power, hence the place-names Worm's Head, Worm's Heath and Worm's bay. A dream of this magnitude shows the dreamer is aware of the more subtle things in life, especially the unseen, unaccountable forces of nature. This awareness will no doubt develop further, depending on the interest this dream has aroused, but one thing is certain. The dragon will be in hot persuit if it is not at least recognized.

23.

Objects, Roles and Occasions

Objects and the roles played by individuals are often found in dreams to symbolize conflicts, relationships, obstacles, states of mind, and even other objects. A dagger, for example, usually warns of danger but in the Freudian sense, the shape of a dagger suggests a penis so it then takes on a sexual connotation. Similarly, a mountain may represent an obstacle to one dreamer but depending on individual circumstances and the context in which it appears, a mountain may represent the pinnacle of achievement to another.

Virtually anything can be used in a dream to denote something or someone else. Royalty have been used to indicate snobbery and 'keeping up with the Joneses', and watches and clocks have acted as watchful, alerting signs. But watchful alerting signs of what? Usually they point out that time and the dreamer's life is ticking wastefully by, but they can also symbolise the beating of the heart with associated emotional disturbances. Again, which it is depends on the individual, plus the context in which the watch or clock appears.

Occasions in life, in particular those associated with insecurity, often appear in dreams as unpleasant sensations and bad experiences. Uncertainty arises from fear — a fear of inadequacy, of not being able to cope, of being a failure, or simply a fear of the future. Most people react to fear in one of two ways: they either fight it or they take flight from it. If a fear is fought, there is no point in dreaming about it because positive action is already being taken, but if it is not faced, then a dream may occur to show that a negative approach has been adopted.

Such dreams include falling dreams and dreams of being chased. Falling or jumping off a high wall or cliff represents a fall or lowering of status or position, either emotionally or even financially. The word 'fall' is used to denote misfortune—we fall into the enemy's hands, we fall upon hard times, and we fall into bad ways. It is, therefore, the context of the metaphorical meaning that has to be interpreted.

Being chased in a dream expresses an insecurity involving a situation which is catching up on the dreamer. Usually the pursuer is an aspect of themselves, or even a manifestation of their fearful thoughts in the form of a person or creature. Whichever it is, running away is the message and although it takes courage to stop, turn round and challenge a fear; this is the action the dream is suggesting.

The images of objects, roles and occasions formed from these impressions and memories collected on the journey through life have both individual and traditional meanings. It is up to the dreamer to decide which it is, a decision which is not difficult once it is remembered that they were formed at the dreamer's own instigation, with a specific purpose and meaning in mind.

'Fell or Pushed?'

I was standing on the edge of a precipice and without moving I fell over the edge. I felt myself hurtling down, but awoke before I hit the bottom. Thinking about this dream afterwards has made me wonder if I was pushed by someone or something.

To be on the edge of a precipice shows the dreamer is about to encounter a dramatic fall of status or loss of some sort. And to actually go over the top warns of the imminent possibility of this. If it is not too late to act upon this warning, the event might be avoided, especially if a pushy sort of person or pressurising circumstances are recognized.

'Crashed Plane'

In this dream I as a passenger on a Jumbo jet. Without warning it suddenly plunged to the ground and I felt myself becoming weightless as I went down with it. Hitting the ground was not as I expected; in fact, when I was told we were down I could not understand why there had not been a terrible impact—there had not.

This is unlikely to be a literal, warning dream. Symbolically, it shows the dreamer has high-flying ambitions and is riding high at present, but her dream is telling her that she should have her feet more firmly on the ground. If she does not come down to earth of her own accord she will probably be forced to do so, but this will not be a bad thing.

'Chased by a Monster'

This dream recurs every few weeks and has done so since I changed my job. What happens is that a cupboard door opens and out comes a creature I cannot describe. I don't wait to see what it looks like—I just run away from it as fast as I can.

One clue leading to the meaning of this repeated dream lies in the fact that the dreamer has experienced it only since she changed her job. The cupboard suggests a usually closed secretive hiding place in her mind, housing a memory, but this has been let out due to the new job. Probably someone or something there reminds her of a past fear, so if this person or thing could be linked with whatever this was, it could be faced and the ghost laid to rest for ever.

'Snapping Crocodile'

A crocodile came after me snapping at my heels. I ran away from it and nearly fell over but managed to keep going. I must have escaped in the end but when I woke up I wondered what I had done to deserve such a fright.

A crocodile is a cold-blooded creature representing inhuman instincts of a hostile nature. It is up to the dreamer to decide if the pursuer is a ruthless characteristic within this own nature, or if it is someone whom he sees as a pitiless assailant. Whether he deserves to be chased or not is, again, for him to decide.

'Teeth and Sweets'
I was enjoying a lovely toffee when I discovered my teeth were becoming loose. One of them actually came out and I seemed to be chewing it along with what was left of the toffee!

Loose teeth in dreams symbolically indicate considerable changes are taking place in the dreamer's life. Eating sweets is an enjoyable thing to do so the changes for this dreamer are going to be for the better, so long as he chews things over well before hand. The literal message, however, warns that eating too many sweets may damage his teeth.

'Loose Teeth'
While brushing my teeth before going to school, they all became wobbly and loose. It was so real I was relieved to discover they were still firmly imbedded when I woke up in the morning.

These loose teeth tell the dreamer that he is leaving his childhood behind, even though he is still at school, and is about to enter the adult world which is full of responsibilites and problems. The change will be emotional as well as physical and it will be a maturing experience that is inevitable.

'The Prince and the Princess'
In this dream I was at an exciting social gathering and found myself sitting with the Prince and Princess of Wales. We were talking as if we were old friends.

Children are brought up on fairy tales where the prince and princess always live happily ever afterwards so it is not surprising to see this myth running through dreams. As a romantic notion it is really a hope for a happy future but this dreamer also seems to see herself as a rather important person—which she is, to herself. Should she confuse this inner personal realization with outer reality, however, her dream warns her that she would be entertaining ideas of pseudo-superiority and grandeur, so she should beware of living in her dreams.

'Royal Garden Party'
I was at a large garden party at Buckingham Palace. The Queen and other members of the Royal Family were there, but it was the Queen who was the centre of attraction.

A queen represents the Mother Goddess as well as the dreamer's mother and all her own feminine characteristics. As head of State, the Queen personifies these qualities, so it is up to the dreamer to decide whether she associates herself with the Queen as a symbol of high society, or as representing one of the more esoteric aspects attached to the image of a queen and femininity as a whole.

'Dead Boss'
I was looking into a coffin and saw a dead body of a man. At first I did not recognize the person but then I realized it was my boss. Having had a row with him the day before this dream I felt I should not have had the cross words with him that I did.

Although this dreamer is not murderously hostile towards her boss she still none the less would like to see him out of the way. Her dream, therefore, is a symbolic reflection of what she unconsciously would like to happen rather than a guilt dream. If he were do die, he would be conveniently removed from the scene and her problem would be solved. In the Freudian sense, this is a typical wish-fulfilment dream.

'Death Day'
There was this tombstone and newly inscribed on it was the date 25 April 1987. I was interested in the date because it was six months ahead, and then I noticed the name of the deceased. It was my name. This date has now passed and I am still here so what did or does it mean?

To see oneself dead or read ones' own obituary means that the end of a particular phase in life is imminent. It rarely symbolizes the final phase, death, as was proved by this dream. The date this dreamer saw told him that after that time he would begin to make a new life for himself, and experience a rebirth. Traditionally, it is said that to dream of death is good for those who are fearful, for the dead have no fears.

'In the Loo'
I went to a public lavatory and as I was sitting there discovered that the walls were made of glass and everyone could see me.

This dream reveals several things about the dreamer. First, she is a private person who likes to keep herself to herself, secondly, she is afraid of what others might think about her, and thirdly, she is very vulnerable to the world as a whole. Having seen herself in this symbolic light she should try to improve her position by protecting herself through an increase of self-confidence.

'Looking for ''the Ladies'' '
Many of my dreams feature a desperate search for a ladies' lavatory but the latest on this theme was rather frightening. Having found one eventually, I went in, locked the door, sat down then noticed a small parcel on the floor. Before I could bend down and look at it, it exploded and I woke up.

Lavatorial dreams generally reflect the down-to-earth basic needs in life. Seeing these dreams recur indicates that the dreamer does not realize she is suffering from a form of insecurity where she is afraid to venture too far from home or stray from convention. The explosion means a situation is likely to blow up so the message is: 'Don't just sit there, do something about it'.

'Toys'
There were several toys scattered around the room and I was wondering which one I

would like to play with. I didn't actually touch any of them but seemed to spend my time just looking at them.

The room in which the dreamer found these toys represents a particular aspect of her life which needs careful consideration. She may feel her attitude towards this aspect is childish. On the other hand, she may be toying with ideas which might help her solve or better understand things.

'A Past Life'
In this dream I was a man dressed in a coarse hessian-type coat and trousers with leather binding and thonging. I soon found out I was a soldier in charge of the horses. There was great tension in the air as we—myself and a company of others dressed similarly—prepared for a battle. The next thing I knew was that I was charging on a large warhorse into the fray. Suddenly, there was a dull, heavy thump in the area of my left chest and shoulder and I fell to the ground, dead. This caused the scene to change instantly, like changing a slide in a cinematograph and so I was able to view myself lying there being trampled upon by what seemed like hundreds of horses.
   I was myself in this dream, but I was not the same person I am today. For one thing I am a woman. Another intriguing thing is that when I was born the muscles in my left arm were withered.

Who can say if this dream is an action-replay of a previous life or not? If it is, it may explain the origin of the weakness to the dreamer's left arm. If it is not, it symbolically tells her that she needs to be more assertive and allow her animus to express itself from time-to-time. The thump on the arm is a reminder that any physical weakness is no reason to be trampled on, underfoot, by others.

'An Old-Fashioned House'
I am in an old-fashioned house which I feel needs modernizing. There is an iron grate with a kettle on the hob and standing by it a lady dressed in what I think are Victorian clothes. It seemed like home at the time of the dream but I have never been in a place like this when awake.

This scene is either a reflection of a previous life or it is purely symbolic. Whichever it is, it is telling the dreamer that she is living in the past and needs to bring herself up-to-date. The grate and the hob represent the heart of family life and the rather genteel lady obviously about to make tea is the establishment-minded home-maker within the dreamer. Probably she wants to break away from convention but finds this very difficult to do. Her dream, however, shows she can have the best of both worlds but alterations will have to be made if she is to achieve this.

'The Table'
I was sitting on a large table while the rest of the family were indulging in a conversation. They did not involve me in this and felt I was left out of things.

Traditionally, a table symbolizes self-sacrifice. It is said to be the sacrificial altar of the mind. Feeling left out of things in this dream is a reflection of how the dreamer feels towards the rest of her family. No doubt she has happily sacrificed herself for their interests in the past but the warning is that she must not make herself into a willing martyr now.

'Candlelight'
There was a large candle in a gold candlestick on a window ledge. Each time I lit it, it went out, even though there was no breeze to do this.

A candlestick and candle represent the dreamer's altruistic feelings and their position on a window ledge means these could have far-reaching effects. The light from the candle symbolizes life and the flame itself is the spirit. Seeing it was difficult to light tells the dreamer not to give in but to try, try, try again to achieve her aim.

'In Court'
I was in court in a witness box being cross-examined about my conduct. The outcome must have been good because I woke up feeling much happier than when I went to sleep.

'Sleep on it' has always been good advice. Obviously this dreamer has a problem in some way related to his behaviour so his dream is saying that he should ask a few searching questions, swearing to tell himself the truth, the whole truth and nothing but the truth. Having been honest with himself, albeit unconsciously, he should now be in a position to face and deal with whatever it is that is causing the trouble.

'Winds of Change'
The window in my bedroom flew open and the curtains flapped madly. I got out of bed to close them and had great difficulty in doing this, but managed it in the end.

Changes are to be expcted which will bring with them a breath of fresh air. Although things may seem to be out of control for a time the dreamer will eventually get to grips with them.

'The Ladder and the Scaffold'
I climbed a ladder and at the top was shocked to find myself on a rather insecure platform or scaffold

Clearly, this dreamer is going to climb the ladder of apparent success but, once up there, will realize that the circumstances are unstable and even potentially dangerous. The warning is that the higher he rises, the further he has to fall.

'A Nasty Injection'
I was taken down in a lift, put in a dark place and given an injection. It was a very nasty dream indeed and left me feeling worried and anxious for days.

Going down in a lift suggests submission and the dark place is fear of the unknown. An injection represents an invasion of personal privacy so overall the dream reflects a situation whereby the dreamer is 'put down' verbally. Somehow, she must rise above all this and protect herself against any such attack.

'Eggs'

Eggs were everywhere around me and some were on the point of hatching out. They seemed to be rolling about and although there were cracks in the shells and I could hear loud chirping inside, the chicks did not emerge.

Eggs represent potential life as well as the potential achievement of the individual. The message in this dream is loud and clear—get cracking. If the dreamer does not make an attempt to help himself, all his past efforts will be wasted and come to nothing.

24.

Nightmares

A nightmare is named after Rhiannon, the legendary Mare-Demeter, who with her two sisters ran wild and devoured her son Hippasus (a foal). As the prophet Job said of this mare, 'She dwelleth and abideth upon the rock. Her young ones also suck up blood'. Appropriately it was once believed that in a nightmare the dreamer was abducted to the mare's nest, a terrible place littered with the jaw-bones and entrails of poets.

A nightmare is an expression of extreme anguish. This originates from physiological disturbances within the physical body or from distressed emotional states churning around in the mind. The severity of a true nightmare, or 'incubus attack' as it is traditionally known, is sufficient to wake the sleeper. In a bid to escape from this night terror the dreamer, especially if it is a child, often sleepwalks and cries out for help.

Nightmares caused by physiological disturbances usually occur during the earlier part of the night, in total absence of any emotional tension, fear or worry. These arise from pain, discomfort and from fevers. For example, if a knife-like pain is present, in sleep it can be transformed in a dream into the ghastly experience of being stabbed over and over again. This scene gives the dreamer a symbolic picture of his or her painful symptom.

Similarly, a child or an adult with a high temperature may suffer hallucinations and find themselves existing in a frightening, unfamiliar world. And in later life, hormonal changes in the body are believed to be responsible for the panic which produces palpitations, sweating, choking sensations, and feelings of suffocation. Hormonal changes bring about an imbalance of the body's chemistry and it is this upheaval that is symbolically represented as disturbing scenes.

Nightmares resulting from emotional states also produce physiological disturbance. The heart pounds rapidly and the body may sweat. The fears responsible for these nocturnal attacks are symbolized as personal attacks, drowning or other very unpleasant ordeals. Sometimes it is a dark figure lurking in a corner, sometimes it is a torturing experience taking place in a dark dungeon, but whatever the nature of the experience one thing is certain. A nightmare is not intended to terrify the dreamer.

Certain nightmares act as emotional innoculations against the traumas of life which cannot be faced when awake, or which may have to be faced in the future. Having experienced it once in a dream, if and when the real thing occurs the shock is reduced considerably. Other ordeals in bad dreams, whether in the form of self-torture arising from unrecognized fears, feelings of guilt, seething anger, the scared anticipation of a real threat, or resulting from a physical source, are intended to draw attention to an immediate physical condition or emotional situation.

Unfortunately, the fear produced by nightmares usually overshadows their purpose so rarely is their message recognized and therefore acted upon. Fortunately, however, the scenes in these bad dreams rarely come true.

'Black Moon'

I can still remember the terrible nightmare I had as a child as if it were yesterday. I slept with my two sisters in a room that led off our parents' room. Between the two rooms were three uncarpeted wooden steps so whenever anyone came down into the room you always heard them coming. In this nightmare I saw a black thing that I later called a 'black moon' at the top of the steps. I knew that if it came down I would hear it, but to my horror it did come down but silently. I woke up screaming as it came nearer and nearer to my bed. Needless to say I feared going to sleep for years after that experience in case it came back.

This dreamer still wonders what this horrible thing was but fortunately she has long since stopped being afraid of it. Maybe the clue to its origin lies in the fact that she *is* no longer afraid of it, which suggests it could have been a projection of a fear encountered during the day which she misread in some way or could do nothing about.

'Terrible Noise'

At the time I had this ghastly dream I was ill in bed with measles. It was the terrible noise that alarmed me and set my heart pounding rather than anything I saw. Somehow this noise was in everything as well as in my head and I thought that at any moment some enormous machine was about to destroy the house with me in it.

Probably this pounding noise was an amplification of the dreamer's heartbeat itself, due to the high fever and a symptom of measles. The thought of the house being destroyed symbolically reflects the damage the illness was doing to her, and even the possibility of her being completely demolished—dying.

'Things that Creep Out at Night'

Virtually every night my daughter woke up screaming and some nights she actually came downstairs while still asleep. When I asked her what was wrong she always said that horrible tiny little things crawled out from a dark corner of the room and came after her.

This dreamer was eight years old when the nightmares began. They were so bad they kept her awake at night and as a result she was away from school for days at a time and when she was there she could not concentrate. It was suggested she saw a psychiatrist, which she did, but things did not improve in the slightest so her mother asked me for help.

The girl and her mother came to see me and the three of us talked about these nasty little things. Emphasis was put on how little they were, which belittled them. I then gave her a sheet of white paper and coloured pencils so that she could draw these things. She chose black and grey crayons and drew ugly, squiggly things which were meant to represent them. I told her to draw hats on their heads which she did. They now looked really funny so we all laughed. Finally, it was decided that they did not like sunlight so she coloured all over them with yellow and orange crayons. I told her to put her drawing in the corner of her bedroom and then see if they came out dressed in their new hats. They never appeared again.

'Dead Child'

I have this nightmare too often for comfort and every time it is virtually the same. I see my daughter of 13 face-down in one of those old-fashioned granite drinking troughs for horses, drowned. Sometimes I simply cannot find her and I think someone has murdered her and I wake up in a terrible state and run into her room to see if she is there.

There are several reasons for this sort of dream. One is the dreamer's fear that someone will murder her daughter. Having heard about this happening on rare occasions to others she is closely identifying herself with the unfortunate parents of such a victim and in her dream experiences it for herself. Another reason for this morbid nightmare is that once children grow up, they become more and more independent of their parents and so the original image of the child no longer exists. This can be compared with 'I've *lost* a son or a daughter', an expression occasionally heard at weddings when an offspring gets married. Finally, seeing a drowned child represents emotional pressures at school and socially, where the forming of relationships outside the family is just beginning for the adolescent child. This her mother notices, probably unconsciously.

'The War'

This dream recurs and recurs and has done so for years. In it I am back in France in 1940 and I see all the horrors of the war I saw then, as real as when they happened. I never think of them during the day but during the night I am constantly reminded of things I want to forget, with a result I do not sleep well so always feel tired.

It is not surprising that events this dreamer witnessed during the war produce nightmares. Maybe if he thought about these before going to sleep he would save himself the trouble of re-enacting them in his dreams. At least he might sleep more peacefully. Although these horrific scenes are clearly engraved deeply in his memory, they usually fade with time; however, there is always the exception to prove the rule.

'Chased and Caught'

In these dreams I am being chased down narrow streets with no means of escape. Whatever or whoever it is who is chasing me catches me but I wake up before anything more ghastly happens.

Fear, whether in a dream or in real life, produces the fight or flight response.

In this case the dreamer is taking flight from someone—and that someone is herself. Symbolically, it shows she is running away from something she will not face, but it is impossible to run away from yourself, therefore she is always caught. This experience will continue until she stops running, turns round and looks bravely at an inner fear which is making life a nightmare.

'Broken-Hearted Lover?'
I wake up,—or at least I believe I am awake—and standing next to my bed looking at me is my fiancé who was killed in the war in 1944. After he was killed I vowed I would never marry anyone else but I did in 1950 and ever since then this nightmare has plagued me.

Having told herself, and probably stated in public, that she would never marry anyone else, this dreamer made a pledge, but having broken it she now feels disloyal to her former fiancé. This nightmare could, therefore, be a projection of her self-guilt, the ghost of a memory and not the phantom of a broken-hearted lover at all.

'Terrifying Monster'
A fierce monster, a cross between a wolf and a wild boar, charges out of a corner of my bedroom and chases after me. At first I believe it is a dog, but, although I am very frightened of dogs, this creature is a hundred times worse. Sometimes I cannot move; I feel paralysed, but fortunately I always wake up before it rips me to pieces.

The clue to the cause of this nightmare is probably the fear the dreamer has of dogs during the day. All fears come into their own at night and take on even nastier images, so if she feels this monster could be a symbol of a fierce dog then she is one step towards stopping them. On the other hand, this creature may be her own top-dog, that aspect of herself which dominates her finer feelings and causes her to land in the dog-house when she does not really deserve it. Gives a dog a bad name....?

The feeling of paralysis is due to the fact that during certain phases of sleep we are paralysed and sometimes it is useful to incorporate this into a dream, especially a chasing dream.

'Tunnel of Life and Death'
I can still remember the nightmare I had regularly from a very early age until I was about 15. There was this long dark tunnel and I was being sucked down it into some awful place at the end. Sometimes I felt as if I was suffocating and sometimes drowning; it was so awful I always woke up screaming. It stopped when my mother told me that I nearly died when I was born so that tunnel must have been the tunnel of death that many seem to travel down to get off this planet.

The tunnel of birth or the tunnel of death, there seems to be little difference in dreams, yet this nightmare could well be a memory of the dreamer's actual birth experience emerging not into another world but into this one.

25.

Problem-Solving, Healing, and Precognitive Dreams

Interpreting a dream means discovering its message but this is only the first step towards fulfilling the purpose of that dream. Written into every dream-message is advice and often a solution to the problem the dream reflects, suggesting that dreaming is fundamental to problem-solving. This has been confirmed by psychologists who have recently noticed that people who sleep for eight hours or more each night, and hence dream more, are more creative and better able to solve their problems than those who sleep and dream less.

Sometimes a problem is solved spontaneously in a dream but sometimes the right dream needs to be incubated. There again, inventive dreams and some healing dreams seem to be a progression or extension of logical thought which manifests in symbolic form. Other healing dreams, however, often have an element of surprise or shock about them. In these the cure following such a nightmare seems to be due to a surge of energy that brings about beneficial changes within the body.

It is generally accepted that images in dreams are crucial to our thinking process but the reasoning used to transform an image into a solution has been discovered to be neither logically linear nor lateral. A totally different pattern of thought is revealed, linked with intuition and creativity. By using the technique of problem-setting, it has been found that a subject's dream symbolism often produces vital clues towards problem-solving.

'Anagrams'
One problem given to a subject just prior to sleeping was an anagram—SCNACEDELIHSKR—with the solution CHARLES DICKENS. They arrived at the answer through a complex chain of reasoning beginning with a dream about the television programme *Dempsey and Makepeace*. The star of the programme had a hairstyle like a friend of the subject's, a woman called Carol. Carol reminded her of *A Christmas Carol* written by Charles Dickens, and so the dreamer arrived at the right answer.

'Lost and Found'
In this dream the dreamer not only found his umbrella through a chain of reasoning commencing in a dream but managed to find himself a fiancée as well. In the dream he was getting ready to go to work and looked out of the window and saw it was raining. He also noticed a brick wall and written on

this in red was one word—NAAN. When he woke up the name *Naan* meant nothing to him, but it was raining just as in his dream. This reminded him that the last time it rained he had been to a friend's house, which then reminded him that his friend had borrowed his umbrella but had not given it back. Later that day he phoned his friend and arranged to collect the umbrella from him in a pub next day. They met and the dreamer reclaimed his umbrella. With his friend were two girls, and one of these the dreamer fell in love with and is soon to marry. Her name was not NAAN but an anagram of this—ANNA.

'Professor Kekule'
The classic example of the progression of logical thinking extending into a dream is probably the dream Professor Kekule had after struggling without success to discover the molecular structure of trimethylbenzine. In this dream atoms gambolled before his eyes. Smaller groups kept in the background but he particularly noticed larger structures in long rows, sometimes closely fitting together, sometimes twisting and turning in snake-like motion. Suddenly one of the snakes took hold of its own tail and the form whirled mockingly before his eyes. In a flash he woke up. By the snake taking its tail into its own mouth Professor Kekule was able to transform this image into the closed chain or ring theory underlying the constitution of benzine, a discovery that was to revolutionize organic chemistry and prepare the way for the internal combustion engine.

And now, some more entries from Dream Diaries.

'The Knitting Pattern'
I had been battling with a particularly complicated knitting pattern all evening and went to bed frustrated and very cross at the thought of not being able to master it. During the night it seemed as if I was dreaming about it in a jumbled-up way—knitting needles, dropped stitches and wool haunted my sleep. Next evening I sat down once again to attempt to unravel the complicated pattern. It was an amazing feeling but even before I re-read the instructions I knew I would be able to understand them. And I did. Somehow I must have worked it all out in my sleep.

'Tonic Water Cure'
I had been suffering from a mild fever for a year or more even though doctors had tried everything without managing to get rid of it. One night I dreamed that I saw a clear glass bottle labelled 'tonic'. On waking I decided, more in desperation than for any other reason, that I would go to the chemist and ask him for a tonic but on the way there I passed an off-licence and noticed some clear glass bottles in the window labelled 'Tonic Water'. I went in and bought half a dozen bottles and drank two bottles a day. At the end of three days my fever had gone. It was not until I found out that tonic water contains quinine, an antidote for certain tropical fevers, that I realized my fever could have been due to a mild form of malaria.

'Pain-Relieving Nightmare'
Five years ago I had an extremely painful elbow and my doctor suggested an injection into the joint to relieve the agony. I postponed this for a month but the pain grew

worse so I made an appointment to have the dreaded injection. The night before I was due to have this I had a nightmare and in it the doctor injected my arm with a pain-killing drug, which caused a violent pain to surge up my arm. When I woke up the pain had gone so I cancelled the appointment. I have not had any pain whatsoever from that day to this.

'Spirit Surgeon'

When I was in hospital waiting to have a malignant growth removed, I dreamed that the face of a surgeon loomed over me and told me that I would still be alive in 20 years time. When I told the nurses this after the operation they did not laugh but told me they had heard other patients say similar things. The description I gave them was that of a surgeon who had retired from the hospital and died years ago. I believed him, whoever he was, and I also believe he healed me. All this was nearly thirty years ago but I shall never forget that dream.

'Dream Cure For a Dog Lover'

A widower dreamed up an amazing cure for a brain tumour that paralysed the left side of his body. He awoke in his hospital bed in London with a start after a vivid nightmare and found he could move his left arm and leg again. In his dream his sole companion, his dog called Rufus, was to be put down because there was no one to look after him. This caused him to wake up with a cry as a jolt and big shock went through his left arm and leg. Immediately following this he got out of bed and amazed the nurses by picking up a chair. The doctors said they had never heard of anything like it before and six days after this nightmare he was well enough to go home to his dog. 'It was my corgi that cured me. In the dream I was convinced he was going to be killed and it shocked me back into action again', he said.

'3-Part Serial'

One night I had a vivid nightmare in which I knew with absolute certainty that a savage tiger was in the next room. It was snarling and tearing at the door as if it were determined to get at me. The feeling of fear and apprehension this caused stayed with me all the next day. That night I again dreamed much the same thing although this time the tiger was not quite so savage. It was quieter and did not tear at the door so violently. Again, the dream haunted my waking hours and I began to wonder if the tiger was not really a tiger but something else that I feared.

I had always been afraid of a particular boss who visited my place of work on occasions and I realized he was soon to pounce on us with one of his unwelcome visits. The more I thought of this as a reason for the nightmares the more it made sense, then on the third night it happened again. This time the tiger was out of the room and although it looked menacing enough it did not take as much notice of me as I feared it would.

It took these three dreams to show me I was unreasonably afraid of someone who was not really as aggressive or dangerous as I thought. By the time this man arrived a few days later, all fear concerning his visit had gone and the event passed without any problem.

'The Sound of Music'

I always know when something good is going to happen to me because I hear music in a dream a few days before. There is usually a sign in the dream as well telling me something about this forthcoming event. Recently I had my music dream but was woken up in the middle of it by my baby crying. I was anxious to see the rest of the dream so, once the baby had settled down, I began to go over and over the half-finished dream until I finally went to sleep, and once asleep I picked up the threads and got back into the dream. The music was playing and then I saw a car, the seaside and sand, the signs I wanted.

Next weekend my husband suggested a picnic in the country but I knew it had to be by the seaside—which it was.

'Taking Control'

A series of four linked dreams changed my life. In the first dream I was running to catch a train but I arrived at the station just in time to see it going out. The next night I was again running to catch a train but this time I missed it only by seconds. On the third night yet again I was running for a train but this time I caught it. On the fourth night not only did I arrive in time for the train but the driver invited me into his cab and asked me if I would like to take the controls.

To me, these dreams meant I was trying to catch up with things in life but never quite managed to do this. It also showed me that I was not really in control of my affairs. Seeing I eventually caught that train, and was even offered the chance to drive it, told me that if I altered in some way I could eventually be my own driver. Since these dreams I have begun to catch up and have already received a small promotion in my work, which must be more than a coincidence.

'Bullets—and the Day After'

In this dream someone was shooting at me. Bullets were hitting me but I could not tell where they came from because it was dark. The wounds they inflicted were not painful but I was most disturbed by the idea that a sniper, especially an unseen one, should do this to me.

Next day when fully awake I kept going over and over the dream and then, quite by chance, I found myself continuing with what had happened in the dream, in a daydream. My imagination took over from where the dream left off and in it I saw something that revealed the source of the bullets and the identity of the sniper. Apparently the bullets, shots in the dark, were a verbal assault from someone I recognized as a rival. Taking this as a warning I took cover and had the pleasure of seeing this person completely missing his target!

'Incubate and So Shall You Receive'

I had a very personal problem and in desperation decided to try and incubate a dream that would help me. After four or five attempts, I had a dream that was quite horrific but on reflection decided it was extremely helpful. In this dream I was urged to look in a cupboard and in it I discovered a head. On looking closely I found it was *my* head. Looking back on the dream I realize it could have been a plaster model because my nose looked as if it had been broken off.

I took the message from this to be that if I was not very careful in the way I handled things, I could lose my head as well as cutting off my nose to spite my face. This warning fitted the situation perfectly so all that was needed was the overcoming of my pride. Fortunately I swallowed this and now feel at peace with myself and someone else.

'The Jigsaw Puzzle'

Having successfully incubated dreams before, I thought I would try to have a helpful dream concerning my future career. The dream I received was a bit of a puzzle, not least because in it I was actually doing a jigsaw puzzle. This was an easy one but towards finishing it I realized that the table was too small for it.

Next day the symbols sorted themselves out a little and eventually I decided that the jigsaw puzzle represented my life which was fairly simple and successful so long as I did not over-extend my aims. If I did I would end up with an unstable career. The choice I now have to make is—do I find a larger table (or to use another cliché, cut my coat according to my cloth)? I intend to seek further advice from another incubated dream in six months' time.

'Through the Wall—Lucidly'

In a lucid dream I had I was well aware I was in a dream state and so I was able to ask myself what I should do to demonstrate that it was my dream and that I could manipulate it. It came to me that I should walk through the wall so I pressed myself tightly up against it and slowly but surely I slithered through it, rather like thick yoghurt goes through a nylon sieve. Although this did not offer a solution to any particular problem, at least it gave me the satisfaction to know that I had some command over my own dreams in a conscious, albeit dream-conscious, way.

'Lucid Solution'

My problem was not particularly pressing or important but I thought a lucid dream might help put things in perspective for me. I am very untidy in the office where I work and I know others find this irritating. In the dream I created my office with its desk and the chaotic mess of papers all over it. I looked at this and said to myself, 'Why can't you manage to keep all this tidy and in some order?' 'You can so do it now,' came the reply. I lined everything up, filed dozens of letters and generally did a good job all round. I then told myself that I would do exactly the same in real life when I woke up.

Whether it was the positive programming of my personal computer-brain or whether I was going to be tidier anyway, I don't know, but it is a fact that my office desk has never been so orderly and I have never before felt so efficient!

Precognitive Dreams

Maybe our souls do travel to other dimensions or maybe it is an inner journey they take, where it is found that everything and everyone exists within, not without at all. Whichever it is, time—linear chronological time—does not exist in dreams as it does when we are awake.

The ancient races made a distinction between two very different concepts of time and called them *'chronos'* and *'cairos'*. Chronos is to experience time in seconds, minutes, hours, days and years, in chronological order; cairos is to participate within time itself, living in the timeless moment. To exist in cairos is to experience the eternal now where there is no past and no future, only the present.

Metaphysical though this explanation is, it explains how, in dreams and in certain psychic experiences, we overcome chronological time and find that just as we can look back in time, so too can we look ahead.

Many dreams do reflect the future and come true. One of the memorable dreams in this respect is that experienced by Mr A. Johnson, a Norwegian fisherman. Two nights before the *Titanic* sank in November 1907 he dreamed that a voice told him quite distinctly that a large ship called *Titanic* would sink after being in collision with an iceberg. Mr Johnson woke up but returned to a light sleep where the dream continued with its terrifying theme. He says he became very uneasy and felt icy ocean waves breaking over his body.

Mr Johnson was not alone in this precognitive warning. Many other people throughout the world also dreamed of that terrible disaster, on the night of the tragedy or sometime before the event. But precognitive dreams, dreams giving foreknowledge of an event, are by no means always associated with collective disasters. The majority reflect extremely trivial events, so trivial in fact that most of them pass unnoticed and unrecognized. Yet it is often heard said 'That has broken my dream' when something in a newspaper, a conversation, or an unexpected encounter suddenly jogs the memory and the event is linked with a dream.

Whether the event is profound or insignificant, the ability to dream out of time occurs far more frequently than is generally realized. 'To be forewarned is to be forearmed' is an appropriate slogan to apply to these precognitive dreams, but unfortunately even being so armed it is not always possible to avoid certain consequences. If, however, warning dreams are taken seriously, and where possible acted upon, they may remain as warnings and not become prophetic.

'Assassination of the Prime Minister'

Precognitive dreams have been recorded throughout history from earliest times down to the present. One of the comparatively recent dreams of this nature concerns the assassination of the British Prime Minister, Spencer Perceval, on 11 May 1812. Eight days previously a man living in Cornwall dreamed he saw a small man enter the lobby of the House of Commons, dressed in a blue coat and a white waistcoat. He then saw another man, wearing a brown coat with ornate metal buttons down the front, pull a gun from under his coat and shoot the first man. Others present grabbed the assassin and the dreamer asked who had been shot and was told it was Mr Perceval.

The dreamer was so impressed by his dream that he wanted to warn the Prime Minister but was dissuaded from doing so. Eight days later the Prime Minister was assassinated. Print-shops in London displayed coloured pictures of the Prime Minister and his assassin, and the clothes they were wearing were identical to those seen in the Cornishman's dream.

'Charles Dickens and Miss Napier'

I [Charles Dickens] dreamed that I saw a lady in a red shawl with her back towards me. On her turning round, I found that I didn't know her and she said 'I am Miss Napier'. All the time I was dressing next morning, I thought—what a preposterous thing to have so very distinctive dream about nothing! and why Miss Napier? For I have never heard of any Miss Napier. That same Friday night I read. After the reading there came into my retiring-room Miss Boyle and her brother, and the lady in the red shawl whom they presented as Miss Napier.

'The Flying Scotsman'

In the Autumn of 1913 John W. Dunne, author of 'An Experiment With Time' and researcher into dreams and time, dreamed he saw a railway embankment. He knew in the dream that the locality was just north of the Firth of Forth Bridge in Scotland. There was open grassland below the embankment with people walking in small groups. The scene came and went but the last time he saw it a train going north had fallen over the embankment. Several carriages were lying towards the bottom of the slope and large blocks of stone were rolling down.

On 4 April 1914 the *Flying Scotsman* mail train jumped the parapet 15 miles north of the Forth Bridge and fell on to the golf links below. The scene was almost exactly as John Dunne had seen it.

'The Bishop's Dream'

On the night of 27 June 1914 Bishop Monseigneur Joseiph de Lanyi dreamed he received a black-edged letter bearing the arms of Archduke Ferdinand, heir-presumptive to the Austro-Hungarian throne. On opening the letter he saw a street scene with the Archduke and his wife seated in a motor car, facing a general. Suddenly two men appeared and shot at the royal couple.

The letter itself read: 'Your Eminence, dear Dr Lanyi, my wife and I have been victims of a political crime at Sarajevo. We commend ourselves to your prayers. Sarajevo, 28 June 1914, 4 a.m.' The next day the Bishop received news of the assassination of the Archduke and very soon after this the First World War began.

'Derby-Winner'

Mr J. H. Williams was a staunch opponent to gambling, yet on 31 May 1933 at 8.35 a.m. he woke from a vivid dream about the Derby. The dream was a radio commentary on the race, that was to be run at 2 p.m. that day. It gave details of the race and the first four winners but Mr Williams could remember only the first two—Hyperion and King Salmon. Mr Williams told a neighbour and a business colleague about the dream and although he had never listened to a horse race before, that afternoon he did. The commentator used exactly the same words used in the dream, and the first four horses to win the race were those he had heard earlier. The two men Mr Williams had told about his dream that morning confirmed that he had done so.

'Punters' Dream—Bookies' Nightmare'

John Godley, later Lord Kilbracken, found he could dream precognitively when he was at Balliol, Oxford, in 1946. The theme running through these dreams was horse-racing. On 8 March he dreamed he was reading the racing results and that two horses—*Bindal* and *Juladin*—won at 7–1. That morning he went to a café in town and met a friend, Richard Freeman, and told him about his dream. They discovered that *Bindal* was running at Plumpton and *Juladin* was running at Wetherby that afternoon. *Bindal* won at 5–4. John Godley put his winnings on *Juladin* which also won its race.

In April that year he did it again. In this dream he was looking at a list of winners and the only one he could remember when he woke up was *Tubermore*. He told his family this at breakfast. *Tuberose*, a name close enough, was running in Grand National that afternoon so he and his family backed it. The BBC news at 6 p.m. told them Tuberose had won.

John Godley's gift lasted for twelve years during which time he continued to dream of winners.

'Dream Home'

In 1945 while living in Lytham St Annes I dreamed that I was sitting upstairs on a green bus travelling from Croydon towards Warlingham. As it passed through Sanderstead it slowed down, giving me time to look closely at the houses. On the right, the far side of the bus, there was open country. On my left there was a row of modern terraced houses with gardens sloping fairly steeply away from the road. There were about four houses to a block, two end ones and two in the middle. My attention was drawn to one of the houses in the middle. It had a very large tree in the front garden. In 1949 I moved into that house. The large tree is a horse-chestnut and, although I do not live there now, everytime I pass it, as I often do, I am reminded of the dream that came true.

'Amber'

While on holiday in Italy I had a vivid dream about Amber, the Welsh mountain pony we had left at home. I told the family about it at breakfast on the Tuesday morning so that they could not then accuse me of making it up if what I had seen in the dream was true. In this dream I saw Amber had managed to force her way out onto a footpath running behind the house. She was covered in mud as if she had been rolling in it.

When we returned I discovered that Amber had broken down the fence and got out on to the path exactly as I had seen in my dream, and she had rolled in the mud. She may have done this the day before I had the dream or the day after, so I am not sure if this was a prophetic dream or a telepathic message. Either way, she had never done such a thing before, nor ever did again.

'Forgetful Milkman'

Many incidents I see in my dreams come true although most of these are everyday events that do not mean anything in particular. I dream of people I have not seen for years, then they turn up on my doorstep unexpectedly, or I receive a letter from them after having dreamed about it the night before. Recently I dreamed that the milkman left only one pint of milk on the very day I had ordered three. This came true a week later. I had invited a neighbour with her three small children to tea and discovered to my horror that, although I had ordered three pints of milk, the milkman, just as he did in my dream, left only one! Not a disaster, but I could have avoided this if only I had listened to my warning dream.

'Auntie's Back-Yard'

Having visited an aunt living in America for the first time, I returned to England and soon after had a vivid dream about her. In this she was pacing up and down her back-yard, as she called it, in an agitated and angry state. She was carrying on about a man called Grayson. This dream made such an impression on me that I wrote to her at once asking if she had been upset by a man of that name. She replied saying she was not angry nor did she know anyone called Grayson.

Two years later she came to London and on meeting me she produced the letter I had written to her about my dream. Apparently, a year after I had dreamed this, she found herself re-enacting what I had described. She was pacing up and down her backyard, carrying on about a man called Grayson.

When I dreamed about this she did not know anyone of this name, nor did her husband, but a year later he had a new boss who decided that all the older men should be made redundant. Understandably, this made my aunt furious so to vent her feelings she went out into her backyard. The name of the new boss? Grayson.

'Goodbye Mr Finch'

I do not often remember my dreams but this one was so real it haunted me all day until the evening when I had to find out if it was true. Sadly it was. In this dream I saw an old neighbour who had moved from the house next door to a bungalow some ten miles away. I have never been to this place but in my dream I was standing by Mr Finch's bedside. He sat up and said that he wanted to say goodbye because he was going on a very long journey. I knew what he meant. In the evening I telephoned and his wife answered the phone telling me that her husband had died in his sleep during the night.

'Sally Burton'

All I can remember from this dream was that Richard Burton was looking handsome and happy. With him a woman I did not recognize. I woke up and put on the early breakfast-time television. As I did so the presenter of the programme was just about to introduce a guest. It was Sally Burton, the woman I had seen in my dream.

26.

Psychic Dreams

Dreams, by definition, are psychic experiences. Whether literal, symbolic or archetypal, they all occur within the dreamer's psyche, defying logic and time yet with powers and sagacity far beyond waking perception and reasoned intellect.

Premonitions, warnings, telepathic communications, astral travel and the re-enactment of past lives are only a few of the unaccountable things manifesting in dreams, but not all of these experiences are enlightening and reassuring. Some are frightening in the extreme, in particular those involving malicious psychic attacks for no apparent reason.

Certain houses and rooms are renowned for an unearthly presence that latches onto sleeping victims in an evil and possessing way, causing a suffocating sensation and feelings of imminent danger. Many old Inns in Britain have their haunted room where unsuspecting guests all have a similar unpleasant experience in their sleep.

These experiences are known traditionally as incubus or succubus attacks, that is an intrusion by a male or female demonic entity which is said to attempt to possess the sleeper, body and soul. This could perhaps explain why many external invasive influences, from ghostly spirits of the dead to harmful thoughts of the living which take on horrible forms, disturb sleepers in this way.

An atmosphere and even an emanation from an article or a piece of furniture may also account for these psychic attacks. Psychometry, the ability to intuitively read the history of an object by making contact with it, has been proved to be accurate on many occasions, but this has never been investigated from the standpoint of sleep and dreams. During sleep, sensitivity increases, therefore influences—whether in the form of a noise outside or an emanation from an object, entity or atmosphere—are intensified.

'The Egyptian figure'
Influences received in this way may account for the dream a woman had while holding an Egyptian figure in her hands, just before going to sleep. In this dream she found herself at the foot of one of the Egyptian pyramids, an experience that was so real she was certain she had been transported not only thousands of miles in distance but also back in time over the centuries. Although association of ideas may account for some experiences of this nature,

the revelation of facts unknown to this dreamer before the dream seemed to prove, at least in this case, otherwise.

If this dream was in fact the result of psychometry, one wonders how many of our more mysterious dreams are the result of objects seen or contacted during the day, through the transference of information and memory in this way.

'Wolves and the Grandfather Clock'

Spontaneous psychometry may account for the repeated nightmares experienced by a child whenever she stayed in a certain house in France. As a child she was taken on holiday each June to a house in Alsace. In the hall of this house stood a large old grandfather clock, and from the first night she spent there the nightmares began. In these, wolves ran out from the clock and chased her.

An explanation for this may be that the clock was made from wood cut from trees in a forest where wolves once roamed. Enquiries proved that this was possible, if not highly probable. Until a hundred years ago the area was thickly wooded and was known to be the haunt of numerous wolf-packs. These were reputed to have snatched children and babies from the few families then living in the forest.

'The Pills'

Psychic transference could also explain the dream a patient had after taking pills given to her by her doctor. In this dream she was on a frozen lake watching skaters speeding along on the ice. She then saw a Negro boy on a sledge, flying out towards the edge of the lake, hitting the side and dying. This so disturbed her that she told her doctor about the dream on her next visit.

The day before the patient had this dream the doctor had been beside a frozen lake watching the skaters. Among them was a Negro boy on a sledge. This boy had tied his sledge to a rope which was attached at the other end to a pivot embedded in the ice. This allowed his sledge to revolve around the pivot at great speed. Suddenly, the boy was thrown off the sledge and hurtled to the side of the lake, where he died almost instantly. That evening, as the doctor was making up pills for a patient, rolling them between his fingers, he related to a friend what had happened that afternoon. His patient's dream was an exact reproduction of what he, the doctor, had seen and described while making up her pills.

Psychic Protection

Nocturnal attacks of a psychic nature were, until this century, well recognized and acknowledged as experiences needing to be guarded against. As a form of protection, the Victorians used prayers which called upon the Lord to bless the house. These were often embroidered into cross-stitch motifs and hung above their bedheads. Pictures of Jesus and crucifixes were also placed in bedrooms for this purpose, but today such signs are rarely seen even though the need for protection is just as great now as it was then.

There is, in addition to asking for divine protection, a simple and effective psychological ritual that will keep out unwanted negative influences. This involves strengthening the aura, an energy-field that surrounds all living things. This is comprised of energy in various forms ranging from that recognized as heat radiated from the body and sounds emitted by the various physiological systems, to electrical impulses produced by muscular contractions and brain activity. In addition to these energies the aura contains energy of a subtler nature which is apparently scientifically unrecordable.

When a person is tired, run-down or depressed, the energy level in their aura is low; if this happens, the aura loses its effectiveness as a natural protective barrier. By comparing this loss of energy with a run-down battery it can be seen that, by recharging it, its efficiency and protective powers are restored. The aim of this exercise is, therefore, to do just this.

The Protective Exercise

This exercise should be carried out before going to sleep each night.

Lie flat on your back in bed, close your eyes, and when you feel warm and comfortable you will be ready to begin relaxing physically.

To do this turn your attention to both feet and clench up your toes for a second or two, and then let them go. Now turn your toes up towards your head, tensing the calf muscles in your lower leg as you do so, and then let them down. Turn your attention next to your hands. Clench your fists tightly, and let them go.

This tensing and relaxing of the muscles in the extremities will remove much of the tension in your physical body.

The next step is to concentrate on your breathing for a minute or two.

Take in a breath to the count of two, and let it out slowly to the count of four or five. Repeat this exercise three times.

This breathing pattern imitates the rhythm of breathing adopted during sleep, so it unconsciously puts you into a particularly receptive state of mind in readiness to carry out the psychological ritual, which is simplicity itself.

All that is needed for this is the power of your own controlled imagination. Using this, see yourself surrounded by an aura of pure light. The light symbolizes your protective energy field. Different colours may appear as you do this, so if they do, try to single out the blue, gold or white light. Pay particualr attention to your head and in your mind's eye see the light encircling this, in the form of a halo.

If you remember to do this before going to sleep, you will remain safe and secure throughout the night, even in the most haunted of rooms.

Communal Dreaming and Telepathy

The merits of shared dreaming were recognized and valued in the past by most cultures. The North American Indian tribes, in particular the Hurons and the Iroquios, held regular dream festivals which often lasted weeks, depending on the material collected. By pooling their dreams a distinct pattern emerged and this was then used to help construct future tribal policy.

The Maoris in New Zealand, the Zulus in South Africa, the Eskimos around Hudson Bay, and the Patani people from as far away as Malaysia, still hold the belief that during sleep the soul leaves the body and returns with useful information which benefits the dreamer and the community in which they live. And the Temiar tribe, part of the Senois in Malaysia, are said to pool their dream experiences which collectively reflect their future.

In Europe, the Corsicans are extremely dream-conscious people. Here whole villages have similar dreams on the same night, as if a collective psyche controls them telepathically during sleep. While on holiday in Corsica on 1986, a British family of four all dreamed exactly the same dream. At breakfast, the mother, father, son and daughter could not believe that the scene each had seen in their respective dream had been a shared vision. At that time they had not heard of the communal dreaming practice of the islanders, and it was only by chance that they learned of this later.

Groups of people studying dreams often pool their dreams as an exercise or to receive special collective guidance. At a meeting in 1980 of 'The Atlanteans', a highly altruistic society based in Malvern, 35 members attended a weekend dream workshop. Although group-dreaming had not been suggested, when discussing the first night's dreaming after all had slept under the same roof, 20 or more members had experienced the same theme and historical time. The theme was a river, the Thames, and the setting was Tudor London. Henry VIII, his wives and courtiers had provided them with an amazing collection of colourful and extremely interesting dreams.

Telepathic Dreams

Heraclitus, the Greek philosopher, is said to have taught his pupils that in dreams, visions of strange places, men, women, animals and objects are brought to the dreamer's attention without the assistance of the senses or personal memories. This fragment derives from a profound theory, the greater part of which has been lost, but clearly telepathy (*tele* = far off, and *pathos* = feeling and suffering)—communication between minds at a distance without the agency of the senses—is involved.

If this transference exists, and there is plenty of evidence to suggest that it does, it explains why certain dreams contain visions and information that could not possibly have come into the dreamer's head in any other way. It also explains mutual or twin dreaming.

Investigating the nature of mental and vital transference seems to show that there is a form of energy transmitted from one source to another, or from one soul to another, and there is a 'tuning-in' or harmonizing of systems. These two processes are fundamental principles underlying all psychic phenomena, whether occurring during sleep or when fully awake.

The following dreams are accounts of mutual dreaming shared by two or more people. In some cases their dreams are similar, in others they are serialized, with one dreamer providing the first part and the other dreamer continuing with the theme.

'The Letter'
In this dream I received a letter from a man I have not seen for some years, but in all honesty I had longed to meet him again. In his letter he said he would meet me in a motorway service station of Monday. On waking I was distraught because the letter had not said which motorway, let alone which service station or which Monday. Giving this considerable thought throughout the next day (in fact I thought of nothing else), I worked out the possibilities. Knowing something of this man's movements, I guessed which motorway it could be and worked out the time he would arrive there if he were going from A to B as I surmised. As for which Monday, I trusted myself and my own dream, believing that it would not be so stupid as to make it one in the distant future, so I plumped for the next Monday.

The dream occurred on Wednesday night. The anticipation and excitement between Thursday—the day after the dream—and the Monday was tremendous. The day arrived at last and I drove to the motorway services, getting there at least an hour before the time I estimated he would arrive. After two hours I began to panic—and then it happened: in he walked.

My dream had come true, but the amazing thing was that this man had dreamed of *me* the previous Wednesday. Unfortunately, he could not remember any details of this beyond the fact that it had been a very happy dream.

'Call For Help'
Several horses were pulling a cart that was too much for them. The man driving them called to me to ask if I could help. When I got close to him I was amazed to discover it was my husband.

When I told my husband about this dream in the morning, he told me that he had experienced a very similar dream, only there were no horses in it. In his dream he was pushing his car that had broken down and he called to me to come over and help him push it. We agreed that our dreams had the same message–that my husband needed support–but we found they had used different scenes to point this out. It was sometime afterwards that we realized that this was a telepathic call from my husband to me, asking for help.

'Lover's Link'
When my husband was abroad for eight months at a time, we discovered that we communicated through our dreams. At first we thought the dreams were just ordinary dreams but we then discovered that we were seeing in them places each of

us were visiting. On one occassion I went to Wales unexpectedly and climbed the foothills of Snowdon. My husband did not know this but during the weekend I spent there he dreamed that I was walking in open, mountainous country. He saw an overhanging cliff with me trying to climb up it. In actual fact I did not climb a cliff but sat under one thinking of my husband.

'Mother And Daughter'
This dream was so real that when I woke up I knew that what I had seen must be true. Quite clearly I saw my daughter with what at first I thought was a white pillow tied to her leg. I moved closer and saw it was a plaster cast. My daughter and her family live 50 miles from me and we see each other from time to time, and telephone each week. Although I had spoken to her only two days previously, I could not rest until I had spoken to her again and was sure she was alright.

I phoned at 8.00 in the morning but there was no reply. I tried at 8.30 but again no reply. By 10.00 there was still no answer so I prepared to go over to see what had happened. Just as I was about to leave the phone rang. It was my son-in-law to say that my daughter was in hospital, so were their two children, and he had spent the night there too. Apparently they had been involved in a car accident the evening before. Fortunately, none were badly hurt. The children were shocked and my daughter had a suspected fracture of her left leg.

At the time I had the dream the accident had happened, but my daughter did not have her leg in plaster until the following day.

'Counterpart Dreams'
My school friend and I often dream about the same things on the same night. We began to make notes of all our dreams and discovered that one of us sometimes had the counterpart to the other's dream.

On one occasion I dreamed that we were riding our bikes in the country, as we often do, and I had a puncture in one of my tyres. We seemed to be miles from anywhere and we were staranded beside the road. At this point I woke up. To my surprise my friend had also dreamed that night that we were out on our bikes. Her dream began where I had a puncture and also that we were miles from anywhere. We did not have a puncture outfit with us so in her dream we stuffed the tyre with grass and in that way managed to go on our way.

Meetings with the Dead

Closely related to telepathic dreams, where a message is passed from one dreamer to another, are those dreams in which a deceased person appears to the dreamer and gives them a special message or a word of comfort. Sometimes it is the deceased who comes to the dreamer, sometimes it is the dreamer who goes to the deceased. Whichever it is, dreams of this nature, where there is contact between the living and the dead, provide sufficient evidence for those who have experienced the encounter to be absolutely certain that their loved ones not only still exist, albeit in dream-form, but are able to contact them before they meet again for good.

'Dream of Phil'
My son was accidentally killed in 1980 whilst at sea in the Merchant Navy. I did not

know the details of the accident and have often wondered about this, but since having this dream I now feel I know the truth.

It is evening and I am in the sitting-room when in walks Phil. It is so wonderful to see him, and I am fully aware in this dream that he is dead. He beckons me to come into the kitchen and he hugs me. I tell him it has been such a long time since we saw each other and he says 'Yes mum, it has, but it's all right now'. He has something in his hand—I cannot see what it is but I believe it to be a key. He tells me that to be dead is like being in another room in the same house but the doors between the two sorts of rooms are usually locked. I remember thinking in the dream that he held the key to those communicating doors.

I then ask him why he died and if anyone was to blame for what happened. 'No one else was to blame,' he said, 'we all disobeyed the safety rules'. The breaking of rules was never mentioned at the inquiry but what he said about this explained everything to me.

'Hello Dear'

Since my husband died four years ago I have felt his presence around me in the kitchen and living-room where we lived happily together for over 40 years. In this dream he was real and as alive as he ever was. I turned round and said 'Hello Dear' just as if he had been out for a walk. He was wearing his overcoat and hat as if he was waiting for me. He told me to get ready and leave everything I was doing and go with him. But I felt I was not ready and had to polish the dinner plates before I could go. He stood there silently and then I realized he was dead and I was alive, and he was asking me to die. Death holds no fear for me now and I am even looking forward to it because I know my husband will be there to meet me.

'A Mother's Warning'

My mother who died some years ago walked into my bedroom as she used to do and sat on the bed. I knew she was dead in this dream but it seemed quite natural that she should be there talking to me. Suddenly she altered and became cross or anxious, I don't know which, and said 'Do you know your fiancé has been married before?' I was shocked by this and when I woke up I was thinking more about what my mother had said than about seeing her so clearly in the dream.

When I met my fiancé later the next day, I tried to give him the opportunity of telling me he had been married before by talking about past events and holidays, but I did not ask him outright. From this conversation I discovered gaps existed in his past and this made me suspicious. Eventually, I found out that what my mother had told me in my dream was true but no one in Britain at that time, other than my now ex-fiancé, could possibly have known this.

'Holiday Spirit'

There is one dream from childhood that I shall never forget. We were on holiday in the Isle of Wight and sleeping in the bedroom with me was my sister. In the dream I saw an old lady dressed in a frilly sort of dress standing by my bed. She had a terrible look on her face, and there was a strong smell of violets. I woke up screaming. The next night I had the same dream and again woke up in a state, so it was decided that my sister and I should sleep in our parents' room and them in ours. That night, my father, who said he never dreamed, dreamed of this same woman. When he told the landlady about this, she told him that we were not the first to have been disturbed by her in this way.

It was thought that this woman lived in the house during the 1914–1918 war and during that war her husband had been killed, an event that had greatly disturbed her.

'Grandmother's Warning'

In this dream I was driving my car fairly speedily round a bend. A voice that sounded exactly like my grandmother's almost shouted in my ear and said 'There's something round that bend, don't be a fool'. It was a short dream but a very vivid one. The sequel to this is that next day it came true—at least driving my car round that bend at speed came true. It was a *déjà vu* experience; then I remembered my dream, and at that moment remembered my grandmother's warning. I slowed down immediately, something I would never have done had it not been for my dream. Round that corner, broken down almost in the middle of the road, was a large removal van. It looked as if its back axle had broken because it was tilting over at a dangerous angle.

Even at the reduced speed I only just managed to avoid a collision, so if it had not been for my grandmother's warning there most certainly would have been an accident. Feeling I had been so fortunate to escape, possibly with my life, I realized the danger others were in so I ran back and placed my road-safety red triangle in the middle of the road.

This dream cost me that red triangle because I left it in the road but I like to think that my grandmother saved not only my life but, through me, others too.

'The Garden of Eternal Life'

The dream began where I was walking over the open Downs. I came to a garden gate and on the other side of this gate stood a man smoking a pipe. At first I thought it was my father who died last year, but then I realized it was not. He asked me if I would like to come in and see the garden. I told him I would, although I did not have to speak to tell him this.

I found myself looking at a curious but beautiful scene. It was a square walled garden with a stone floor, and at intervals in this were planted rare trees and plants. I thought of myself 'This is the Garden of Eden, what am I doing here?' The man asked me if there was anything I wanted to see in particular. I thought about the people who looked after this garden, and as I did into the garden came several figures who can only be described as more real then real. They were so real they were unreal, if that makes sense. This is where the saying 'larger than life' comes from, I thought. It was then that I realized they were all dead people, yet so alive. I did not recognize any of them and the man with the pipe must have known what I was thinking because he said I would have to come again and next time he would see that those I wanted to meet would be there.

I have not yet dreamed of this place again but, even if I do not, I know I shall go there one day.

'Playtime'

I have had just one dream about my little girl who died when she was only three. It was not the usual sort of dream; there was something about it that made it strange, but ever since then I have seen life and death in a new light.

It started off in a hospital where there was a huge screen. I went behind this and found a long, long corridor which I ran down. At the end of this was a room, rather like those in church halls where playgroups are held. I went in and there were about ten or more children there, playing with all sorts of things. I wished I could see my little girl playing like that but I knew she could not, because she was dead. Then I looked again and there she was among the others. The leader, who looked rather like a nun, told me not to disturb her or call her name because she was happy with the others.

'Heavenly Pets'
My cats died years ago but I always felt very close to them and they were close to me. All the family loved them too so everyone was very upset when our last feline friend died. Recently, I dreamed that I was with them again—at least with two of them, the third was not there. They were living in a heavenly sort of cattery where it was warm and the whole place was devoted to idleness and laziness. Cats where just lying about purring happily.
The next morning I told my daughter about this dream and she could hardly believe it because she too had dreamed about the cats. In her dream the scene was much the same as mine but somehow she knew that one of the cats had come back to life. She took this to mean it had been reincarnated and that we were to look out for his spirit inside the new body of a kitten. This explained why I saw only two cats and not three, so now we have to find that new kitten, who is really our old cat.

Astral Projection

Astral projection, or an out-of-body experience, is a state whereby the dreamer's consciousness apparently moves outside their body. Once free it is possible for this centre of awareness to receive information and impressions which would normally be impossible to perceive from where the physical body rests at that time.

The word 'astral' relates to a second body which is said to exist within the physical body. It is reputed to be composed of a subtle form of energy but has the same shape and apppearance as the physical body. This astral body, or 'ghost in the machine', is capable of separating itself from its physcal counterpart and travelling freely, passing throught walls and objects, and surviving death.

Astral projection during sleep occurs spontaneously as opposed to the consciously-contrived experience attempted when awake. When experienced in sleep it is often described as a 'flying dream' where the dreamer flaps his or her arms and rises weightlessly up to the ceiling. From that position they can then look down and see themselves lying asleep in bed. Sometimes the experience begins outside on a lawn, where the dreamer runs a few steps then takes off and soars above houses and tree-tops like a bird in flight.

Maybe the astral body which projects in this way has complete mobility and the ability to merge with similar bodies, or maybe it is a personified concept created by the dreamer for the purpose of inner development leading to evolution of the spirit. Whichever it is, the realm of this transient figure appears to be that of the multi-dimensional, archetypal realm where consciousness and understanding extend far beyond the barriers of reality.

Once free, great distances can be traversed instantly. Sometimes the destination is recognized, sometimes it is not only a foreign land but a place where the inhabitants are so unfamiliar that the dreamer may well be on another planet, galaxy or even in a different dimension. On these astral journeys meetings with great spiritual beings, aliens, fairies and gnomes, as well as with the living and the dead, are possible. Such encounters have been known to alter the dreamer's life completely and at the very least give an added dimension to life itself.

Astral projection has a strong personal significance for those who experience it, suggesting the existence of an awareness beyond that of physical consciousness and even beyond the concept of unconsciousness. Although it is impossible to prove conclusively, the experience seems to provide evidence of individual survival after death as well as bringing back proof that such unshackled travel does occur.

Experiences of this nature are not, however, always enlightening and positively exciting. Some dreamers are afraid to go to sleep fearing that they will leave their bodies and meet terrible extra-terrestial forces encountered on previous occasions. Others have found that once freed in this way, something indescribably horrible prevents them from returning to their body.

By placing a psychic protection around yourself, as described earlier, it is possible to protect and prevent yourself from projecting astrally.

'Low-Flying'

In this dream I flap my arms furiously knowing that doing this will enable me to take off and fly a few feet above the ground. The dream recurs fairly frequently and each time I have it I manage to improve my flying skill a little and gain height.

This experience could be described as low astral flying compared with the astral flight that takes the dreamer to faraway places. Stong links with the physical body, a natural form of protection, prevent great distances being covered at present. Slowly but surely confidence is increasing so eventually he will be able to fly higher and further and with this will come an elevation of ideals and aims.

'OBE'

I suddenly rose about six feet above my bed and seemed to glide up a long narrow staircase which opened out onto the stars. With a minimim of effort I flew way out among them, returning with an exhilerated, wonderful feeling.

Many nocturnal experiences in sleep are not dreams in the accepted sense, and this is one of them. Known as an out-of-body experience, OBE for short, this dreamer's 'ghost' soared among the stars and returned invigorated. Symbolically, it shows the dreamer can rise above his problems in the real world.

'Two Me s'

I was seeing myself lying in bed, as if viewed from above. As this realization came to me I began to hear a strange hum that shook my body, so I voluntarily returned to my body on the bed. The thought of there being two me s has intrigued me ever since.

This dreamer astrally projected and became aware of the separation of his subtle aspect from his physical body. The strange hum has been noticed by others who have projected similarly and it is thought to represent or be due to a form of psychic energy.

'Proof'

I floated up towards the ceiling, then I came down to the level of the window and passed through it as if it were not there. Once outside I flew over some rooftops and swooped down into the park just at the end of the road. It looked exactly as it does when I take my dog there each day except that three workmen were digging up the path, searching for a broken gas main.

I was able to return at will to my bed and soon after waking I got up and went straight to the park to see if what I had seen during the night was true. There was no one at all in the park at that early hour and I felt disappointed but when I returned later I discovered to my delight three men searching—not for a gas main but for a burst water pipe. They were digging up the path in exactly the same place I had seen them digging in my nocturnal visit.

This experience gave proof to the sleeper that it is possible to travel astrally during sleep. It also shows that an individual has the free will to make assumptions, wrongly in this case—it was not a gas main, it was a water pipe— in a hyperconscious state as well as one does consciously, when awake.

'The Tunnel To Heaven'

In this dream I flew out of my bedroom window into a long dark tunnel which must have been perfectly straight because I could see a light at the end. This light became brighter and brighter and when I emerged from the tunnel I was surprised not to be dazzled by it. Bathing in this light was an amazing experience because with it was an overpowering silence. This took on the form of a man whom I knew to be God. On each of His hands were stars, the creation of the Universe.

This tunnel has been experienced by many who have been near death and it is thought to be the connecting link between this world and the next, earth and heaven, life and death, and conscious and unconscious awareness. The light is the hope for the future, either in this life or in the next and the vision of God is the projection of the dreamer's own image of the Creator. Galaxies are the Creation, and each individual is a part of this.

'The Devil's Castle'

After travelling out into space at great speed I came to a vast castle in the sky. The door opened and I went inside. The feeling was terrible and I knew it was the castle of the Devil so I made myself as small as possible and flew back to my bed.

This is probably an astral experience warning that such trips beyond the physical world are fraught with unknown dangers and risks. Since out-of-body projections during sleep are spontaneous they are beyond conscious control, so this dreamer should place a psychic protection around himself before going to sleep. A projection or not, the image of the Devil is still a warning telling the dreamer that the Devil is also an aspect of himself. It is an image he does not wish to see, let alone face, but the time has come for some self-searching questions with honest replies.

'Electric Lady'
When I was seriously ill in hospital recently, one night when I was asleep I levitated above my bed. I could see all the other patients in different sleeping positions and I could see the nurses sitting round a desk with a table lamp on it. One nurse got up and came over to me and told me to come down because she had a special drink for me. She was dressed more like an Edwardian lady than a modern nurse. I came down and as I took the cup form her I felt a great electric shock run through my body. When I woke up in the morning I was so much better I could not believe it. When I asked the nurse who it was who gave me a drink in the night she did not seem to know what I was talking about and thought I must have been delirious, but I know I was not.

If it is true that everyone has an astral counterpart that is capable of freeing itself from the physical body and then meeting up with other astral forms, then it is also possible that a transference of energy takes place which has the power to heal. Healing is energy and energy is the key to recovery, and in this experience the energy was interpreted as electric.

'The Godmother'
In this dream I ran across the beach, jumped into the air, and found I could stay up if I peddled an invisible space-bike. Once I was airborne the sky looked different. It was full of what I first thought were birds but they turned out to be the spirits of the dead. They looked like those white alabaster statues seen in cemeteries. One of them came up to me and said my godmother was coming down to help me. She arrived and said there was no need for me to go any further, and that when I got back I would find everything was alright.
   At the time of this experience I was depressed and had considered suicide, but the very next day my life changed for the better. It was as if my godmother arranged for things to go right for me.

Perhaps we can all draw comfort from this experience which shows that there is someone, somewhere, who has our interests at heart. But who can say for sure who or what this godmother was. Maybe she was the spirit of the dreamer's godmother or maybe she was the godmother within the dreamer, or there again perhaps the two are one and the same. The important thing is that she existed when she was most needed by the dreamer.

'Pillars of Strength'
Having been rushed into hospital following a coronary I dreamed I was flying in heaven. I had feathered wings and I moved about by flapping these in a bird-like way. Heaven was a church in the sky. It was a magical building with a tower and a spire but above all it had many marble pillars. When I woke up I thought it meant I was going to die but now I believe I was shown a glimpse of what it will be like when I do eventually go there.

The angelic form and the church in the sky are images from the dreamer's personal belief system reflecting existence after death, but seeing them does not necessarily mean death is imminent. As positive signs they tell the dreamer that he himself is a pillar of strength and that the sky is the limit, so he should concentrate all his efforts on recovering form his heart attack.

'Golden in the Garden'
Soon after dropping off to sleep I thought I was awake because I found myself getting out of the window. Once over the ledge I became weightless and could manoeuvre myself in any direction I chose. The sun was setting so I decided to go into the centre of this. It was white hot but it did not burn me, and once through it I found myself in a perfect garden full of flowers of every colour, including a wonderful golden hue. During my stay in the garden I became a rainbow and although this sounds ridiculous in the harsh light of day I know that the experience healed me and altered my entire life for the better. I have never had an experience like this again.

Life depends on the sun and its white heat is a combination of all the energies that go to make up the golden cosmic rainbow. The garden was the dreamer's own Garden of Eden, a haven she can return to at any time through her imagination. Overall, this was a self-healing experience through the merging of the individual with the whole.

PART III
A–Z DREAM DICTIONARY

The Dictionary

Each dream is unique and has its own symbology based on the dreamer's personal experiences. It is, therefore, impossible to collate a dictionary which gives an interpretation of the actions and objects found in dreams. What is possible, however, is to translate the collective, traditional symbols and metaphors that are also found in them. These go to make up the language of dreams and are self-explanatory once they are recognized as representations and plays upon words; they are, accordingly, no more mysterious or difficult to understand than when they are encountered in everyday language.

It is these translations that, when related to the dreamer's own personal circumstances, become meaningful messages. A dream dictionary is not, therefore, a dictionary of dream interpretations at all. It is a dictionary which gives the meanings of collective, traditional symbolic and metaphorical word-pictures, found in dreams.

Abandoned

To be abandoned means the dreamer can and must rely only on himself or herself. This is a step towards independence.

Everyone is alone in this life but many do not realize it until it is seen in a dream.

To be abandoned does not mean loneliness.

For someone else to be abandoned in your dream means you would like to drop them from your circle of acquaintances, or that you see this person as someone who does not take responsibility for themselves.

Abattoir

This is a warning sign. The dreamer is aware of a life-threatening situation or unfair domination.

The inevitable is to be expected.

Abbess

A woman with high ideals.

Abbey

This is a special Mansion of the Soul, housing spiritual beliefs.

Abbot

A man with high ideals.

Abdomen

The state of the abdomen is important. An enlarged abdomen foretells great expectations. A diminutive abdomen warns against persecution and false friends.

A situation cannot be 'stomached.'

Abortion
Plans will go awry, abort.
To contemplate an abortion means regrets later on.
To be party to an abortion warns against persuasive enemies. Beware of a miscarriage of justice.

A-Bomb
A highly explosive, dangerous situation is looming up.
Collective dreams of the A-bomb show there is a collective awareness of the dangers to the planet as a whole.

Abroad
Unexpected travel is indicated. Foreign or unusual experiences are to be expected.

Abundance
Riches which have been well-earned are in store for the dreamer. Life will be rewarding.

Abyss
Emotionally, this shows the dreamer is in the depths of depression. It is the bottomless pit in life, the dark night of the soul.
Things cannot get worse so efforts must be made to climb out. Psychically, the abyss is an initiation, a test of inner strength.

Accident
An accident is a warning sign. Whatever the accident is, it may become prophetic if steps are not taken to heed the warning.
It also means the dreamer is not to blame for something that has happened. Take extra care when involved in activities resembling the accident in the dream.

Accounts
Apart from the warning of not overspending, accounts remind the dreamer that they will have to account for their actions sooner or later. This should be applied to personal circumstances.

Ace
Success is certain.
A favourable win or triumph is on the cards.

Ace of Clubs
To see this card in a dream means financial security is assured.
A wealth of friends and a wealth of understanding will pay dividends.

Ace of Diamonds
Careers and business ventures are under scrutiny at present.
Now is the time to launch new businesses and projects.

Ace of Hearts
Love and romance will play important roles in the dreamer's life shortly.
Friends will be supportive in times of need.

Ace of Spades
This card in a dream warns of immovable objects. Obstacles and trouble are to be expected.

Acorns
Acorns are excellent signs showing the future holds spreading potential. A single acorn is a sign of fertility, so the woman who wishes to become pregnant can expect her wish to come true.

Acrobat
An acrobat warns the dreamer that difficulties can only be overcome in a roundabout way. They must be prepared to perform the impossible, but it can be done.
The dreamer will be called to account for their actions.

Actor/Actress
Life is a stage with each individual playing his or her part.
Recognizing the part an actor or actress is playing in a dream helps the dreamer to see how they should play that role,

and how they can play it better.

Adam & Eve
These archetypal figures of man and woman symbolise future potential for the human race.
Fundamental feelings concerning relationships with a member of the opposite sex should be carefully considered.
Perfect harmony is possible.

Adultery
Adultery warns of adulteration—contamination.
Also a sign of guilty feelings.

Advertisement
This means the dreamer wishes to draw attention to him or herself.
Also a cry for help.

Aeroplane
To see an aeroplane flying in the sky means the dreamer has high-flying ambitions.
If the plane crashes it means plans should be brought down-to-earth or they may turn out to be nothing more than 'pie in the sky'.
Travelling in an aeroplane shows the dreamer's life is speeding up and they will soon reach their destination.

Africa
Exotic experiences are to be expected.
Dark secrets may be unveiled.

Afternoon
A dream set in the afternoon relates to a specific time.
It represents middle age.

Age
When age is a dominant sign in a dream, the dreamer should take extra care of their health.
When a dreamer appears as an old man or woman, it is the inner image of wisdom and experience.

Aggression
Aggressive figures in a dream warn of resentment.

The dreamer may be the aggressor or may be the victim.
This is a self-destructive influence manifesting as an unknown person.
In a woman's dream an aggressive man often symbolizes the threat of sexual dominance or assault.
In a man's dream aggression and violence may be due to passive homosexuality.

Air
Fresh air indicates renewed vigour and recovery from an illness.
Misty-air means an inspiration will provide a solution.

Airport
To be at an airport shows the dreamer has completed a phase in life and is preparing for the next, in readiness to take off again.
Speed is involved so beware of hasty decisions.

Airship/Air Balloon
Great adventures and flights of the imagination could carry the dreamer off on romantic, scenic, inner journeys.
Artistic dreamers will return to earth with brilliant, original ideas.

Aisle
To walk down a narrow aisle means there is no choice in life but to go forward.
As a pun, an aisle becomes an isle, warning of isolation.

Alien
An alien figure may be the dreamer's own shadow, reflecting an unrecognized quality, talent or defect of character.
An alien from outer-space symbolizes a threat to personal security.

Alligator
To see an alligator is a serious warning concerning overpowering opposition.
Considerable difficulties will have to be overcome.

Almonds
Beware of harbouring bitterness.

Altar
Traditionally an altar symbolizes self-sacrifice.
It warns the dreamer not to become a self-imposed martyr.
From a spiritual standpoint an altar means the dreamer is prepared to sacrifice his or her interests for others.

Ambassador
The dreamer is capable of self-representation.
The dreamer enjoys authority.

Amber
As a colour it reflects a magnetic attraction.
As a stone it symbolizes healing qualities.

America
Unless the dreamer has personal associations, practical and materialistic matters are under consideration.
Duality, twin situations, and repetitions are likely.

Amethyst
Peace of mind is to be expected.

Ammunition
Dangerous messages and cruel words.
Do not pass on unworthy comments concerning others.

Amputation
To lose a limb means severe restrictions may be imposed on the dreamer.

Amulet
This is a sign of protection. No harm can come to the dreamer.

Anagram
Look for hidden meanings and messages which are really obvious all the time.

Ancestors
The dreamer is interested or concerned about cultural roots and origins.
Ancestors are the dreamer's guardian angels who protect and help them.

Anchor
Strong attachments to a person or to a place.
If the anchor is above water and is clearly seen, it is a sign of good fortune. If it is below the water, it indicates a disappointment.

Angel
Freedom and purity.
These unearthly beings are messengers of good tidings as well as death.

Anima
This is the feminine, emotional, intuitive side of a man's nature.
All women in the dreamer's life, beginning with his mother, have helped to form this image.
In dreams the Anima appears in many archetypal forms, from feminine deities in mythology to the Egyptian Cat Goddesses and the Queen of Heaven.
The Anima is the dreamer's 'woman of his dreams'. He tries to superimpose this image on the woman whom he believes to be his soulmate.

Animals
The basic nature in man and woman, with its physical and instinctive craving for sex and food.
Psychologically it is the taming and harnessing of personal potential.
Unconscious energy of which the dreamer is becoming aware.
Prehistoric animals represent a memory from the remote past which may not be understood unless in the right context.
Wild animals warn of dangers from certain people or from destructive emotional forces.
Eating an animal is the assimilation of energy.
Killing an animal shows the dreamer is ruthless and could destroy his own vitality.
Fear of an animal indicates lack of self-awareness.
Superior animals such as the owl (wisdom), the elephant (memory), the ox (strength), represent superior qualities in man.
Baby animals—kids, lambs and chicks—

represent children.

Young animals represent people who are immature, selfish and insensitive.

Animus

This is the masculine, dominant and practical side of a woman's nature.

All men in the dreamer's life, beginning with her father, help form this image.

In dreams the Animus appears as many archetypal male figures, from heroes in mythology to Sir Galahad and handsome princes.

The Animus is the dreamer's 'man of her dreams' and she tries to superimpose this image onto the man whom she believes to be her soulmate.

Ankh

One of the oldest forms of the cross, known also as the cross ansata—the cross with a handle.

It is a combination of male and female symbols, representing the union between heaven and earth, Father Sun and Mother Earth.

It is the archetypal symbol of life.

Ant

As with all insects, this is a warning sign of some irritation.

It is a symbol of industriousness, ordered community spirit and virtue.

Emphasis is on work for work's sake, so workaholics beware.

Antelope

Traditionally these creatures indicate the dreamer's love of nature and the countryside.

A longing to travel away from civilization is indicated.

Antenna

A desire to communicate important information.

Antiques

Forgotten but valuable hopes and ambitions will be rediscovered.

Anvil

The forging of a friendship.

Physical strength is on the increase, possibly following an illness.

Ape

An image of regressive tendencies, childish bad habits and unknown ugly thoughts.

To see an ape in human surroundings warns of imitations which do not flatter.

Apostles

Fishers of men, spiritual leaders.

Applause

The dreamer is looking for praise and recognition, maybe for compensation, maybe for a boost of self-confidence.

Apples

The fruit with which the serpent is said to have tempted Eve, therefore an apple means temptation.

To eat an apple means a disappointment is to be expected.

Apricots

Good health and good fortune are indicated.

Arch

Unification of two principles, a marriage of ideas, a wedding.

To pass under an arch means that many who fomerly ignored the dreamer and their ability will seek their help or advice.

Archbishop

To see and recognize one means the dreamer will receive encouragement from those in high places.

Archer

A person who knows what his or her aim is in life.

Someone born under the astrological sign of Sagittarius.

Ark

Protection in times of trouble

A special haven.

Arm

Traditionally an arm is a member of the family.

As a pun it is an indispensible member

of the family or group.

Army
Tremendous opposition.
To be a member of an army indicates lack of individuality and a blind follower of the blind.

Arrow
As a weapon it represents a primitive or basic way of fighting.
As a sign it indicates direction in life where the goal is in sight.
Pointing left or right shows the way, pointing upward towards heaven means aims and ambitions will be achieved, and pointing downward warns of serious consequences should the dreamer continue to follow the present trend or path.
As a symbol it is one of Cupid's arrows, and the male libido.

Artist
The creative aspect within.

Ascend
Progress is being achieved.
Ascending in a lift or walking up steps means obstacles will be overcome.
Hopes are raised.

Ashes
Past memories
Reduction of self-confidence, as in 'sackcloth and ashes'.
Debasement.

Asia
Personal associations apart, this represents the unknown, mysterious and exotic things in life.

Asparagus
There is a forging ahead at the spearhead so keep up with the rest.
A warning concerning laziness.
To eat it means social success.

Ass
Beware of making a fool of yourself.
To see an ass carrying burdens means success but only after considerable hard work.

If an ass pursues you it means you will be the victim of ridicule.

Assassin
To see an assassin in a dream is a serious warning against known and unknown enemies.

Astronaut
An adventurous, youthful and hopeful sign.
Masculine immaturity.

Atoms
The pattern of life and destiny.
Too much attention to detail is unnecessary.

Attack
A warning of bodily harm.
A psychological or emotional attack.

Attic
The top room in the Mansion of the Soul where high ideals are stored.
The spirit, intuition, instincts, intellect, conscience, altruism.

Auction
Beware of swift disposal of assets and friends.
Bartering and competition.

Aunt
A supportive, feminine influence.

Audience
The need for attention.

Australia
Personal associations apart, this continent represents youthfulness, new beginnings and opportunities.

Automobile
The energy and the driving force within.
To be driving an automobile shows life is speeding up.
If one breaks down it warns of health problems through overdoing it.
To be run over by or escape from one warns someone will cross your path.

Autumn
Time is running out so make the most of

life. Be bold, be positive.
Reap what has been sown in life before it is too late.

Avalanche
A strong warning of being a victim of circumstances.
Family and social structures are fragile.

Aviator
In a woman's dream a male aviator is her Animus or dream man.
In a man's dream a male aviator is a hero figure.

Baboon
An image of regressive tendencies.
A particularly childish person who is selfish and materialistic.
To see a baboon face to face may be a reflection of the dreamer, therefore he is trying to tell himself something.

Baby
The birth of a new idea possessing great potential for the future.
The dreamer's brainchild; their own creativeness.
If the baby grows quickly it means a certain venture will expand; if it is sick, problems are to be expected.

Bachelor
For a man to dream of a bachelor is a warning telling him not to become too involved with women.
For a woman to dream of a bachelor means she is searching for her dream man, a male-virgin who fits the description of her animus.

Back
To see only the back of a person warns the dreamer not to jump to conclusions.
A bare back traditionally means loss of power or control over a situation.
For someone to deliberately turn their back on you warns of a rebuff.

Avocado
Better health is to be expected.
An increase of social activities.

Awaken
To awaken in a dream means the dream is trying to impress the dreamer with an important message.
Self-awakening and increased awareness of life are to be anticipated.

Axe
This is a warning of redundancy.

Badger
A nightworker who works hard for little reward.
A fear of going bald.

Bag
A prostitute or an unpleasant woman.
A heavy bag when carried by the dreamer is a sign of continuing heavy commitments.

Bagpipes
Earthy vibes which stimulate physical energies.
Indications of marching, incitement and possibly battle.

Baggage
A difficult wife.
To carry heavy baggage warns the dreamer to begin to shed responsibilities.

Baker
A good omen indicating all will turn out right in the end.

Balcony
To be on a balcony means the dreamer is in an advantageous position to take stock of his or her position in life.
For lovers to dream of a balcony warns of a sad adieu.

Baldness

A bald-headed man warns that the dreamer needs to keep his wits about him.

If a woman dreams of a bald-headed man it warns her of an over-sexed man who will try to force his attention on her.

Ball

The whole world.

A golden ball, as in fairytales, means great understanding and enlightenment.

Ballet

Ballet, dancing and music symbolizes a facet of the dreamer's life which is harmonious.

To see a ballet performance in a dream means the dreamer will have many opportunities to enjoy the finer things in life.

Too artistic an approach to life may not be practical so the dreamer should try to keep his or her feet more firmly on the ground.

Ball Games

The game of life. As serious as life is, it is metaphorically regarded as a game, especially when the dreamer wishes to make light his or her burdens and become philosophical.

Team ball games show lack of self-confidence to 'play' alone.

Competing with oneself, the conscious self v. the unconscious. Such competition sharpens the wits.

Balloon

A festive balloon instructs the dreamer to make light of a problem and if possible rise above it.

To travel in a balloon shows the dreamer can rise above their problems and is often in an excellent position to view their circumstances in relation to others.

Banana

As a fruit 'a fruitful' period of development is indicated.

Symbolically the elongated shape of this fruit represents the phallus.

Bandage

A warning concerning injuries, physical and emotional. Protect and guard against accidents and become 'thick-skinned' when verbally attacked.

Bandit

Beware of those who feel they are above and beyond the law.

Bank

Physical and mental resources from the past, in the form of 'a wealth of experience', deposited in the memory bank.

Emotional security resulting from past experience.

Bank of a River

To be standing on a river bank warns the dreamer that life is passing them by. Get into the swim of things or bridge them.

Bankruptcy

Usually associated with depression, bankruptcy shows that the dreamer's 'store' or 'bank' of personal resources is depleted. Not enough reserves have been built up from past experiences.

Banjo

Association with country and western lifestyle. Beware of recklessness in others as well as in yourself.

Symbolically it represents the head and neck.

Banquet

Momentarily pleasure and self-indulgence will only temporarily satisfy the dreamer's needs.

Bantam

A small but spirited person.

An idea which is not quite ambitious enough. Bantams cannot fly far so they will never really get off the ground. Some replanning or reorganization is necessary.

Baptism

Baptism, a universally ancient ceremony of initiation and acceptance, signifies rebirth; the end of one phase

and the beginning of the next.
Off with the old, on with the new.
An experience which may shock initially but prepares the dreamer for all eventualities in the future.

Baptism of Fire
A warning urging the dreamer to avoid all conflict, physical and emotional.

Barber
If a barber cuts the dreamer's hair, it is a health warning; beware of losing strength, energy and stamina.
Surgery or radical measures may be necessary.

Barefoot
To walk barefoot on soil or rock brings the dreamer into close contact with the truth.
It warns the dreamer to tread extremely cautiously over certain ground.

Barge
Travelling on water in a barge means life will be uneventful and boring.
As a pun it warns the dreamer not to barge into others.

Bark
If the bark on a tree is damaged in any way it warns of vulnerability and lack of protection.
If the bark is healthy and strong it indicates that the dreamer can proceed with every confidence.

Barking
To hear dogs barking warns that trouble is approaching and danger lies ahead.

Barley
This grain represents health and strength.

Barn
A store for memories of the past, to be recalled in times of need.

Barometer
Beware of mood swings and changes within yourself and in others.

Barrier
An obstacle that has to be overcome in one way or another.

Basement
The lowest or deepest level within the Mansion of the Soul. The unconscious.

Basket
A vessel within carrying benevolence and sustenance.

Bat
To see a bat means you should become more aware of your location and the direction you are taking in life. And since bats have a special sense of detection, try to 'see' if you can discover that which has so far been hidden from you.

Bath
To take a bath indicates moral purification and the washing away of past fears and indiscretions.

Battle
Prepare to do battle with an aspect of yourself or be ready for an encounter with someone else.

Bayonet
Beware of a physical or verbal attack which strikes home.

Bazaar
An event is to be expected which brings surprises and good fortune.

Beach
A balance has to be struck between earth and water, head and heart, intellect and intuition.

Beads
A chain of social events will bring personal satisfaction.
A broken chain of beads warns of broken promises.

Bear
An overpowering force often of a dominant feminine nature.
This animal also represents the continent of the USSR.

Beard
The strength of personal conviction is under scrutiny.
Beware of outer appearances disguising inner uncharitable characteristics.

Beasts
So-called bestial instincts may be represented by any beast of burden.
Heraldic or mythological beasts symbolize archetypal forces.

Beaten
To be beaten at a game warns of someone over-taking or getting the better of you.

Beaver
An industrious person who will reap rewards from past efforts.

Bed
A resting place.

Bedroom
As a room in the Mansion of the Soul the bedroom represents personal secrets and memories, usually associated with sexual relationships.

Beef
Seen as flesh, the sensual and sexual side of life is suggested.
A carcase of beef without the living spirit represents death and feelings of hopelessness, sometimes associated with the onset of an illness.
As a play on words, beware of 'beefing' about something.

Beehive
When activity is seen within the hive it is a sign of prosperity and success through communal effort.
If the hive is empty, it warns of financial difficulties.

Bees
A single bee is the ancient symbol of royalty indicating an inheritance.
A swarm of bees is a sign of good fortune.
To be stung by a bee warns of an unwarranted attack.

Beetles
As insects beetles represents small but persistent annoyances.
A scarab-beetle symbolizes the dreamer as an awe-inspiring being.

Beetroot
Guilt and shyness may be indicated, arising from associations with blushing and 'as red as a beetroot'.

Beggar
This figure usually represents the dreamer, pointing out feelings of deprivation. Consider personal needs and try to attain them without enlisting help from anyone else.

Beheaded
Beware of 'losing your head'.
Try to keep a balance between the head and the heart, the intellect and the emotions.

Bells
One ring on the door bell is reminding you about something you have forgotten, maybe alerting your conscience.
A peel of bells means good news is to be expected shortly.

Belt
A dividing line has to be drawn between two factions or two aspects of the same problem.

Bereavement
To feel the loss of someone in a dream means you will have regrets unless you make ammends before it is too late.

Berry
A berry symbolizes the fruit of one's labour.
A berry, as a pun, tells you to 'bury' the past.

Bet
Betting tells you to take a calculated chance, remembering that nothing ventured, nothing gained.

Bewitched
To be bewitched tells you that you are

under the domination of someone. This someone may even be an aspect of yourself.

Do not be taken in by others and their illusory affluence.

Bible
To see a Bible means you are searching for the truth.

Bicycle
To be riding a bicycle shows progress in life is due entirely to your own efforts. You are travelling in the right direction and, although the going is sometimes uphill and difficult, you will succeed in the end.

Binoculars
You are trying to see ahead and discover what lies ahead.

Be careful not to unintentionally spy on others or you may have to defend your position.

Birds
A flight of birds symbolizes a flight of fancy, high-flying ideals and hopes for the future.

A single bird represents an inspiration and an aim, often of an elevated nature.

A flying bird symbolizes freedom of the spirit and individualism.

If the bird is in a cage it means you feel caged-in and cannot express yourself fully.

Broken or clipped wings indicate restraint.

In a man's dream, a bird may represent a woman.

Birth
To dream of being born may be an inherited memory of the event but more likely it is pointing out that escape from present circumstances is possible.

To witness a birth symbolizes a rebirth or second chance in life, with a new, fresh start.

The basic message of a birth in a dream is that there is tremendous hope for the future.

Birthday
To dream of your own or someone else's birthday tells you to count your blessings and celebrate.

Biscuits
Sweet memories of the past.

Bishop
Respect is felt for someone but this is tinged with fear.

Black
Black is often associated with mourning, death and gloom.

Black can be warm and comforting when associated with Mother Earth and passiveness.

To be in the dark means something is hidden from view; a situation is far from clear and light needs to be thrown onto it.

Blackberries
This fruit traditionally symbolizes setbacks. Maybe this is because these berries were once thought to be the food of the Devil.

Blackbird
A warning sign concerning the question of territorial rights.

Beware of over-possessiveness.

Blacksmith
Physical effort is necessary if conditions are to improve.

Blanket
Beware of smothering sentiment and over-protectiveness.

Look for hidden meanings.

Blind
To be blind means you cannot see the truth.

Blood
Blood in a dream is a sign of life and animality. It is associated with anger—hot blooded, lust—young blood and fear—blood curdling.

To lose blood is a warning concerning loss of energy, vitality, strength or virility.

Blossom
You can expect happiness and contentment but this may not be permanent.

Blush
Feelings of guilt are reflected.

Boa Constrictor
This snake probably represents a friend or acquaintance who tries to restrict the dreamer's freewill.

Boar
If you ran from this animal be prepared for a disappointment.
It may represent a pig-headed person or someone whom the dreamer considers to be ignorant, selfish, gluttonous or possessing other unattractive qualities. Metaphorically, 'pearls before swine' may apply.

Boat
To be in a boat shows the dreamer journeying across the sea of life on their destinational course. It may be smooth sailing or the going may be rough, depending on other circumstances in the dream.
To disembark indicates the end of a particular phase in life.
To row a boat shows plenty of physical effort is, or should be, put into life.

Body
A body usually represents the dreamer, as a whole.
If it is a dead body it warns of lifelessness, lack of vitality or deprivation.
A nude body means someone's true nature is going to be revealed.

Bomb
A threat of some description. This may apply to the dreamer's physical safety or to an undermining of their way of life.
If a bomb explodes it warns of a sudden emotional eruption.

Bones
Hard times are signified.
It is necessary to get down to the bare essential.

Book
A closed book invites investigation into past experiences and deeds.
An open book means you can learn from past experiences.

Boomerang
A warning against rebounding events. 'Things come back at you.'

Boots
New boots indicate new avenues lie ahead. Old boots mean that attention should be paid to personal matters.

Bouquet
Past work and effort will be well rewarded.

Borrow
Borrowing warns of a dwindling of personal resources, lack of organization and lack of foresight.
If someone borrows from you it means you are regarded as a source of practical help and emotional support.

Bow
A bow without arrows indicates aims cannot be attained at present.
A bow and arrow tells you that now is time to take aim and go for that target.

Bowels
To see bowels may be horrid but it is urgently telling you to get to the bottom of something.

Box
A box often represents a coffin, therefore the death-wish is in the air.
A box also signifies an inner secret or a fortunate surprise.

Boy
In a man's dream, whether recognized or not, a boy represents the dreamer's youthful, childish self.

Bracelet
Bracelets, like rings, symbolise a union or a reunion.
If a bracelet is received as a gift, romance can be expected.

Brain
To see a brain means intelligent thinking is essential if progress is to be made, or a problem solved satisfactorily.

Brake
Whether a brake is applied or not it warns the dreamer to apply the brakes, metaphorically, in relation to a certain situation.

Brambles
Hindrances and minor difficulties may be encountered which prevent the dreamer from achieving aims and goals.

Branches
Branches of a tree represent branches or members of a family.

Brass
To see brass ornaments warns against false deals. Financial matters are represented by this metal.

Bread
A loaf of bread represents a spiritual gift: it is food for thought.
To share bread means rewards will be reaped in the future.

Break
To break something warns of finality.
To see a broken object means the pieces should be picked up and then start again.

Breath
To be aware of breath or breathing indicates the need for healing, life-giving energy.

Breeze
Refreshing changes are to be expected soon.

Bricks
Bricks represent different aspects of the overall situation.
Laying bricks warns against empire-building or over-emphasis in one respect.

Bride
She may be the image the dreamer has of herself for the future. Marriage, in one respect or another, is certainly under consideration.
A bride symbolizes femininity.

Bridge
A bridge shows there is a link between two problems, two solutions or two aspects of a particular situation.
To be standing on a bridge shows the dreamer is between two possibilities and finds it difficult to know which way to go.

Brook
A brook symbolizes the free and easy flowing of life's twists and turns.

Broom
Seeing a broom in a dream is a good sign indicating a clean sweep should be made. This will bring certain changes, which will ultimately be for the better.

Brother
If the dreamer is a man a brother introduces the question of rivalry or, depending on the scene in which he appears, family support.

Brown
Much depends on the shape or form brown takes, and personal feelings associated with this colour. To some it suggests depression, yet to others it has a deeply religious, monastic significance.
Traditionally, brown has an earthy association which offers stability as well as financial gain.

Buildings
Buildings, unless exemplifying real buildings, symbolize the person as a whole, yet at the same time highlight a particular characteristic. For example, a factory represents the industrious side of the dreamer's nature, while a church reflects their aspirations and beliefs.

Bull
An angry, uncontrolled person who becomes dangerous when teased.

Bulldog
The archetypal English spirit.
Both defence and protection should be considered in relation to personal circumstances.

Burglar
Beware of intruders, literally.
A burglar may also be an intrusive characteristic which the dreamer tries to keep at bay but once recognized as this, new understanding and maturity could develop.

Burn
To smell burning is a distinct warning. Something dangerous could be smouldering behind the scenes.

Bus
Travelling on a bus shows the dreamer's destiny is shared with others. This is telling them that they should be more self-reliant and stand on their own feet more often.
Waiting for a bus means the dreamer must not miss an opportunity when it eventually does come along.

Butcher
Beware of someone who will metaphorically slaughter and sacrifice others for their own ends.

Butter
Better, richer times are assured.

Butterfly
The psyche.
The spirit of a departed relative or friend.

Cab
A cab—a hired vehicle—indicates uncertainty and lack of self-confidence. Reliance on others should be avoided as much as possible for such support is only temporary.

Cabbage
As a vegetable it represents a vegetating, time-wasting existence.
A dull person may be indicated.

Cage
Whatever the context of this, inhibition and restrictions are clearly indicated.

Cake
Sweet but transient things are under consideration.
Beware of over-indulgence.

Calendar
This signifies the passing of time and serves as a reminder of an important date such as an anniversary.

Calf
Young love is represented by a calf but so too is the dreamer's immaturity.

Camel
Since these animals usually have to work hard and are put-upon, beware of over-burdening either at your own behest or through the instigation of others.

Camera
Personal secrets that do not concern others should be well guarded.

Canal
This relates to childbirth and the delivery of a baby.

Canary
If this bird is singing it has romantic associations so future happiness is promised.
A silent canary warns that danger is in the air.

Cancer
A fear of serious illness.
A person born under the zodiacal sign of Cancer the crab.

Candle
A lighted candle indicates strength and life. An unlit candle warns of deprivation and disappointment.

Cannibal
To see cannibals indicates self-destructive motives.
Cannibalism warns of total domination and possession, either of the dreamer, or of someone else by the dreamer.

Canoe
A canoe, like a boat, signifies personal destiny over the waters of life.
To be alone in a canoe shows the dreamer has control over his or her own destiny.

Canyon
Beware of divided opinion which can cause much harm.
A rift generally.

Captain
A rise in status can be expected but with this comes added responsibility.

Car
This represents the driving force in life. Driving a car, depending on the manner and speed, represents progress, dangers and accomplishments.

Cards
Playing cards symbolize the game of life with each suit representing the four different aspects of life. Hearts are for love and friendship, Diamonds are for aims and ambitions, Clubs are for rewards and wealth, and Spades are for the inevitable obstacles which occur.

Carnation
As a flower the blossoming of personality is indicated.
A rebirth, as in reincarnation, offers new hope and a fresh start in life.

Carols
A good year ahead can confidently be expected.

Carpet
An intricate design on a carpet shows the intricacies of life's rich pattern.
A plain carpet warns of 'being on the carpet'.

Carrots
The Freudian significance of a carrot is obvious but it also has to be seen as an inducement, temptation, bribe or bait.

Castle
As a building a castle represents the dreamer as a person with resolute aims.

Castration
This shows a fear of loss of respect, status and manliness.

Cat
This animal is either representing someone of a psychic nature whom the dreamer knows, or is an intuitive, psychic aspect of the actual dreamer.
A black cat is a fortunate sign.

Catastrophe
Whatever the catastrophic event, it warns of an unheaval. This may be of a practical nature or it may be an emotional disruption. Both bring change, to lesser or greater degrees.

Caterpillar
Seeing one of these insects reflects immediate difficulties and feelings of inferiority but also tells you that the future holds tremendous potential.

Cathedral
This building represents the dreamer's loftiest, spiritual ideals.

Cattle
A herd of cattle represents the majority. Beware of loss of identity and being a blind follower.

Cave
A cave symbolizes the inner realm, the unconscious.
Entering a cave shows a return to pre-natal days, and to past memories generally.

A mythological cave, where a dragon guards the entrance, shows an inner seeking for the hidden treasure of the mind.

Cedar Tree
Family matters are under consideration. This tree has associations with Celtic mythology, so consider Celtic roots.

Ceiling
Although aims have not yet been reached and ambitions not fulfilled, a ceiling has been reached at present. Certain changes are necessary if a breakthrough is to be made.

Cell
A single idea or remote hope.
Fear of imprisonment.

Cellar
As the basement of the Mansion of the Soul, dark thoughts and memories are often found here.
Basic instincts, hidden fears or deep feelings which are not often expressed are coming to light.

Cemetery
A graveyard is often associated with thoughts of departed relatives, friends and the past, which is also dead.
Depression; the fear of dying and loss of hope.

Centre
Recentring the self—finding personal aims and targets.
The centre of a town shows you are close to your goal.

Chains
Invisible but nonetheless strong links bind you to someone or something.

Chair
An empty chair signifies a vacancy. This should be seen as a promotional opportunity, or, depending on personal circumstances, a sad loss.

Chalice
This vessel offers the waters of life which bring healing for the body, mind and spirit.

Chameleon
Beware of someone who disguises their true nature. Alternatively, a particular situation may not be what it seems.

Champion
A champion sportsman or woman is a projected self-image.
Aims, however ambitious, can be achieved.

Chapel
A holy part of the Mansion of the Soul, therefore an aspect of the dreamer which houses special beliefs.

Chase
To be chased by someone unknown shows there is conflict within the dreamer, with one aspect pursuing another.
When a fierce animal chases you, you could be trying to escape from your own angry, basic self whom you have not yet recognized.
Running away from a difficult or frightening situation which cannot be faced.

Cherries
Beware of romantic temptation.

Chess
The game of life where fate, destiny and the will of the gods intervene when least expected.

Chest
A chest, open or closed, symbolizes the mind containing individual treasures in the form of personal potential.

Chicken
A chicken shows aims and ambitions exist but since this bird cannot fly these will be very difficult to get off the ground.
To eat chicken in a dream warns of cowardliness.

Child
The child within the adult, so beware of

adopting a childish attitude.

Progress has already been made towards attaining a certain standard in life.

Several children mean lively and exciting times can be expected.

Chimney

The centre of the family; the person upon whom they all rely.

Chimney-Sweep

Traditionally, this figure is a sign of good fortune and a wedding.

China

Crockery denotes domestic arrangements which need careful handling.

To break china warns of shattered ideals and broken promises.

China

The nation of China suggests an oriental outlook or atmosphere.

Choke

To experience choking in dreams is fairly common and is often due to physiological symptoms, not psychological ones. If persistent seek advice.

Choking can symbolize a situation that is causing considerable worry or sadness. 'Choking back tears' becomes a dream-reality.

Christ

To dream of Jesus means protection and help are at hand, thus faith should be totally restored.

As the archetype of perfection, immortality of the spirit and healing of the body is promised.

Christmas

This is a symbol of reunion, forgiveness and happiness, as well as good news from near and far.

Church

The religious aspect of the dreamer; beliefs and moralistic ideals.

A place of safety and a sign of peace within.

Cigarettes

To see cigarettes, or to be smoking one, means you need a diversion in life and need to relax more.

Cinders

Past memories which can be recalled but not relived

Circle

The innermost self surrounded by the cycle of life.

The world, the universe and time.

Circus

Life itself, especially in relation to strange encounters.

Beware of going in circles.

City

The outside world and the dreamer's relationship to it.

Clean

Clean, as opposed to dirty, offers comparisons between two situations.

To see clean clothes reflects moral standards.

Climb

To climb stairs, a hill or a mountain shows life is an uphill struggle but progress is definitely being made.

Striving to rise above a problem or climbing the social ladder.

Cliff

To be looking into the distance from the top of a cliff shows the dreamer is comparatively safe at present but if care is not taken danger could lie ahead.

To be at the bottom of a cliff means you are facing an obstacle of considerable proportions.

Cloak

To be wearing a cloak means you are protected from harm and verbal attack.

To see someone else wearing a cloak tells you they are covering up something they wish to hide.

Clock

Time assumes importance in your life.

Maybe it is later than you think.

Cloth
Cloth symbolizes the fabric of life. Patterns reflect the intricate experiences woven into it and the quality of the cloth relates to the 'roughness' or 'smoothness' of such experiences.

Clothes
The personality and façade of the dreamer as seen by others.
To be putting on clothes shows a change of image, especially in the eyes of others.
To have no clothes on at all means the dreamer keeps himself to himself (or herself to herself) and does not want others to pry into his personal affairs.
Old, tatty clothes means you need to improve your image.

Clouds
The present could be clouded with negativity in some shape or form.

Clover
To see clover growing or being picked is an encouraging sign.

Clown
Beware of making a fool of yourself.

Coal
To see a coal mine or lumps of coal indicates great potential energy and inner strength.

Coat
The personality put on for certain occasions, perhaps to impress others or to protect against their cold attitude.

Cobweb
Any restrictions around you are minor ones so should be brushed aside.
Beware of entangling circumstances which may be difficult to escape from later.

Cock
As with chicken, limitations are indicated.

In the Freudian sense lust is definitely indicated.

Coffin
There is no escape from a certain situation.
To see yourself lying in a coffin means you have reached the final stages of a particular phase in life and should begin at once on the next round.
Metaphorically, a coffin means 'I wish I were dead' a statement not to be confused with a true death wish.

Coins
Financial improvement can generally be expected but coins also signify wealth of opportunity, wealth of understanding and wealth of happiness, all assets in the bank of human experience.

Cold
To feel cold points out feelings of neglect, emotional hard-heartedness or sexual frigidity.
An unrecognized, freezing fear.
A cold landscape indicates a bleak environment where the dreamer's surroundings lack warmth and love.

Collision
Arguments and head-on encounters are warned against.

Colours
The intensity of colour sets the backcloth of a dream. Dullness indicates depression and a negative setting, whereas brightness shows improvement of a situation can be expected. This also reflects the dreamer's mood or state of mind.
Black and white dreams are thought to have been 'in colour' originally but as with dreams generally, this fades from memory.
Each colour symbolizes an energy or principle in life, with its good and bad aspects:

Black
Shades of mourning and death, gloom and depression.

The dark earth, passive, receptive and motherly.

Blue
Great hope and inspiration through spiritual energy.
Cold and calculating.

Brown
Devotion to duty
To some it indicates a depressing mood.

Gold
Sunshine and happiness.
Over-dominant masculinity.

Green
Relaxation through natural, vital things.
Jealousy.

Orange
Intuitive reasoning as well as cheerfulness.
Triviality.

Pink
Warm, pleasant things.
Transient happiness and superficial feelings.

Purple
Vitality.
Rage.

Red
Physical energy and strength.
Anger.

Silver
Moonshine and romantic emotions.
Over-dominant femininity.

White
Illumination, innocence and purity.
A colourless life.

Yellow
Inspiration.
Cowardice.

Comet
A warning of future problems.

Computer
The brain and intellectual, logical thinking.

Confetti
Apart from its association with weddings, confetti means social success.

Cooking
Plans are being made, cooked-up, which will transform a situation.

Corn
Prosperous times ahead.

Corpse
Metaphorically, a lifeless sort of person. To see oneself as a corpse means a new phase in life should be started immediately. The old you is dead.

Corridor
There is a connection between two situations or circumstances but certain limitations are imposed along the way.

Cot
An empty cot represents unfulfilled hopes.

Cottage
A mature personality surrounded by a peaceful existence.
A dream of the future.

Countries
Foreign experiences are likely. The nature of these is symbolized by the national characteristic of the country seen in the dream.

Cousin
Help can be expected from a member of the family or from a close friend.

Cow
A female whom the dreamer dislikes.
A woman with bovine characteristics.

Crab
Devious manoeuvring.
Renewal of hope.
Someone born under the sign of Cancer.

Cripple
Someone who needs practical help or emotional support.
A fear of being incapacitated.

Crocodile
Beware of underhand dealings and dangerous situations.

Cross
The archetypal sign of Christianity as well as the four elements of creation and the balance of nature.
A sign of protection.

Crossroad
A point in life has been reached where an important decision has to be made, concerning which way to go.

Crow
Messenger of the dead.
Bran, the spirit of Britain.

Crowd
Other people generally who do not think or see life as you do.

Crown
To see a crown is a symbol of glory, recognition and crowning success.

Crystal
Spiritual illumination and healing potential.

Cup
A source of life-supporting energy which will sustain in time of need.

Cupboard
If closed, a cupboard represents a closed attitude of mind, or it could contain the proverbial skeleton.

Curtain
An obstacle which prevents progress and obscures the view, but can easily be brushed aside.

Daffodils
Welsh associations.
Spring and fresh hopes for the future.

Dagger
Beware of treachery and a verbal stab in the back.

Daisy
A symbol of love, affection and kindness.

Dam
An emotional outlet is needed to allow blocked-up feelings to flow freely.

Dance
A prelude to love-making.
Relaxation and social activities are on the increase.

Darkness
Depression concerning unknown factors. Feelings of being kept in the proverbial dark.

Daytime
The present time is indicated.
A specific time of day relates to the dreamer's age. Morning: youth; afternoon: maturity; evening: old age.

Date
To see a specific date means that by that time you should have accomplished or completed something.
To see the date of your own death is not prophetic. It urges you to make the most of every available moment so that by that date you will have something to show for all the effort you have put into life.

Daughter
In a woman's dream her daughter is an image of her former self, suggesting a more youthful approach to life is adopted.
In a man's dream she is an image of his anima.

Dawn
With the new day comes new hope,

even when the dawn looks grey.

Death
Death in dreams is usually metaphorical and not a death wish or a premonition. It signifies the end of a phase. 'Off with the old and on with the new' is the message.

To see your own death tells you that you should put an end to a particular way of life and take on a new image or role. A definite change is necessary to do this and bring about a rebirth.

Seeing someone dead, a parent, relative, friend or acquaintance, may indicate hostility towards them.

To see a spouse or partner dead warns that love or liking for that person is dead.

Debt
Someone owes someone something, but it is not money. A karmic debt has to be paid.

Deep
Deep water, deep caves or a deep shaft represent unplumbed depths of the unconscious mind.

Deluge
A downpour or flood warns of being swamped by emotions.

Descending
Whether walking down a hill, walking downstairs, going down in an elevator or lift, going down a mine or pothole, the meaning is the same. A descent is necessary in order to establish a firm footing. This may bring a lowering of standards, temporarily.

Delving into the unconscious where past memories are buried.

Desert
This arid place warns of desolation and loneliness but time here should be turned to advantage: find the real you.

Devil
To see the Devil is a distinct warning concerning evil influences. These may be from without or they may originate from within.

Diamond
The inner, many faceted personality. The self.

Dice
Do not take chances.

Digging
A search for an answer is revealed by this action but the chance of discovering what you are looking for is unlikely.

Disaster
Whatever the nature of the disaster it warns of trouble in some shape or form. Evasive action is necessary.

Disguise
Try to see through someone (or something), because they are not what they seem.

Distance
Seeing into the distance tells you to look ahead positively and with confidence.

Ditch
Something has to be overcome before an aim, ambition or goal can be achieved.

Diving
Diving into the unconscious mind for answers, help or information.

Divorce
To dream of your own divorce is probably a fear but symbolically it warns of split ideals or principles. This separation may be between the dreamer's own ideals and principles, or between his or her ideals and those of someone else.

A bid for independence and self-reliance.

Doctor
An authoritive father figure to turn to in time of need.

The self-healer within.

Dog
If the dog is friendly it symbolizes a friend but if it is not it may represent a dog-in-the-manger type of person or someone with a dogged nature.

Doll
An object of affection, albeit a one-way affection.

Door
Above all else a door symbolizes an opportunity. If the door is locked it means you should find the key. If it is open, make sure you do not miss an excellent opportunity.

Dough
Money.

Dove
The spirit within.
The Holy Spirit.
Hope and help are near but a personal sacrifice may be necessary before complete peace of mind is found.

Dragon
This mythological creature symbolizes an inner fear beyond human comprehension.
An archetypal force to be reckoned with.

Drama
A play, film or television programme representing an episode from the dreamer's own life.
The theatre of the mind where, in the imagination, future plans or fears, as well as past dramas, are enacted and re-enacted.

Dream Within a Dream
To dream you are dreaming doubly reinforces the meaning and message of the dream.

Drinking
Sustenance, in one form or another, is needed. Drink in the atmosphere or drink from the fount of wisdom and knowledge.

Driving
To be driving a car or other vehicle shows you are making your own way along life's destinational highway.
To be driven by someone else means someone is steering the same course as you but beware of them mapping out your destiny completely.

Drowning
To feel you are drowning warns that you are in danger of being overpowered by emotions and the over-all pressures of life. This tells you that you must rise above all this to survive.

Drugs
These warn of misleading influences.

Drum
Someone is trying to tell you something but you have not yet understood what it is they are beating out.

Drunk
To see yourself drunk warns that you are intoxicated with your own exuberance.

Dying
To see someone, something or yourself dying warns that life and effort has to be put into a relationship or venture if it is to survive.

Dusk
This time of day indicates that it is later than you think.

Eagle
Extremely high-flying aims with dominating characteristics.

Ear
Listen for good news, avoid gossip and do not pass on that which could cause trouble.

Earring
An unusual distinction will be bestowed

upon the person who is seen to be wearing an earring in the dream.

Earth
A basic, elemental principle associated with Mother Earth, therefore the feminine principle is significant. Fundamental principles of life.

Earthquake
A disruption bringing change. Old attitudes and beliefs are overturned as the mind is prepared for a new way of life.

East
The sun rises in the east so new hope is dawning.

Eating
There is a basic need for fulfilment and satisfaction in life generally.
Eating with others shows there is a sharing and an assimilation of ideas, with information and knowledge being inwardly digested.

Echo
To hear an echo warns against repetition or repeating something that should not be perpetuated.

Eclipse
Beware of standing in someone's way. Conversely, be careful not to stand in the shadow of someone else.

Eggs
The embryo of an idea which has a great potential for the future.
Easter, therefore a time for the renewal of hope.

Electricity
Energy, in various forms, surrounds you but be careful when trying to tap this. Beware, too, of forceful people who could make the sparks fly.

Elephant
Someone who is large but gentle.
A motherly, dependable characteristic.

Elevator
To ascend in an elevator or lift means you will rise above problems and experience a sense of achievement.
To descend in an elevator or lift warns of loss of status, and depression.

Elf
A spirit of the elements acting as a dream messenger.

Embroidery
To see embroidery warns against exaggeration.

Emerald
This stone can have a psychological healing effect.

End of the World
To dream of this event shows the dreamer's fear of failure and the end of a particular phase in their life.

Engine
To see an engine in action represents the pumping or beating of the heart. Depending on other circumstances in the dream, the physical or emotional state of the heart and mind can be discovered.

Envelope
If the envelope is sealed it means unseen dangers or problems exist but if the envelope is open, all will be revealed shortly.

Eruption
To see a volcano erupt warns that a quarrel may develop soon.

Evil
A warning against someone or something that is distinctly bad.

Evening
The latter part of life, meaning that there is not much time left to do all the things planned.

Excrement
This is a fortunate sign even though it is considered to be dirty; 'filthy lucre' is an example of this.

Expedition

To see a party of explorers is a reminder urging that 'every avenue should be explored' if an underlying cause is to be discovered.

Faces

Faces, familiar and unrecognized, often appear in early sleep. These are known as hypnogogic images and are thought to be identikit faces representing types of people rather than individuals. Many are nasty.

A particular face reflects the dreamer's mood.

Factory

As a version of the Mansion of the Soul a factory reflects the mundane, repetitive aspect of the dreamer's lifestyle. To be working in a factory shows life to be routine and boring.

Fairy

Nature's dream messenger.

Falling

The feeling of falling occurs in early sleep and is not a dream; it is the sensation of 'falling asleep'.

To dream of falling off a cliff or from a high building indicates insecurity and a fall from power or grace.

Family

Relationship with the rest of the family is under scrutiny.

Loves and rivalries, within the family, are symbolized.

Farm

The domestic scene generally.

Father

The male archetype in the eyes of the dreamer, therefore a reflection of himself.

A symbol of authority and dominance. In a woman's dream he is a reflection of her animus.

Explosion

Be prepared for explosive situations and surprises.

Eye

Inner sight and wisdom. The all-seeing eye of the soul.

Feast

Now is the time to count blessings and make amends.

Feathers

These represent protection and the good things in life.

Feet

Be careful where certain paths in life lead. Always try to keep both feet firmly on the ground.

To walk in bare feet means a good balance has been found in life.

Fence

An inhibiting factor. Self-made limitations have been imposed which cause frustration.

Ferns

Natural remedies and cures.

Ferret

Protection is needed against prying eyes and viciousness.

Ferry

For someone else to ferry you over the water warns against allowing others to do too much for you.

The link between life and death.

Field

The 'field' of interest such as art, science, etc.

Green fields foretell better times ahead.

Figs

Enlightenment—Buddha sat under a fig tree and there was one in the Garden of Eden.

Fighting
A physical struggle can mean mental conflict.

Figures
Often the neglected aspects of the dreamer's nature.
Shadowy figures are various characters whom the dreamer does not know very well or understand, even though he or she thinks they do.

Film
Whether the dreamer is watching a film or acting in one, it is usually an action replay of an earlier event in their life, albeit dramatically and symbolically represented.

Film Star
When the film star or pop star or actress is the same sex as the dreamer, it is someone they greatly admire and unconsciously mimic.

Fingers
Dextrousness, thus pointing a way towards a practical career or rewarding hobby.
Beware of getting your fingers burnt so do not meddle in the affairs of others.

Fire
Usually powerful emotions and passions are roused; fire is the natural expression of burning love, hate and desire.

Fireplace
The home. A place of emotional warmth.

Fish
The spirit of the dreamer, sustenance and the power of renewal.

Flames
Beware of uncontrolled passions.

Flag
Nationalism and patriotism.

Flood
The destructive side of the emotions which inundate. To be overwhelmed by this shows that certain beliefs long held dear have been swept away.

Flowers
The beautiful things in life, along with the blossoming of friendship and love. Crushed flowers warn of sorrow.

Fog
To be in a fog is self-explicit. The truth or whatever it is you seek is at present hidden from view.

Flying
To experience weightlessness and rise above the ground is known as astral projection. In this state the spirit is thought to temporarily leave the body. Those who experience this can also rise above their problems in life so rarely become depressed.

Font
A source of spiritual sustenance from whence springs energy for self-healing.

Food
Food for thought, not for the body.
Satisfaction with oneself, sexually.

Footsteps
Following in others footsteps means lack of originality.
To see footsteps invites you to follow a particular path in life.

Foreign Land
Foreign, unfamiliar events and experiences are to be expected.

Forest
Metaphorically, make sure you can distinguish the wood from the trees.

Forge
Reliable people will restore confidence.

Fountain
To see, and especially to drink from a fountain, is to drink the healing waters of life itself.

Fright
To experience a fright in a dream is self-

explanatory but as a warning it has to be related to something specific, so that evasive or protective steps can be taken.

Frog
Complete transformation of character, as in 'frogs to princes'.

G

Gale
Better times ahead. Any trouble at present will soon blow over.

Galloping
An increase in the pace of life is to be expected.

Gambling
Now is the time to take a chance.

Games
Life is a game full of winning, losing, and competing against yourself and others.
Each experience is a separate game related to different aspects of life and each of these is an exercise in sportsmanship.

Garden
Personal Garden of Eden.
The surroundings of the Mansion of the Soul, therefore it is the dreamer's environment. The state of the garden is important for it reflects this.
Trespassers in the garden are intruders in the dreamer's private life.

Gargoyles
Psychic guardians.

Garlic
Protection against illness is needed; consider immunisation and taking medical advice.

Gas
To smell gas warns of an invisible danger.

Funeral
The end of a phase in life, or of a friendship.
Metaphorically, 'it is their funeral'.

Furniture
As well as reflecting the personality, furniture represents personal possessions and home comfort.

Gate
A gate, like a door, is an opportunity.
An entrance to the other world and a connecting link between the conscious and the unconscious.

Germs
Health problems may be signified if germs are seen in a dream.
Germs warn of the invasion of personal rights.

Ghost
To see a ghost standing by the bedside is a visitation from the dead.
The spiritual nature of the dreamer.

Giant
A memory from childhood when, by comparison, adults seemed gigantic.
An archetypal, forceful principle.

Girl
In a woman's dream a girl is her former self, also an image which is forever youthful.
In a man's dream, a girl he does not recognize symbolizes his dream woman.

Glass
A clear yet fragile situation.
To break glass warns that ideals and hopes are in danger of being shattered.

Gloves
A certain situation needs careful handling.
To be wearing gloves shows the dreamer is averse to something and does not, metaphorically, want to dirty their hands.

Gnome
A spirit of nature who is a guardian of the home and personal property.

God
To see God reflects the dreamer's concept and image of the Creator.
A need for divine help and protection.

Gods and Goddesses
Gods and goddesses personify archetypal forces and principles encountered in life.

Gold
A precious memory of great value to the dreamer.

Golf
To be playing golf is a reflection of life, showing it to be a solo effort with handicaps and a few prizes.

Gorilla
Maybe a gross image of someone whom the dreamer dislikes or sees as uncivilized.

Haemorrhage
To lose blood is a warning concerning loss or the draining away of energy, strength and vitality.

Hair
Depending on the state and type of hair, degree of virility and attractiveness to the opposite sex can be assessed.

Half
Halfway towards something.

Half Animal, Half Man
A mythological creature symbolizing two human potentials in one figure: the instinctive and the intellectual.

Hand
If a hand appears from the clouds it is said to be the hand of God, assuring you that help is at hand.

Grain
Grain symbolizes rewards which will be reaped from life's rich harvest.

Grass
Green grass is an excellent sign of fresh pastures but parched, brown grass shows you will have to work very hard to make ends meet.

Grave
The past, which should remain buried.

Gravestone
Self-appraisal or self-analysis.

Great Mother
The archetype of the earth. The feminine principle within individuals and found throughout nature.

Guest
An unknown guest is unrecognized potential.

Gypsy
To see a gypsy, and a gypsy camp, is a warning sign.
Show respect for hidden talent.

To see hands means industriousness, and a labour of love.

Handbag
Thoughts and private opinions which are extremely personal.

Hanging
To see a person hanging indicates, or warns against, loneliness.

Harbour
Look for a safe, sheltered place in order to reorganize yourself and so regain confidence.

Hare
To see a hare on the move means you are following a mystical path where intuition and spiritual insight take great leaps forward.

Harness
To see a horse in a harness shows you are a workaholic.

Harp
A Welsh, as well as a heavenly influence.

Hat
A sign showing the dreamer wants respect and recognition.

Head
Intellect and conscious intentions.

Heart
Intuition and unconscious awareness.

Hearth
The centre of the family where warmth and affection will be found.

Heaven
The dreamer's own version of paradise.

Hedge
A restriction, but not of the dreamer's making, so it can be fairly easily overcome.

Hell
To glimpse this in a dream warns of a terrible time ahead.

Hen
A black hen means personal sacrifices will have to be made if you are to attain an aim, ambition or goal.
A white hen means success will be yours soon.

Herbs
Herbs are an urgent reminder telling you to take extra care of your health.

Herd
To see a herd of cattle warns you not be one of them.

Hero/Heroine
The self.
Someone the dreamer admires and unconsciously mimics. Sometimes a celebrity or famous person is used as a model to symbolize this ideal.

Highway
Destiny, the road through life.

Hill
To be climbing a hill shows progress is being made towards attaining an aim or goal.
To be going down a hill warns against losing ground in relation to something.
To be on top of a hill shows you have reached a pinnacle in life and can now see things much more clearly.

Hive
A hive symbolizes many people working together for a common cause.

Hole
A distinct warning either not to put your foot in it, or not to fall into the depths of depression.

Holiday
A break from the routine way of life is indicated.

Home
Feminine, motherly comforts should be appreciated and if necessary enhanced in some way.

Honey
A symbol of plenty.

Hood
A hooded figure is traditionally known as the figure of death.

Horse
Whatever the action, a horse symbolizes horsepower—personal energy. If you are riding a horse it shows you have control over driving forces within.

Horseshoe
This is the symbol of the moon goddess who traditionally rules romance.
It is a sign of good fortune.

Hospital
Hospice and hospitality. Take this as a warning sign indicating you need someone to help, entertain or look after you for a while.

Hot
To feel hot in a dream warns of becoming too closely involved with a certain person.

Hotel
To be in a hotel shows the desire to lose personal identity and become one of a crowd.

House
Usually a dream house is a composite house made up of your childhood home and present abode. Symbolizing the dreamer as a whole, body and soul, it is the Mansion of the Soul with each room, corridor, staircase, cellar and attic representing different aspects and approaches to life.

Hunger
To experience this feeling means you hunger, and probably thirst, after knowledge, understanding or an explanation.

Hurricane
Destructive forces are in the air.

Hurt
To feel the pain from an injury symbolizes an emotional hurt.

Hymns
To hear hymn-singing shows you have divine protection.

Ice
Total lack of feeling, emotion and sensitivity.

Iceberg
Beware of what lies beneath the surface.

Icicles
Apparent danger will soon melt away.

Icon
This sacred image may symbolise the dreamer's worship of someone they love.

Idol
Do not place anyone, or someone in particular, on a pedestal.

Illness
To feel or be ill in a dream should be taken as a literal health warning.

Impostor
The impostor is probably yourself, so above all be true to yourself.

Impotence
Probably a fear of such a thing but symbolically it warns of powerlessness and helplessness.

Incense
Healing and help are represented by the smell of incense.

Injury
To experience a physical injury in a dream warns against emotional injury.

Ink
Writing in ink tells you to state your case or voice your opinion clearly.
An ink blot means any trouble at present was caused by your own hand.

Inoculation
To receive an inoculation protects against future trouble and unhappiness.

Insects
These represent small but none the less extremely annoying incidents. Brush them aside.

Intestines
To see these could indicate digestive problems, as well as worry.

Inventor
The dreamer. This person shows that you have latent talent and originality.

Invisibility
Unseen possibilities, as well as unseen problems, should be sought.

Iris
This flower represents the goddess Iris who is one of the messengers of the gods.

Iron
Will power, endurance and strength of purpose will be tested.

Island
Isolation and the feeling of being alone. An ideal state of complete self-sufficiency.

Ivy
Beware of an emotional hanger-on.

Jade
Do not rely on the opinions of others.

Jasmine
Feminine qualities, especially in a healing capacity.

Jay
This bird is said to be a messenger from the dead.

Jerusalem
A symbol of eternal hope.

Jellyfish
A mysterious concept or situation that defies logic.

Jesus
God within the dreamer and God without.
To receive a visitation from Jesus in a dream gives hope, healing and confidence.

Jewellery
Self-adornment for the express purpose of attracting attention.

Jewels
Usually treasures of the mind; a crystallized plan or a brilliant idea.

Jockey
An individual who is well in control of their own drive and destiny.

Joker
This card should not be taken at face value. Do not be deceived by jocular behaviour; the person this card represents has a very serious side to their nature.

Journey
Whatever the mode of transport, destiny—the way through life—is symbolized.

Judge
This is a 'judge-not lest you are yourself judged' symbol.

Jug
Life holds more than you realize so look forward to much happier times.

Juggler
Plans for the future should be rearranged, not abandoned.

Jump
To jump from the top of a building or cliff tells you there are other, safer ways of climbing down, other than those you have in mind.

Kangaroo
An elusive, restless person who hops around.

Kennel
Unless the dreamer is involved with dogs, a kennel signifies the proverbial dog-house.

Kerb
To step off a kerb and suddenly wake up is known as a myoclonic jerk, a muscular contraction.
Muscular contraction occurs in early sleep and is often incorporated into a 'stepping off the kerb' dream.

Kettle
Beware of trouble brewing, or the boiling-over of particular circumstances.

Key
The 'key' to a problem, or the 'key' to happiness, depending on the circumstances in which the key appears.

Killing
To witness the killing of a person means extreme hate is felt for someone.
The figure whom the dreamer kills is a personification of one of his or her unpleasant traits. This is an attempt to get rid of it.

King
The archetypal father figure as well as a dominant, ruling principle.

Kiss
A sign of recognition through the bestowing of a kiss.
Affection, love and genuine friendship.

Kitchen
When a dream is set in a kitchen it means the theme is concerned with the home and domestic matters.

Kite
To see a kite in the sky has the same metaphorical message as not to hide one's light under a bushel.

Kitten
To see a kitten playing may be an inducement to have a cat. On the other hand, it may symbolize a kittenish, skittish person.

Knee
Attention being drawn to a knee or knees in a dream is traditionally taken to mean that the dreamer will meet an important person.

Kneel
A humbling symbol, suggesting more respect is needed for others.

Knife
Quarrels and rows are possible as well as verbal stabs in the back.

Knight
The chivalrous, gallant image of the self.

Knitting
Depending on other signs in the dream, knitting shows the pattern of your life is emerging, or conversely, things are getting rather in a tangle.

Knocking
To hear a knock is a warning sign, alerting you in readiness for a surprise, or a shock.

Knot
Traditionally, a knot symbolizes a union or marriage.

Labyrinth
A mystery or puzzle in life needs to be solved. This can be done only by following the thread, the causal chain, back to its origin.

Lace
A closely guarded, or veiled, secret.

Ladder
The connection between the conscious and unconscious minds.

Ladybird
Although an insect, a ladybird does not signify an annoyance. It means success, albeit in a small way, is possible.

Lake
Smooth sailing and easier times ahead, but remember, still waters can run deep.

Lamb
Self-sacrifice.

Lame
To see a lame person warns that progress will be slow and painful.

Land
The environment and surroundings relating to a particular situation or circumstance.

Lantern.
If the lantern is hanging, it is to be seen as a warning sign. If it is resting on a shelf or table, it is a welcoming sign.

Larder
This symbolizes emotional reserves which fortify you with food for thought.

Laughter
A happy sign, but it also means you should laugh only at yourself and not at others.

Laundry
Whether a laundry, or clean laundered clothes, the meaning is that a fresh, new start in life can now be made.

Lawn
Try to cultivate a calm and serene outlook.

Leaf
If the leaf is on a tree life will prosper, but if it is on the ground hardship will follow.

Leather
An unfortunate, materialistic sign.

Lecture
Be ready for the person who will speak down to you.

Leek
Like onions, a leek is an excellent sign of good health.
A symbol of Wales and the Welsh.

Left/Right
A comparison between two concepts or choices.
Dream scenes are mirror images of reality. The left is, therefore, the right and vice versa. This is seen clearly when driving a car. The steering wheel and driving seat are on the opposite side of the car, unless you are driving in a foreign country.

Letter
News from afar. Expect to receive a letter or communication from someone you have not seen for some time.

Lettuce
Problems will be short-lived.

Lift
Ascending in a lift or elevator means inspired thoughts will help you to overcome difficulties.
Descending in a lift or elevator means you will be brought down to earth and may feel somewhat depressed.

Light
The light within, the spirit.
To see the light, metaphorically, means you will come to a realization or understanding.

Lighthouse.
A version of the Mansion of the Soul, where towering ambitions are housed. These will be able to withstand the roughest of life's storms.

Lily
The symbol of the Great Mother and the Holy Family.

Limbs
To feel paralysis of the arms and legs is a

physical state experienced in early, light sleep. When this is incorporated into a dream it is one in which you are rooted to the spot and cannot run.
You feel isolated, out on a limb.

Lion
A couragous person, but none the less one that should not be tested too far.

Lizard
Someone is not as formidable as they appear.

Lobster
Shyness—a trait that should be overcome.

Lock
Unless a key is in the lock, this is a warning sign denoting an obstacle.

Maggot
Considerable changes are to be expected.

Magnet
Sex appeal and personal attractiveness are symbolized by this.

Magpie
Traditionally, one magpie is said to be unlucky, but seeing two of these birds signifies good fortune.
Black and white plumage introduces a 'yes or no' situation.

Man
In a woman's dream he represents her ideal man, her animus.
An unpleasant man symbolizes a masculine trait she fears.
In a man's dream he represents a particular aspect or characteristic of himself.

Looking Glass
Reflections of the past as well as the present.

Lose
To lose an object means you are mentally distracted and should take more care with personal matters.

Lost
To be lost in a town, or elsewhere, shows you feel insecure. This is because your plans for the future are uncertain, or even non-existent.

Luggage.
Luggage, like baggage, is traditionally linked with marriage.
It also signifies that superficial, personal qualities hamper your progress.

Lynx
A quick-witted person.

Mansion
The whole person, body, mind and spirit.

Manure
The cycle of life where nothing is ever lost.
Wealth and plenty.

Map
Destiny and the future are mapped out for you.

Marble
To see marble in any shape or form is a monument to the past.

Marigold
A symbol of the Mother Goddess.

Market
Choose carefully from a selection of options.

Marriage
A union of two compatible opposites;

the mystical marriage of the soul.

Marsh
Beware of unseen difficulties and dangers.

Martyr
Distinguish between willing self-sacrifice and grudgingly martyring yourself.

Mask
This is the face of the dreamer as seen by others.
Beware of deception and deceit.

Mass
When this ceremony is seen in a dream it is a healing experience for both body and mind.

Mast
A signpost to direct you on your way through life.

Mat
When walked upon a mat shows you are down-trodden, but when it is seen alone it means discussion with others will be very beneficial to you.

Maze
This represents the path you are taking through life, your destiny.

Meal
Sharing a meal with others shows a need to communicate and share knowledge and ideas with others.

Meat
To eat meat, flesh, shows you are assimilating the ideas originated by others.

Medicine
To take medicine shows retribution at work, metaphorically showing you taking your own medicine.

Medium
A spirit medium is a dream messenger.

Melon
Events will take a turn for the better.

Mermaid
A water spirit symbolizing a lost love.

Metal
Beware of rigid thoughts which eventually have limiting effects.

Meteor
A warning sign concerning unrest in the future.

Microscope
Try not to see too much in a situation or it will appear out of all proportion and therefore greater than it really is.

Milk
Human kindness and support can be depended upon.

Mill
Water and windmills indicate a peaceful, prosperous future.

Mirror
The truth is reflected in this so you will probably come face-to-face with yourself.

Miser
A mean, miserly streak in yourself or seen in someone else.

Mistletoe
Apart from indicating Christmas as a time of personal significance, this plant represents a poisonous thought.

Mole
A spy, so beware of someone whom you cannot trust.

Money
Things of value, but not money in the bank or financial assets.
To discover or receive a sum of money tells you that you will receive a reward for the deeds you have done in the past.

Monk
A dream messenger and the wise man within.

Monster
A monster symbolizes a monstrous fear.

Monsters appear frequently in children's dreams. To be chased by one means you are running away from facing the frightening truth.

Moon
Femininity and the maternal realm, closely associated with the unconscious. Emotions need to be carefully controlled.

Morning
This time of day relates to youthfulness and the early stages of life; it also relates to the beginnings of a new project or career.

Moth
Fleeting happiness can be expected, especially after dark.

Mother
The Mother Goddess, feminine principles and maternal instincts.

Motor Cycle
Destiny and life are speeding up considerably.

Mountain
An obstacle which seems immovable. It also represents a pinnacle in life, a position which is not easily attained.

Mouse
Try to be insignificant, keep quiet and lie low until a danger has passed.

Moving
Take steps to alter your image by moving away from the one you have of yourself at present.

Mud
Mixed blessings will result from a situation that is causing worry and trouble at present.

Museum
Old, antiquated ideas should be dropped or at least kept more in the background.

Mushrooms
Mystical connections will explain certain things to you.

Music
To hear music symbolizes life with its harmonies and discords, and its high and low notes. Metaphorically, maybe you have to face the music, or on the other hand perhaps someone is playing on your emotions.

Nail
To see nails warns of dangers from external sources which slow progress along life's destinational path.

Naked
To appear to be nude shows the dreamer's real self, personality, characteristics, habits and secrets are all bared for others to see.
All pretence is dropped and the truth is revealed.

Names
Friends and acquaintances may play a role in a dream, solely because of their names. This, in turn, reminds the dreamer of someone else.

Narrow
A narrow path or corridor indicates certain limitations at present. There is no choice but to go on.

Neck
Do not take any chances with anything.

Needle
Continue to make amends.

Negro
Richness and colour will enter your life.

Neighbour
The self.

Nest
The home.

Net
An obvious trap, so beware of walking into this.

New Year
This time of year in a dream tells you to start again with renewed hope for the future.

Niece
Youthful femininity and loyal family support.

Night
For the dreamer to be aware of the dark shows he or she 'is in the dark' so should try to throw some light on whatever it is that is troubling them.

Nightmare
This is a bad dream based on fear arising from many different sources, from an illness which is symbolised as a devouring creature, to a real, frightening situation, represented by a terrifying marauder.

North
Darkness, winter and the colder things in life are symbolized, including death.

Numbers
The dreaming mind is an unconscious calendar so dates, anniversaries and future appointments are indicated by numbers.
A specific number will relate to a number of years, days or months, as in the Pharaoh's dream of the seven kine and seven ears of corn. Usually this can only be verified and proved after the event.

Nun
A very special person loved and respected by all.

Nymph
A nature spirit and a dream messenger.

Oak
This tree represents steadfastness within the family.
Druidic influence.

Oar
Direction and the effort put into life.

Oats
Sexual appetite.

Objects
Objects usually symbolise subjects or situations. A cup, for example, represents a source of nourishment therefore the feminine principle is indicated. And a cracked cup may represent a flaw in the mother/offspring relationship.

Observatory
Look well beyond the present horizon to see the whole picture.

Ocean
Vast emotional potential reflected as shallow, deep, turbulent or calm feelings.

Office
When not taken literally an office represents the filing room in the Mansion of the Soul—the memory.

Ogre
An archetype of the threatening father figure.

Oil
To see oil tells you to act as peacemaker

and pour oil onto troubled waters.

Ointment
Healing balm.

Old Man
The wise old man within who has learned from past experience.

Old Woman
The wise old woman within who is healer and comforter.

Olives
Healing, and a connection with the Holy Land.

Opal
A warning of unfortunate circumstances.

Operation
Interference and a calculated invasion of personal rights.

Opium
Beware of being duped into submission.

Orchard
As part of the Garden of Eden, rewards

will be reaped from the harvest of life.

Orchestra
Be sure to keep in tune and in harmony with others.

Orchid
Passionate love.

Ornaments
These represent false standards.

Ostrich
Do not bury your head in the proverbial sand.

Owl
A symbol of the Mother Goddess as well as a sign of wisdom.

Oxen
Mundane tasks and heavy burdens carried in life.

Oxygen
Inspiration and headiness.

Oyster
The world belongs to you.

Pain
To feel pain in a dream can be a warning concerning physical health, but it can also relate to a painful, emotional wound.

Parachute
An escape is possible but this could be a very dangerous way to bring things down to earth.

Paralysed
The feeling of paralysis in sleep is not a dream but an awareness of physical immobility which occurs naturally during the early stages of sleep. When this paralysis is incorporated into a dream it seems as if you are rooted to the spot.

Parcel
To see a parcel means you can expect a happy surprise.

Parents
Inherited attributes as well as inferior qualities. These are exaggerated in dream-parents, in the hope that they can be recognized in oneself.

Parrot
Repeated, worthless chat.

Parsley
This herb has traditional links with the feminine principles in nature, hence the belief that only the wife who is dominant in the marriage partnership can

grow parsley.

Party
Social activities and the meeting of new friends.

Pattern
The thread of life's rich pattern as it weaves in and out of various experiences.

Peach
Bitter-sweet memories.

Peacock
Male dominance and a sign warning against boasting.

Pearls
Tears of the Moon Goddess.

Peas
A choice has to be made but this will be extremely difficult due to the similarity between the two options.

Pen
The pen is mightier than the sword.

Penguin
Birds that cannot fly indicate that limitations are imposed on high-flying aims and ambitions.

Photography
A reminder of someone or something.

Picture
A situation can be seen in two ways—abstractly or symbolically.

Pig
A degraded person, at least in the eyes of the dreamer.

Pigeon
Town and country influences to different locations.

Pillars
Support will always be there for you.

Plants
Life itself. Success, growth and health are symbolized by the state of the plant.

Plastic
Plastic objects warn of artificial or false feelings.

Play
A play relates to an episode from the dreamer's life.

Plough
All the effort that has been put into ploughing ahead in life, especially when the going was hard, will be rewarded.

Plums
Ideal conditions are ahead and these will bring all round improvement.

Police
Authority, law and order are signified by this force. Depending on the circumstances in the dream it can be discovered whether these relate to the environment or to the orderliness within the dreamer.

Pond
Happy feelings and emotions.

Potatoes
These represent human responses to the basic problems of a so-called earthy nature.

Prayer
A call for help and guidance.

Pregnant
To be pregnant, or see someone who is, means ideas have been conceived which have great potential in the future.

Primrose
Romantic relationships and passionate love affairs need very careful handling.

Prison
Life can seem like a prison. Self-made rules and restrictions can create inhibitions.

Puppet
A warning that someone is pulling your

strings, so beware of this over-bearing influence.

Pyramid
A symbol of Egypt, but from a personal point of view a pyramid tells you that, to reach that point you are aiming for, you should start from a firm basis and work your way slowly but surely to the top.

Python
This snake is a dream messenger for traditionally it symbolizes the Pythea, the Greek oracular priestess.

Quarry
Make every effort to discover the truth for, as the saying goes, 'the answer lies in a stone'.

Quartet
The fourfold nature of life and the four elements of the creation.

Quay
Make the most of the present calm, before a storm blows up.

Queen
The queen at present on the throne, or a historical queen, represents the feminine principle and Great Mother nature. To socialize with the queen shows feelings of familiarity with royalty.

Queue
To see a queue shows great patience is needed but you will receive that which you seek, eventually.

Quicksand
This is a distinct warning indicating danger ahead, so beware of being swallowed up by some awful situation.

Quoits
This game represents the skilful game of loving, in the Freudian sense, and living, from the point of view of chance and good luck.

Rabbi
To see a rabbi suggests thoughts concerning the Old Testament. A Judaic influence.

Rabbits
Fertility and breeding instincts.
A white rabbit, like the one in Alice in Wonderland, leads the dreamer into their own inner world.

Race
The pace of life is increasing unnecessarily.
Rivalry between the dreamer and his or her parents, or some other competitor.

Radio
Telepathic messages and external influences generally.

Raft
To be on a raft shows you have been rescued from a bad situation, but beware of drifting into further trouble.

Rags
Poor circumstances can be improved but personal effort has to be exerted to attain this.

Railway station
Destiny and the line of direction is under consideration at present so stop

and wait a while before continuing on your way. You may need to take a different direction entirely.

Rain
To see this is a good sign showing all fears, anxieties and troubles will soon be washed away.

Rainbow
Hopes, with the proverbial pot of gold at the end.

Ram
Masculine over-dominance.

Rape
Apart from the obvious warning try to avoid anyone who attempts to force you to do something against your will.

Raven
A crow. Bran, the spirit of Britain.

Recipe
A guide or prescription for better health is needed.

Religious Experiences
Spiritual beliefs require expression, possibly in a practical way.

Reservoir
This represents a store of physical, emotional and spiritual energy.

Restaurant
Food for thought, a source of energy from an exterior source is needed.

Revolving door
An opportunity has been missed.

Rhinoceros
Traditionally, this creature is a sex symbol.

Rice
Good news on the domestic front is to be expected.

Riding
Riding a horse or any other animal means mastery and conquest of a person, talent, energy-drive or even of a handicap.

Right
see 'Left/Right'.

Ring
A ring means a long, unbroken friendship is anticipated, as with the giving of a wedding or engagement ring.

River
Life is flowing by, sometimes swiftly and dangerously, sometimes serenely.

Road
The road through life with all the hazards and joys encountered on the way.

Robber
Fear of losing face, identity or credibility.

Robin
A message from a loved one who is now dead.

Rocks
The meaning of seeing rocks or 'being on the rocks' is a self-explanatory warning of impending danger.

Room
One room or aspect in the Mansion of the Soul. Depending on the room—the bedroom, sitting room, kitchen, cellar or attic—the particular characteristic or outlook can be discovered.

Roots
Stability, confidence and strength of purpose.

Rope
A strong attachment to a person or to a place.

Roses
These signify a message of true love.

Rooted to the Spot
see 'Paralysis'.

Running
You may be running towards a goal, or running away from something you cannot face.

S

Sack
To see a sack shows that the future holds more than is apparent at present.

Sacrifice
To see a sacrifice being performed means you should not be afraid to sacrifice your own interests for others.

Saddle
To be in the saddle is a sign showing you are in control of your own destiny and so you should know where you are going.

Sage
This herb symbolizes physical healing.

Sailing
Sailing on smooth water tells you that you can expect better times ahead, but if there is a strong wind blowing, or the water is rough, take this as a warning sign.

Saint
A saint is someone who can be relied upon, whatever the circumstances.

Salad
Food for thought of a philosophical or spiritual nature.

Sale
To be at a sale means you can expect bargains in life.

Salmon
This fish was sacred to the Celts. Celtic origins should be investigated.

Salt
Traditionally, salt is the essence of life.

Sand
Dry sand represents annoyances which are trivial and not lasting.

Sapphire
This stone, along with all gems, reflects the inner self, the soul.

Satellite
Watch out for those on the periphery who could take over a situation.

Saw
To be using a saw means you will be cut down to size.

Scar
A scar shows that an emotional wound from the past is healed but is not forgotten.

Scent
An influence manifesting through the sense of smell. This is usually associated with certain smells which, in dreams, bring back past memories.

School
Schools symbolize life which is made up of various lessons from which we are supposed to learn and thus evolve.

Scientists
The head, the intellect rules; intuition and the heart need to be expressed.

Scissors
Any unnecessary links or ties should be cut.

Sea
see 'Ocean.'

Seeds
Great potential for the future, provided the seeds are sown at the right time.

Serpent
A serpent, especially if it twists and turns, symbolizes an emotional en-

tanglement which is difficult to throw off.

Sewing
Industriousness.

Sex
From the Freudian point of view, impotence, homosexual tendencies or some other deviation from so-called normality, are always suggested.
It can represent a guilty feeling in no way associated with sex.

Shadow
Usually this represents the neglected side of the dreamer but, depending on the circumstances in the dream, it may symbolize a fear cast by someone else.

Shapes
The basic language of the mind. Life itself, which conforms to strict patterns.

Sheep
To see sheep tells you to be individualistic and not to be easily lead.

Ship.
The voyage of life with its rough crossings, deep waters and even a warning of missing the boat.

Shoes
You are being encouraged to follow in someone's footsteps.
Try to see someone else's point of view as if you were in their shoes.

Shop
To see a shop tells you that there are several choices, so do not make up your mind too hastily.

Sight
Intuitive insight.

Silk
Riches, luxury and an easy or easier life are on the way.

Silver
This metal is associated with the mind, and flashes of illumination.

Singing
A sign of encouragement and help from a superior level.

Sister
Feminine support generally.
If there is disagreement with a sister it means lack of harmony exists within.

Skeleton
Usually a skeleton represents the proverbial skeleton in the cupboard.
Get down to the fundamental problem, the bare bones.

Sky
The sky is the limit so be confident and go for that aim or goal.

Sledge
Like other vehicles, this represents the dreamer making his or her way through life. Since sledges do not have brakes it warns of the dangers of starting something in life and then not being able to stop it.

Slide
To slide on something, or to see a slide, warns of losing control.

Smoke
Slow, twisting smoke is a warning of death.

Snakes
These reptiles represent human energies in various forms, from sexual demands to ruthless, ambitious drive. They also symbolize healing.

Snow
Emotional coldness, bleakness and lack of warmth.

Soldier
He may symbolize the dreamer's hero. On the other hand, the military discipline this image conjures up warns of certain compulsions and restrictions in life.

South
Sunnier, warmer times are forecast.

Sparrow
A chirpy person, possibly a cockney.

Spider
The feminine figure with a devouring affection. The mother who denies her family freedom of expression.

Spirit
A spirit is either a memory of the past, or the ghost of a person who has died.

Square
This shape symbolizes a situation on 'an all square basis', showing a well-regulated and stable lifestyle.

Stag
A bachelor.

Stairs
Going up stairs indicates a rise in status, promotion, success and acclaim.
Going down stairs shows loss of recognition and confidence.

Star
Destiny.
The birth of a baby.

Statue
Someone the dreamer has put on a pedestal and idolizes.

Stones
Cold-heartedness and lack of compassion.

Sun
A sign of hope, brilliance and happiness.

Swan
A sign of the White Goddess, the Mother aspect of creation.

Swimming
Effort put into life on an emotional level.

Sword
A sign of defence rather than attack.

T

Table
An altar upon which lie the dreamer's beliefs, thoughts and hopes.
Self-sacrifice.

Tap
To hear a tap means someone wishes to contact you or draw your attention to something.

Tarantula
This warns that you are probably your own worst enemy.

Taxi
Take advantage of help offered by others but know that in the end it is that which you do for yourself that is the more valuable.

Tea
An innocent friendship is represented by drinking or serving tea.

Teacher
A teacher is an aspect of the dreamer—the wise self within.

Tears
A warning of sadness or frustration.

Teeth
Changes in the pattern of life are to be expected.

Telephone
Getting in touch with your inner-self for advice or help. Listen to the quiet voice within.

Temple
A private place within yourself; the place to retreat to and reflect on the outer world.

Thread
Fate, karma and destiny.

Theatre
The theatre of the mind, where images act out thoughts.

Thunder
A powerful warning voice from an authoritative source.

Tide
The ebbing and flowing of emotions tied to external events and circumstances.

Tiger
A sign of physical energy, drive and enthusiasm.

Time
Hours, days, weeks, months or years signify the passing of time, warning that it is running out fast.

Toilet
Lavatories represent the basic needs in life, especially the more personal ones. They also signify the elimination of unwanted memories linked with bad experiences.

Tomb
A warning indicating restrictions which surround the dreamer. These should be broken down as soon as possible.

Tower
Towering ambitions which tend to isolate the dreamer in a world of their own making.

Train
Travelling on a train symbolizes the journey or destiny through life.

Treasure
Priceless, unique ideas and treasured thoughts and memories.

Trees
Family matters

Triangle
Stability and protection are assured.

Tunnel
A connection between this life and the next, and the conscious and unconscious.

Twins
The dual aspect or both sides of a problem or situation.

U

UFO
The individual search for the inner light and illumination.

Umbrella
Seeing this in a dream means the dreamer should look for shelter from life's intermittent storms.

Uncle
A reliable, experienced friend in time of need.

Undertaker
To see an undertaker means you have an unpleasant task to undertake.

Undressed
Personal secrets may be revealed unless care is taken to cover them up properly.

Unicorn
The archetype of purity, virginity and altruistic beliefs.

Uniform
A respect for authority.

University
A university represents ancient seats and centres of learning inherent in the dreamer.

Urine
To see this is an expression of relief following a tense time.
To have urine poured over you is a sign of denigration.

Urn
An urn, when it contains ashes, is a symbol of reincarnation.

Vaccination
To be vaccinated means you are immune from emotional and verbal attacks.

Valley
Life is restricted at present and there are few, if any, choices but to go on.

Vegetables
Basic necessities in life.

Veil
The truth is there but it needs uncovering.

Velvet
Beware of what lies beneath the surface. This warns of the iron fist in the velvet glove.

Vest
If the vest is inadequate, it shows confidence is lacking and a fear of exposure.

Village
Good foundations exist but these are only the beginning of something greater.

Vine
Spiritual inheritance.

Vinegar
Do not be deceived into thinking something is wrong, bad or awful. It is, in fact, the reverse.

Voice
Most voices heard in dreams are those of the dreamer.

Violets
These flowers symbolize the spirit.

Violin
Emotional harmony can confidently be expected.

Volcano
An explosive situation is to be expected, probably of an emotional nature.

Vomit
An unpleasant situation will resolve itself soon.

Voyage
Travel abroad is the traditional meaning of a voyage, but it also symbolizes life's journey over troubled and smooth waters.

Vulture
Beware of a vicious competitor waiting to move in and take his or her pick.

Waiter
To be a waiter in a dream shows the dreamer's role is one of service to others.

Walking
Walking symbolizes the dreamer making his or her way through life.

Wall
This is an obstacle which should be 'got over' or 'overcome.'

Wallet
The masculine equivalent of the handbag therefore personal beliefs, ideals and private thoughts are represented.

Wallflower
The odd man, or woman, out.

Walnuts
The dreamer will be well provided for but will have few luxuries.

War
Conflict and aggression.

Washing
Wash away the past.

Wasp
A warning that enemies are close at hand.

Watch
A watch alerts you to the fact that time is marching on.

Water
The unconscious self. Heartfelt emotions and deep feelings. The spiritual waters of life.

Wealth
To be wealthy in a dream shows the dreamer has an accumulation of wisdom.

Weaving
The pattern of life woven in time through experience.

Web
Beware of a trap from which escape is virtually impossible.

Wedding
A union of opposites, of the conscious and the unconscious.

Well
Depth of feeling.

West
Towards Atlantis—hope for the world. 'Gone west' warns of failure.

Whale
The feminine self and instincts. The womb of Mother Nature.

Wheat
Fertility and plenty.

Wheel
The cycle of life, but beware of going in circles.

Whistle
A warning sign.

Willow
Family problems associated with temporary sadness.

Wind
The breath of life and of the spirit. Changes are to be expected.

Winter
A quiet, resting time.

Witch
Disenchantment with someone or with oneself.

Wolf
Beware of hard times.

Woods
Families and communities as a whole.

Wool
Protection from verbal blows.

Worm
Terrestial energies.

X-Ray
Unseen, energetic forces are at work which bring considerable changes.

Xylophone
Try to keep in tune with others and with life generally.

Yawning
An outlet is needed to escape from a boring situation.

Yeast
Nature will take its course.

Yew
Nothing can be done to alter certain facts relating to the family.

Zebra
There is an equal chance of success or failure.

Zodiac
Fame and fortune are in the balance.

Zoo
The world, populated by the many different races.

Conclusion
Life is Only a Dream

'Again, no one is sure, apart from faith, whether he is awake or asleep, seeing that during sleep we believe that we are awake as firmly as we do when we are awake. We believe we see spaces, figures, movements; we experience the passage of time, we measure it; and in fact we behave just as we are awake. We spend half our life asleep, in which condition, as we ourselves admit, we have no idea of truth, whatever we imagine, since all our perceptions are illusory. Who knows, therefore, whether the other half of life, in which we believe ourselves awake, is not another dream, slightly different from the first from which we awake when we suppose ourselves asleep?

'If we dreamt in company and the dreams, as often happens, chanced to agree, and if we spent our waking hours in solitude, who doubts that in such a case we should believe matters reversed? Finally, as we often dream that we are dreaming, and thus add one dream to another, life itself is only a dream upon which other dreams are grafted and from which we awake at death, a dream during which we have as few principles of truth and goodness as during natural sleep, these different thoughts which disturb us being perhaps mere illusions, like the flight of time and the empty fancies of our dreams.'

From Pascal's *Pensées*—unfinished at his death in 1669.

Index

Of further interest ...

The Dreamwork Manual

A step-by-step introduction to working with dreams

Strephon Kaplan Williams

This unique manual is a complete dreamwork course designed for both individuals and groups. It contains over thirty tried and tested dreamwork methods by which we can actualize our dreams and thus *experience* their meanings. The methods are based on two major approaches: the Jungian journey towards individuation or wholeness, and the idea of altering the dream state and using dreams to benefit individual and community life — attributed to the Senoi people of Malaya — the so-called Dream People. The techniques provide a means of renewing and creatively transforming our outer world into a state of harmonious wholeness. Manual also contains information on:

- Transpersonal dreamwork
- Working with nightmares
- The dream ego
- Sexual dreams
- Dreamwork and ritual

- Lucid dreaming
- Dreamwork and healing
- Meditation for creative dreaming
- Symbolism
- Seven basic archetypes

A practical book covering all aspects of dreaming and showing how the power of dreams can be harnessed to develop and transform our lives.

Your Dreams And What They Mean

How to understand the secret language of sleep

Nerys Dee

The ancients saw dreams as messages from the gods, but today psychiatrists regard them as reflections and expressions of our innermost selves and deepest urges. This fascinating and popularly written book explores the mysterious world of dreams and shows how we can learn to understand and make use of them. Nerys Dee begins by describing some famous dreams—such as Jacob's and Joseph's—in history and goes on to describe current scientific research into dreams and brain wave patterns. The main focus of the book, however, is on types of dreams—symbolic, psychic, psychological, lucid and request dreams—and the decoding of dream language. Topics covered include:

- Inventive dreams
- Nightmares and what they signify
- Dream messages
- The healing power of dreams
- Warning dreams

- Sexual symbolism in dreams
- Daydreams
- Jung and Freud on symbolism
- Making sense of your dreams
- How to remember your dreams